"In the right culture, hourly w  remarkable things. *Stop the Sh* that culture. Great Job, Scott!"

          -Peter **....../CEO, Jersey Mike's Subs**

"In *Stop the Shift Show*, Scott's expertise shines through once again, just as he's done from the stage with our Great Clips franchisees and salon managers. He offers practical, powerful insights and tools for those leading and developing hourly employees. Scott will help you unleash the incredible potential inside your employees and allow you to build a stronger and more successful business."

          -Rob Goggins, President, Great Clips, Inc.

"*Stop the Shift Show* provides a framework for business owners and managers to build teams that excel, and even more importantly, teams that last."

          - Whitney Knight, Brand Management Director, Hilton

"With authenticity, candor and a bit of humor, Scott Greenberg calls us all on our s***. Stop the excuses. Stop wishing for the good old days and embrace the new reality: To win we must create a loving, supportive environment for our leaders and teams – doubling down on past efforts. Lofty? Yes, but Scott provides a step-by-step path forward (with case studies) to recruit, to hire and to retain. This is the book we need, now."

          -Monica Rothgery, Chief Operations Officer, KFC US (retired)

"Scott Greenberg's *Stop the Shift Show* is simply great: accessible, actionable, and erudite… Humor & puns? Check! Easy-to-follow tricks to engage and motivate your hourly staff? Check! Management tips from Aristotle? Check! It's a wonderful read and I'm excited to introduce it to my team."

          -Anna Haaland, Global People Business Systems Director,
          Costco Wholesale

"Scott details well strategies and opportunities to win in today's ever-changing labor market - it's about creating teams and getting real buy-in. The right tactics are here for any business that relies on the efforts of an hourly workforce to succeed."

          -Charles Watson, Chief Executive Office, Tropical Smoothie Café

"Kudos to Scott for yet another inspiring guide to leadership that ties together head, heart, and hands. It's filled with practical tools to uplift hourly workers and enhance your organization. A true game-changer for anyone in a leadership role. I remain a huge Scott Greenberg fan!"

-Stacy Anderson, President, Anytime Fitness

"Scott Greenberg's writing takes readers on an enlightening journey, revealing a wealth of strategies that are as powerful as they are relatable. This is the book the workplace desperately needs. I'm excited to share this with as many people as possible!"

-Chris Dull, President & CEO, Freddy's Frozen Custard & Steakburgers

"*Stop the Shift Show* isn't just another management book—it's a resource that could turn your hourly workforce into an absolute powerhouse. Scott delivers practical strategies, offers game-changing insights for business owners and managers, and knows how to elevate a team's performance. Whether you're a new or experienced leader, or at a startup or legacy company, this book can help you build a dream team."

-Jason Feifer, Editor in Chief, *Entrepreneur* Magazine

"Scott Greenberg's book, *The Wealthy Franchisee*, was a game-changer for me helping me understand the dynamics of the franchisee and franchisor as business partners. His new book, *Stop the Shift Show*, changes the game again by being a wake-up call for anyone in a leadership position employing hourly workers. He challenges us to be more purposeful in how we manage, urging us to understand what our employees truly want rather than placing the blame on them. Scott's emphasis on changing your mindset from being a mere manager to becoming a great leader will be transformative to your small business. Become the 'employer of choice' and read this book!"

-Heather Nykolaychuk, President, Budget Blinds

"With indispensable advice and a unique blend of humor and storytelling, *Stop the Shift Show* is a must-read for any leader looking to recruit, retain and develop their hourly workforce into a high-performing team."

-Cathy Susie, Vice President of Human Resources, Schneider Electric

"Scott's firsthand experience and practical takeaways make *Stop the Shift Show* a must-read for anyone in the franchise sector. IFA's research consistently tells us the top challenge facing franchisees is employee retention, and applying Scott's learnings from countless hours of research and practical insights will benefit anyone looking to improve the business they lead and the employees that can make (or break) a business."

-Matt Haller, President & CEO, International Franchise Association

"A refreshing departure from generic management advice. This is the ultimate resource for anyone working with frontline employees."

-Amir Shiekh, Vice President of Operations, Shiekh Shoes

STOP THE SHIFT SHOW

TURN YOUR STRUGGLING HOURLY WORKERS INTO A TOP-PERFORMING TEAM

SCOTT GREENBERG

Entrepreneur Press®

Entrepreneur Press, Publisher
Cover Design: Andrew Welyczko
Production and Composition: Mike Fontecchio, Faith & Family Publications

Library of Congress Cataloging-in-Publication Data
　　Names: Greenberg, Scott (Speaker), author.
　　Title: Stop the shift show : turn your struggling hourly workers
　　　　into a top-performing team / by Scott Greenberg.
　　Description: Irvine : Entrepreneur Press, [2024] | Includes index.
　　　　| Summary: "An essential guide for managers and business owners looking
　　　　for techniques and strategies to transform their hourly workforce into a
　　　　top-performing super team"-- Provided by publisher.
　　Identifiers: LCCN 2023035202 (print) | LCCN 2023035203 (ebook) | ISBN
　　　　9781642011623 (paperback) | ISBN 9781613084731 (epub)
　　Subjects: LCSH: Employee motivation. | Teams in the workplace--Management.
　　　　| Performance. | Corporate culture. | Franchises (Retail)--Management.
　　Classification: LCC HF5549.5.M63 G755 2024 (print) | LCC HF5549.5.M63
　　　　(ebook) | DDC 658.3/14--dc23/eng/20230727
　　LC record available at https://lccn.loc.gov/2023035202
　　LC ebook record available at https://lccn.loc.gov/2023035203

26　25　24　23　　　　　　　　　　　　　　　10 9 8 7 6 5 4 3 2 1

For my children's future employers,
and always,

For Rachel

Contents

PART 3
Coaching for Top Performance

CHAPTER 8
30-Second Leadership™ 131

CHAPTER 9
Coaching in the Green and Yellow 149

CHAPTER 10
Coaching in the Blue 169

CHAPTER 11
Coaching in the Red 185

CHAPTER 12
Putting 30-Second Leadership to Work 201

PART 4
Maintaining Top Performance

Introduction

It's a Saturday afternoon in a Southern California shopping mall, and I'm strolling past the stores, occasionally glancing over my shoulder to ensure I'm not within eyesight of my 14-year-old daughter and her friends. Where I was once my little girl's hero, today I'm her "cringy" chauffeur. I agreed to keep myself invisible to spare her the embarrassment of having a father.

With two hours to kill, I have time to observe the 200 stores, altogether employing more than a thousand hourly workers. I peek inside a Japanese pop culture outlet. One employee apathetically stocks shelves while another at the counter mindlessly swipes on her phone. Next, I visit a busy (perhaps understaffed?) athletic shoe store where frazzled associates are quickly fetching footwear and ringing up sales. Just a few doors down is a bustling tech store, where attentive hipsters proudly demo their phones and computers. At the far end is one of the mall's anchors, a major discount retailer with two floors of merchandise. I ask one of the employees in their distinctive vests where I can find Brita water filters. "I'm sorry, I don't know," she says. "I'm new here." I thank her and wander off to find my filter.

Later I scan the food court to make sure the coast is clear and consider my lunch choices. At a pizza place, a young man who looks like he's already taken 10,000 orders robotically moves through transactions. "Next in line," he murmurs to the humanoid in front of him.

At a nearby counter, three cheerful employees around his same age serve up chicken with smiles. They warmly reply to every thank you with "My pleasure." There's a long line there. I was thinking about pizza, but I patiently queue up for chicken.

I take my tray and scan for a place to sit. A man on the cleaning crew notices me and beckons me to a vacant table. He removes the last person's tray and gives the table a wipe. "Bon appetit!" he jokes, clearly enjoying his work.

As I take my first bite of chicken, I notice the cell phone swiper from the Japanese pop shop on a break. She sits with friends from the mall and engages in lively conversation, completely different away from her job.

It's amazing how under one roof there's this much disparity among employees. Some are happy while others are miserable. Some excel at their jobs and others struggle. Many love their work, but even more endure it. Much of their performance is a reflection of who they are. But there's another factor that often has an even bigger impact on how well they work: the way they're *managed*.

My job is to help business owners and management teams operate at a higher level. I speak at conferences, consult, and consistently interact with people who have a lot of responsibility, from running frozen yogurt shops or managing retail stores to supervising large manufacturing plants and warehouses. I have clients in hospitality, auto care, home services, education, personal care, food service, senior in-home care, fitness, and many other industries. All of them oversee systems, procedures, and technology. But regardless of their industry, there's one responsibility they all share—managing workers. And for most, that's their biggest challenge.

The Workplace *Shift* Show

"Good morning. Mind if I join you?"

It was breakfast time at The Peabody Memphis hotel. I found an open seat at a table of business owners and managers, identified myself as their guest speaker, and asked to join their conversation. I was scheduled to give the keynote address that day for a large retail association. While my main profession is public speaking, most of my work is listening, so I embrace every opportunity to interview audience members before my presentations. I want to know my clients and their struggles, and conference breakfasts are a great time to meet them. As they fill their stomachs, I pick their brains.

"So what's the most stressful part of your business?"

They responded in unison, like a Greek chorus: "Employees."

I had anticipated this answer because that's what I always get, but I asked them to expound.

"We just can't find anyone."

"They don't show up for interviews."

"They're lazy."

"They don't care."

"They're so unmotivated."

"They're constantly calling out."

"They never last."

"They're always on their phones."

Not only have I heard these things countless times, but I've also thought them myself. For more than 10 years I was an owner/operator of two Edible Arrangements franchises in Los Angeles. I had teams of hourly workers and a management staff. I'd been working full time as a motivational speaker for 13 years before opening my first location, and that gave me a false sense of confidence. I believed I'd have an edge over other Edible Arrangements franchisees because I came into the business armed with such nuggets as "There's no 'I' in team" and "No one cares what you know until they know that you care." I'd read countless books on leadership and regurgitated their theories onstage.

The problem was that my employees hadn't read those books. They didn't know how they were supposed to respond to my brilliant Jedi-leadership tactics, and the clichés didn't land as I'd expected. There's no

"I" in team? To them, that was just a statement about spelling. When I talked about how Together Everyone Achieves More (TEAM), their eyes glazed over. I tried brainstorming a list of company values with them. "Are these the rules?" one asked. I explained our opportunity to do something meaningful, to be part of something great. Another hand went up. "Do we have to punch out when we take breaks?"

If you had asked me during those first two years what my biggest headache was running my business, I would have responded just like those retail store operators in Memphis. It was my employees. Despite my determination to be a great boss, some of them ghosted me. Others stole from me. One of the first team members we fired had been calling ahead for others to punch her in when she was running late. Another called out on Valentine's Day (our busiest day) because she had to help her grandmother move. I once checked the surveillance cameras on my phone and found my assistant manager doing an employee's hair. A few succumbed to drug addiction. Several great employees left to make an extra dollar per hour at a business down the street. Many just moved slowly, repeated their mistakes, and topped out at mediocre.

I did everything I could to help my employees succeed. I paid them fairly. I bought them food. I rewarded them with gift cards and praise. I clarified my expectations. I gave them additional training and second chances. I was the cool boss I always wanted when I was an hourly worker. I tried to make our workplace feel like a family. I also tried playing the tough boss: I wrote people up and came down hard. I let them know in no uncertain terms when they weren't working as they should. Good cop, bad cop, tender, tough—none of it made a difference. My business was a total *shift* show.

It was as if everything I'd ever learned about leadership was wrong. These people were immune to my tactics. I had such an ambitious vision for them. I so badly wanted to create a culture of high performers, create the greatest workplace in history, and prove to my audiences that I could walk the talk and get results. If I couldn't do that, what business did I have telling others how to manage?

I also wanted to make money. I took out a big loan against my house to open that first store. I begged my wife to trust me that this was a good investment. But I had no intention of giving up professional speaking, and that entails traveling. I had to build a team I could trust to run things while I was away. I was struggling with the same issues I was paid to discuss onstage. Years of sharing my messages with audiences had conditioned me to think positively and believe in human potential. But these real-world experiences were shaking me to my core. I was becoming cynical. It was stressful enough dealing with employees. But this was calling into question my entire life's work. I felt like a fraud.

I started looking through some of the leadership books I'd collected over the years, searching for answers. As I thumbed through them, I realized something that hadn't occurred to me during my first readings of them: Most discussed leadership in large organizations. The employees they referenced were full time and career bound. Others spoke broadly about employees or team members, lumping engineers with cashiers, as if one-size management fits all. The books were loaded with jargon and models and consultant-speak. Few of them mentioned the kind of employees I had: lower-paid, lesser-skilled, hourly workers. Most of these management gurus had little or no direct experience managing them.

Try Googling the phrase "top leadership experts." You'll see many familiar names. Notice their backgrounds. Most of them come from large white-collar companies. Others are academics or motivational speakers. I don't want to knock these people. There are some brilliant minds there that I deeply admire. But the kind of people they talk about leading are different from the type of worker I was leading—and the type of worker *you're* trying to lead. Even those who founded companies and started from the ground up doing the hourly work themselves have focused their books on high-level organizational leadership.

I do a lot of work in the franchise industry, which is a massive sector (really an industry made up of smaller industries) relying on hourly workers. Most franchise business owners come to their business after exiting other occupations, often corporate jobs. Many people who've led large teams of salaried professionals struggle with managing hourly workers. Their tactics just don't translate.

As I spoke with other business owners operating in my industry, I realized I wasn't alone in my difficulties managing this unique sector of the workforce. Most people I knew who dealt with hourly workers had no idea how to get through to them. They'd stopped trying and basically accepted that employees were a necessary evil of running their business.

I was discouraged but not ready to give up. Seeing how much frustration was out there, I saw an opportunity. Sure, I wanted to resolve my own employee issues. But I also realized if I could figure out how to lead *these* people, I could bring something very helpful to my clients. I could go beyond theory. I could share practical, real-world, on-the-ground tools that could change the game for a lot of bosses.

There's something very powerful about pursuing a higher purpose. I still needed to reduce my headaches, increase my income, and get my work done. But now I had a new mission that was as much about learning as it was about earning. I wanted to solve a big problem. I wanted to find management solutions that applied to this type of worker and make those solutions a focus of my speaking work. If I could figure out how to do that, it'd be great for both businesses.

Thinking in those terms shifted my mindset to something more productive. I replaced my frustration with curiosity and started asking different questions. Instead of wondering, "What's wrong with these people?" I asked, "What *drives* these people?" I had different conversations with Jennifer, my general manager. In addition to reviewing our daily operation and specific team members, we took a step back and discussed what we could learn generally about employee management. The store became a laboratory to experiment with new strategies: interviewing, training, retaining, coaching, motivating, etc. The goal was always to think bigger than our business and find tactics that could help anyone managing hourly teams.

I also changed the way I looked at my employees. My desire to understand them made me less contemptuous of them. I wanted to learn about them and *from* them. When someone was performing well, I paid closer attention to determine why. What were the conditions that brought out their best? Was it something innate to them or was it something we could replicate in other team members?

I developed the same inquisitiveness about my underperformers. Before, I was very judgmental about them and made a lot of assumptions. I blamed their soccer trophies and helicopter parents. I complained about the effects of screens and social media. Now I was eager to go deeper. I wanted to know if there might be other reasons behind their low performance. Were they really from a broken generation? Were they perhaps just a bad fit for the job? What was missing for them?

I began conducting one-on-one meetings, both formal and informal. Instead of just doing standard performance reviews, I used this time to ask bigger questions. I wanted to know what they valued and cared about. What did they want and expect from a job? What made them feel confident, successful, doubtful, and insecure? What put them off? I listened as objectively as I could, seeking only to understand. Every employee was a source of information. We also conducted blind surveys where employees could share their thoughts and feelings and provide feedback with less concern for how their comments might come back to them.

But the biggest change was inward, in me. I realized I might be a major factor in my employees' underperformance. My confidence, my attitude, my tactics—were they really serving me? Was I an asset to my team or a liability? I decided to let go of everything I thought I knew and went back to management kindergarten. I didn't entirely dismiss my knowledge; I just put it on the table for consideration and hit the reset button.

There was so much to do to run that business—operations, marketing, payroll, etc. But I made the people my priority. My theory was that if I took care of them, they'd take care of the business. Most of the time I invested in my store, I spent on them. Over time, that investment paid off.

Slowly, through a lot of trial and error, mistakes, and mis-hires, we saw improvements. We continually refined our approach to management, and we got noticeable results. Employees lasted longer. Sales increased, not just with more transactions, but with an increase in our average ticket size. Online reviews from customers improved. The atmosphere became more pleasant and fun. I could leave town to go speak somewhere and return to fewer problems and more money in the bank. Employees began socializing outside of work. Soon my team won the Edible Arrangements "Best Customer Service" award out of a thousand locations worldwide. The following year, Edible Arrangements created a brand-new award: "Manager of the Year." That inaugural award went to my manager, Jennifer.

Other owners began stopping by to see what we were doing with our team. Many would ask, "Where do you find such great people?" believing that great staffing was just knowing where to fish. Eventually I was asked to speak from the main stage to my peers at the Edible Arrangements convention about what they can do to build high-performing teams.

Soon I was getting invitations from other franchise systems to speak at their events. While those engagements were meant to benefit their owners and managers, I benefited the most. Part of my preparation for any speech is interviewing audience members. I ask to meet their best performers. My first book, *The Wealthy Franchisee*, is based on those conversations. I was especially interested in how they were managing their hourly workers compared to others who struggled. But learning from high performers isn't always easy. Many great bosses don't realize how they're getting great results. They're just leading employees the only way they know how. I usually have to keep asking questions to identify the tactics that distinguish them from everyday bosses. But with enough digging, I always find something unique in their approach. These top franchise owners showed me many things that I could duplicate with my team.

With the help of my employees, our first Edible Arrangements store became one of the highest-volume locations in California, often ranking number one in the state. Then we acquired one of the lowest-performing locations in the state. My team significantly boosted its sales ranking and online reviews and made it profitable within a year—all while keeping labor costs at or below our benchmark.

But I'll be honest: At no point were we without personnel issues. Where there are people, there are problems. Always. Even our best employees can lose focus. They make mistakes, get bored, squabble among themselves, bring personal problems to work. People always need feedback, motivation, and redirection to get back on track. That just comes with managing people. What we had were significantly *fewer* problems and much better performance.

When the timing felt right for me to sell Edible Arrangements, I had a solid enterprise run by a superstar team. Most of my employees at that point had been with me for years. If you had asked me then what was the greatest aspect of running those businesses, I would have told you it was my employees. I'm still in touch with most of that final crew to this day.

I sold my businesses, but my mission to learn about leading these workers has continued. *Stop the Shift Show* isn't just lessons from my own business. In this book, we're going to study a diverse swath of organizations that are accomplishing great things with their hourly workforces, from mom-and-pop businesses to large companies. We'll discuss franchises, restaurants, factories, retail stores, and other industries that rely on hourly help. They're all different, but there are a few characteristics they share:

1. All of them employ and excel with hourly teams.
2. All of them are producing goods and services and are serving customers (external and/or internal) at a high level.
3. All of them have been recognized as great places to work.
4. All of them pay well, but not excessively well.
5. None of them is a perfect employer. They all make mistakes and have occasional struggles with team members. They wouldn't need managers if that weren't the case. Managing people is hard. They just do it better than others.
6. None of them is a perfect organization. If you've heard something you don't like about some of them, don't let that stop you from learning from them. In some way, they're all known for accomplishing great things with hourly workers. See if there's something you can borrow.
7. None of them uses all the tactics described in this book. Not even I did. But all of them use some of them.
8. All of them have tactics you can replicate!

And that's really the point. You can use the methods in this book to make your life easier and your employees' performance better. You won't eliminate all the issues you face, but you can move the needle significantly in the direction you want. You can build a top-performing hourly team, and this book will show you how.

My experience managing hourly workers actually affirmed many of the tactics discussed by those famous leadership gurus. But for those tactics to work in our world, they need to be brought down to earth and made more digestible and practical. *Stop the Shift Show* is intended to be that resource.

By this point, you may be cynical about what's possible. I've talked to many of you over the years, and I know how difficult managing hourly workers can be. Maybe your biggest problem isn't even managing them but finding them. Or maybe you can find them but can't seem to keep them.

Maybe you're tearing your hair out, and deep in your soul, you don't believe it's possible to build a strong, reliable team of hourly workers.

I sympathize, but I can't ignore the results I've gotten, or the results gotten by Chick-fil-A, Starbucks, The Ritz-Carlton, In-N-Out Burger, Trader Joe's, Costco, the Apple Store, and others whose reputations and cultures have been well-documented. And I can't deny the success of the many diverse employers I've personally worked with and interviewed that are also thriving with the help of an outstanding hourly workforce. I've identified what these exceptional organizations have in common and what they do differently. By replicating their thoughts and actions, you can replicate their results. They're not extraordinary organizations—they're ordinary organizations managing employees in extraordinary ways. You can adopt their methods and get the same results.

I've tried to incorporate a variety of hourly work environments into this book. Many are franchises, not just because I know that world well but also because these are independently managed businesses with brand counterparts to which we can compare them. What they're doing well is similar to what's going right in top-performing independent businesses, large retail chains, and other companies. The multi-unit KFC franchisee profiled in Chapter 2 isn't much different from the single dry cleaner profiled in Chapter 5. And both work environments resemble the factory I discuss in Chapter 9 and the grocery chain in Chapter 10. All these organizations employ hourly workers and have a similar approach to achieving top employee performance. Your organization may differ in size, structure, and function, but most of their methods for managing hourly workers will also work for you.

In this book, we're going to buck tradition. We're going to question everything that's been done before in employee management. We're going to dispense with the beliefs, expectations, and practices of the past. We're doing this not to reject them but to quickly sort through them and determine which still work in today's environment and which are outdated. This isn't about coddling the sensitive or being "woke." It's about being *effective*. It's about maximizing your influence over your hourly workforce so you can increase productivity, decrease turnover, have more impact on those you serve, and make more money.

While other employers continue to complain about their teams and struggle to get back to the way things should (i.e., used to) be, you're going to pull ahead. You're going to out-recruit, outcoach, and outgrow your competitors. You're going to become a manager of the future as they struggle to let go of the past. Your teams will outlast and outperform theirs. Your business, your department, or your organization will get better results, and your employees will produce higher-quality work as you enjoy a higher quality of life.

To achieve these results, however, it's going to take some discipline on your part. Great teams result from great coaches. Before you start to work on your employees, we need to work on you. We need to get you thinking like a top-performing manager, reflecting on your beliefs, your biases, and your expectations. We need to reinforce what you're doing right and address what you could be doing better.

That may not be what you're looking for. You might have bought this book hoping for a quick fix to get your team to care. You want to know how to find more employees and how to motivate them to just do their job. You're busy, and you're not interested in changing.

If that's the case, you won't get the full value of the book. Great results must start with you. Maybe you don't believe you're part of the problem, or maybe you do but are just too tired to do anything about it. Many bosses feel that way, and I understand.

But remember that the marketplace for great employees is as competitive as the marketplace for customers. There are a lot of folks out there who are coming for your best team members. They're willing to do the work to become better bosses. I'm here to help them. I'd love to help you, too.

You may question my methods, but I promise you'll be impressed with the results. There's no magic here. This book is not about performing miracles but about increasing influence. It's about making the odds more in your favor. We can't eliminate all your headaches, but we can reduce them. We can make your job easier and your team better.

What to Expect in This Book

Don't look for one management methodology here. Hourly workplaces are too different for there to be a one-size-fits-all approach. Look instead for individual ideas. This book is loaded with them. None of the great leaders you'll meet here does everything we'll discuss. But they all do some of them. This book is a compilation of their tactics. Look for the ones that might work for you. You may be just a few best practices away from totally transforming your team.

Here's what our four-part journey together will look like. Part 1 is about preparing to manage. It's everything you must do within yourself to be capable of elevating others. These chapters are the preparation you need to build a great team. You're probably already in a leadership position, but the ideas in this section are the foundation for all the great things you and your employees will do later. They entail a lot of self-reflection and personal work to ensure you're in the best shape possible to manage. I know you're in a hurry to improve your operation. But if you rush the preparation, the tools you get later won't work as well. Each chapter builds on the next. Invest time in this section, and you're much more likely to thrive.

Part 2 is about designing your culture and building your team. These are two separate but connected endeavors. We're going to dive deep into each one.

Part 3 is all about coaching hourly workers. I'm going to give you a practical, powerful tool for diagnosing employees' needs for a given task and then use our model to determine the best approach to boost performance. My audiences love this tool, and you will, too. This alone will be worth your investment in the book.

Part 4 is about keeping your employees great. How do you maintain their performance? How do you motivate them? How do you measure their progress and keep them engaged? These chapters will help you sustain your culture and your employees' work.

My Promise to You

If you read this book with an open mind and consistently apply these ideas, you'll quickly:

> ⟩ Attract higher-caliber job candidates and identify the right employees for your organization
> ⟩ Improve employee retention and boost performance

❯ Spend less time putting out fires
❯ Provide better service for your customers, whether external or internal
❯ Build a healthier, more enjoyable workplace
❯ Reduce your stress
❯ Create a top-performing hourly team that will help you build your organization
❯ Transform your shift show into a smash hit!

Let's get to work!

PART 1

PREPARING TO MANAGE

CHAPTER 1

The Manager's Role in the *Shift* Show

One of the worst bosses I ever had was one of the *first* bosses I ever had. When I was a senior in high school, I got a job as a front desk clerk at the local Best Western hotel. The manager who hired me informed me on my first day that he was leaving but was already training his replacement, Diane. Diane had had front desk experience at a hotel back in Texas, but this would be her first management position. As I was being trained on my new job, Diane was being trained on hers.

I watched as they went over the reservations system, check-in procedures, and posting room charges. They discussed housekeeping protocols and how to program room keys. They sat together and created the schedule for the upcoming week. He even gave her a tutorial on how to adjust the temperature of the hot tub. They went over everything on how to manage hotel operations. (Diane trained me on some of these things the day after she learned them.)

What I never saw was Diane being trained on how to manage *us*, her team. It might have happened when we weren't watching, but I doubt it. And if it did, it didn't go well. Because Diane really struggled with her employees.

Some days she was extremely friendly and personable, trying hard to connect with us. Other days she was strict and short-tempered. We were never sure which Diane we were going to get. When she showed us how to do something, she spoke fast and got frustrated if we didn't catch on quickly. She herself made a lot of mistakes but would never admit to them. Chatter among the team was that she was "a total idiot." Harsher words were also used. Since this was one of my first jobs, I wasn't sure what to think. I was too worried about how I was being perceived.

Looking back on it now, I feel sorry for Diane. Like so many others who step into management, she was totally unprepared to manage people. She was trained to keep the hotel running but never taught how to lead a team.

A Crisis in Management

Too many new managers come into their role as Diane did. Most are promoted after excelling as an employee but receive little or no training on management. They have tenure and job skills but haven't developed their leadership abilities. Managers *should* have tenure in their industry and know the positions they're going to supervise. But management itself is a discipline that requires training—not just on operations, but on *people*, and certainly before a manager starts.

We see this a lot in sports as well—great players who struggle as coaches. Los Angeles Lakers legend Magic Johnson had a career win-loss record of 670-236 as a player, but his record during his short-lived coaching career (a single season with the Lakers) was 5-11. Wayne Gretzky played 1,487 hockey games, scoring 894 goals, and is considered one of the greatest players of all time. During his four seasons coaching for the Phoenix Coyotes, however, his record was a tepid 143-161 (plus 24 overtime/shootout losses). All-star players often don't become all-star coaches because coaching is a totally different skill set.

Unfortunately, few managers get an opportunity to develop that skill set properly. The average manager works for nearly 10 years before receiving any formal leadership training. Consider all the bad habits that can be developed during that time. In one survey conducted in the United Kingdom in 2021 by LMS provider Digits, more than a quarter of managers surveyed indicated they've never received any management training.

In the franchise industry, franchisors promise new business owners they will be taught everything they need to know to run their business. But attorneys have spooked franchisors from getting too involved in anything employee-related at the franchisee level for fear of taking on the liability of "joint employers." They don't want to be accountable for labor problems (such as overtime disputes, wrongful termination, harassment, etc.) at an independently owned location. Consequently, they prepare independent owners for operations and marketing, but most steer clear of advising them on how to manage people.

This lack of training is particularly problematic for organizations employing hourly workers. Hourly jobs make up almost 56 percent of all work in the United States. In fact, according to the U.S. Bureau of Labor Statistics (BLS), 20 percent of all U.S. jobs are in retail and hospitality (which includes food and beverage). These industries have notoriously high turnover rates. A 2022 Korn Ferry survey of more than a hundred major U.S. retailers found the annual turnover rate for all hourly jobs exceeded 75 percent. Data from BLS (June 2023) from a pool of 21,000 retail businesses showed a monthly separation rate of 4.6 percent, or 55.2% annually. The accommodation and food services sector has a monthly separation rate of 6.2 percent, or 74.4% annually. Monster.com reported that collectively, the turnover for hourly workers is triple that of salaried workers. Most people working these jobs will be gone within a year. That means managers must spend that much more time on staffing.

There are several reasons for all of this turnover. Compared to salaried professionals, hourly workers are more transient. Their families are more likely to be in flux. They're less likely to see their job as part of a career path, and there may not be as many opportunities for them to grow and increase their income. Young workers may seek employment only for the summer or until volleyball season starts.

For these reasons, many employers have lower expectations of them. They see employees as disposable. I can't tell you how many times I've heard bosses say, "If I can get three months out of them, I consider that a huge win."

But the demographics of hourly workers aren't the only reasons for lower retention (or for lower morale and/or performance). Good management and management training are also lacking. Consider the following statistics from the Society for Human Resource Management (SHRM):

> ◈ Sixty percent of employees say they left their jobs because of their managers.
> ◈ A third of employees don't believe their boss knows how to manage them.
> ◈ Eighty-four percent of U.S. workers believe inadequately trained managers create excessive work and stress.
> ◈ Fifty-seven percent feel their boss could benefit from training on how to be a better people manager.
> ◈ Half believe their work would improve if their immediate boss had more training in people management.

While many bosses complain that their employees are their biggest headache, the statistics suggest the feelings may be mutual.

But when hourly workers get better management, the data tells a more optimistic story. Global management consulting firm McKinsey & Company found that frontline employees at top retailers, including grocery stores, big-box stores, department stores, restaurants, and convenience stores, "are twice as motivated in their day-to-day jobs and leave half as often." These retailers also enjoy three additional percentage points of comparative-store sales. Better management gives these organizations a meaningful competitive advantage. That's your opportunity.

If your organization has given you this book, they're among the few who recognize the value of formal management development. They're investing in you. If you bought this book on your own, you're investing in yourself. Either way, the return on that investment will be you joining that elite group of top-performing leaders who are getting great results with your hourly workers. But it takes more than reading about great managers to become one. You must also act and think like them. That starts with breaking down your preconceptions so you can better understand the people you're leading.

Who Are Hourly Workers?

I've already had much to say about hourly workers, but let's clarify whom we're actually discussing. *Hourly worker* describes anyone whose wages are based on the number of hours they put into their job. This system of hourly compensation dates back to the Industrial Revolution, when factory work became a widespread form of employment. Before this, workers were paid by the day or week, or through *piecework*, where employees were compensated based on physical production. When work moved into factories, employers found it more efficient to pay their employees by the hour. Then, in the mid-19th century, time clocks were introduced, allowing hourly work to be tracked to the minute. After many abuses of this system, the Fair Labor Standards Act of 1938 was passed, regulating the length of a shift, overtime, minimum wages, and child labor.

Salary work, on the other hand, was introduced as a way to attract and retain white-collar workers such as managers and professionals. Their contributions were not as easily tracked in terms of hours worked. As a result, businesses began to offer these workers a fixed salary. Over time, salary work evolved and provided more advantages over hourly work. In the mid-20th century, businesses began to offer benefits such as health insurance, paid leave, and 401Ks to their salaried employees. These perks have become important to acquire and retain top talent.

Today the type of work employees do and how they're compensated often depends on their profession. Hourly work is still commonly used for manual labor, such as restaurant work, construction, or retail. Salary work is more commonly associated with white-collar jobs, such as management and office work. While many highly skilled, certified workers can still receive hourly compensation (such as nurses, ultrasound technicians, and tradesmen), the majority of workers under this classification come with fewer skills and earn lower wages.

Hourly Workers vs. Salaried Workers

The difference between these two compensation models is important in order to better understand your hourly team. Certainly there are universal desires all employees share, such as fair compensation and respect.

But some people receive more compensation and more respect. There's status that comes with receiving a salary and not having to punch in. Salaried employees are more likely to work full time, receive benefits, and earn a reliable income, making it easier to plan a life and access credit. (Though they don't typically earn overtime pay.) There's also a perception in salaried work of being on a career path with opportunities for new roles and larger compensation. Salaried jobs feel like they're on a ladder, and people feel they can build their careers as they help build the organization. That lifestyle comes with more responsibility and accountability. Salaried workers may continue to put mental energy into their work in their off time (and receive calls and emails after hours).

In most cases, hourly workers' responsibility ends when they punch out. But there's a greater chance they're going to another job or to school. During tough economic times, their hours may be reduced. And even during prosperous times, their hours may be changed. With a less reliable schedule and income, they must do a lot of shuffling in their life. They're also aware their employer may be no more committed to them than they are to the company. Hourly employees usually have fewer opportunities to grow with the organization, making their relationship with their employer more transactional than relational. With fewer roots in the organization (and without benefits such as health care), it's easier for them to move on to another workplace.

Collectively, hourly workers skew younger. According to a report by hiring platform Workstream, "The Hourly Workforce of 2022," the average age of fast-food workers in the U.S. is 24 years old.

The human brain takes 25 years to develop fully. Teens and young adults are driven by the emotional amygdala, while older adults think more with the rational prefrontal cortex, according to the University of Rochester Medical Center's Health Encyclopedia website. For several years still, their brains try to connect the emotional areas with the rational decision-making ones. To a grown adult, teenagers and even young adults may seem like they're still oversensitive children with no common sense. (On my better days, my dad just called me Scott!) But they're just still in the process of growing up.

Knowing that neurological development continues through age 25, that means there are plenty of people exiting college and even graduate school whose brains are still forming. They're not yet the people they're going to be. They're like raw dough still baking in the oven. They're not quite bread, but they're getting there. Younger workers have much longer to bake.

But it's important to remember that as they grow, they're still human. Their emotions are real. Their perspectives and feelings shouldn't be dismissed. They need to be managed with more patience and compassion and a lot less judgment. When faced with work problems (or personal ones), they may need the help of your fully formed prefrontal cortex to calm their untamed amygdala. But with their youth comes lots of energy and a willingness to learn. They may also have a lot of talent and useful insight into the marketplace. A little understanding will help you tap into their potential and boost their performance.

Another noteworthy difference between salaried workers and hourly workers is the flexibility they've sought since the COVID-19 pandemic. Since that time, more salaried workers have been requesting to work remotely. They want *location* flexibility. Employers were forced to experiment with remote work during the pandemic and many found multiple advantages, making it easier to provide that flexibility.

Not so with hourly teams. Most (but not all) hourly work is on-site. What hourly workers have requested since the pandemic is *time* flexibility. They want more control over when they work and for how long. That's impacted hiring and retention in a massive way. It's also come as a shock to many longtime employers. I've discussed this shift in scheduling expectations with older managers, and their reaction is almost violent: "Who the hell do these entitled brats think they are to tell me when they're going to work?!" It's certainly a different world, even from just a few years ago when I had employees. But those organizations that find ways to meet this expectation will have an advantage over those hoping to return to traditional scheduling practices.

It's important to appreciate the different experience hourly workers have of their jobs compared to salaried workers, and perhaps even compared to *your* experience of work. Hourly teams can be coached into becoming high performers, but not when you expect them to think and behave like those who enjoy the benefits of salaried work and career jobs. To win their loyalty and see them meet their full potential, you must be more purposeful in how you manage them. That point may be more important now than ever because the hourly workplace is going through a massive sea change.

TOP-PERFORMANCE SPOTLIGHT

THE EXERCISE COACH
Twin Cities, Minnesota

Amy Hudson operates three successful studios in the Twin Cities with a team of hourly "coaches" who provide personalized exercise training for clients. She's had success recruiting students from local colleges. Major employers in the area, like Target, are starting employees at 50 percent above minimum wage, so she does, too. For The Exercise Coach, however, the long onboarding and training process for new coaches is riskier. Certification of new team members as personal coaches requires a hundred hours of paid training. With that kind of investment, employee retention is vital. College students have rapidly changing schedules and lifestyles, so longevity is not something they're known for.

Amy struggled with retention during her first year in business, even when paying competitive wages. But she learned what her team members wanted beyond a paycheck. They wanted *growth*. They wanted to feel like they were developing personally and professionally. They wanted a sense of advancement.

So Amy devised a plan to facilitate their forward movement. She created a robust first-year development program where team members earn more money and opportunities as they acquire skills.

TOP-PERFORMANCE SPOTLIGHT, continued

The objective was as much about giving her employees a feeling of growth as it was about helping them improve at their jobs. "People want to feel like they're making progress," she said, "so we built that into our employee development plan." Every organization promotes employees and boosts their wages as they progress, but often the path is unstructured and unpredictable. Amy realized her employees wanted a more formal process where they could track and plan for advancement.

Part of their path forward is three to four performance reviews a year, where managers and coaches together review specific benchmarks. Amy personally participates in every coach's first review and always finds something positive to call out and reinforce.

New managers have weekly check-ins that include filling out a Google document that tracks KPIs. Amy doesn't just want managers who stay busy. She wants them focused on important metrics.

The company conducts monthly meetings for the entire team where every coach is expected to share a success story. They celebrate wins, review their Net Promoter Score, and talk about any concerns from clients and what can be learned from them. "I want to encourage a 'growth mindset,'" Amy told me, referring to Carol Dweck's seminal 2006 book *Mindset: The New Psychology of Success*, which encourages continuous learning and improvement. It's likely her team members would know the reference. The company offers the entire team optional participation in a book club, where together they learn about their industry as well as broader self-development issues. "The things I know in my 40s, I wish I learned in my 20s," she said. "I love facilitating this learning for my team members, and they really seem to appreciate it."

Together they also enjoy quarterly "fun events" and celebrate birthdays with gift cards and lots of acknowledgment.

TOP-PERFORMANCE SPOTLIGHT, continued

Since implementing her development program, retention has improved dramatically, along with employee enthusiasm. Team members now gush about the work environment:

"The last three years have been an absolute blast and by far my favorite job I've had."

"Amy does a great job creating a positive atmosphere at the studios, not only for clients but coaches as well."

"I have never worked at a place where I felt more appreciated and valued."

The entire purpose of The Exercise Coach is to help people be their best selves. Amy has learned to promote this growth in her hourly coaches as much as in her clients. Doing so has enabled her to build and retain her team and grow three profitable locations.

Top-Performance Takeaways:

- ▷ Keep salaries competitive and offer extra on-the-job benefits.
- ▷ Create opportunities to advance (even micro-opportunities) and a formal path for progression.
- ▷ Track progress against specific benchmarks and hold employees accountable.
- ▷ Promote team members' personal and professional growth.
- ▷ Celebrate wins.

The Hourly Revolution

I recently saw a bumper sticker that said, "A bad day fishing is better than a good day at work."

A similar sentiment was expressed by comedian Drew Carey on his sitcom *The Drew Carey Show*: "Oh, you hate your job? Oh my god, why didn't you say so? No, there's a support group for that. It's called everybody, and they meet at the bar."

Job dissatisfaction is nothing new. Ever since the invention of the clock, workers have been watching it, waiting for the workday to end. Gallup's "State of the Workplace" studies have consistently shown alarming rates of unhappiness among workers as well as low rates of employee engagement.

Historically, people have accepted work as something to be endured, and a willingness to suffer has been considered a virtue. The bills have to get paid. No pain, no gain. We must all make sacrifices. Those values, combined with people's need to have an income, have given employers tremendous leverage, especially when jobs are scarce. Many have been able to get by without worrying too much about employee welfare. Employees will stick around. They need the money.

But values change over time and with each generation. Millennials have grown up in a world that talks increasingly openly about mental health issues such as depression, anxiety, and eating disorders, making them less stigmatized. They're more willing to acknowledge these issues and less willing to live with them. Gen Z is even less inclined to "succeed at any cost" if the cost is their mental well-being. I grew up seeking success. Younger generations are seeking *balance*.

These differing priorities have created divisions in the workplace. Many bosses see these workers as overly sensitive, and many workers see bosses as uncaring. That tension has been festering since Millennials entered the workplace.

Then in 2020 the labor market was hit by one of the largest disruptions it has ever seen: COVID-19. It shut down businesses around the world. Employers were forced to let go of workers and jobs disappeared. People lost their lives, their loved ones, their incomes, their social connections. Zoom literally made our personal interactions two-dimensional. When we did venture out in public, half of people's faces were covered. No one knew when normal life would resume or what the new normal would look like. Everyone was scared and isolated. The demand for mental health services far exceeded what the industry could provide. It will be years before we know the full impact of the pandemic on humanity.

But we do know its effect on the workplace. Businesses reopened and invited workers back, only to find they didn't come. Having had time to think and reflect, a lot of people decided they didn't want to return to the same work environment they had before. Some believed this was because people preferred to stay home and collect free money from the government. (What could be better than getting paid to chill on the couch and watch *Tiger King*?)

But when that money stopped coming, the labor shortage continued. It turned out the "Great Resignation" was more complicated than initial assumptions. A combination of factors affected the labor market. Experts have cited a reduction in immigration and migrant workers—an aging population—and the start of mass retirement, child-care issues, and other concerns.

But here's the reason most relevant to our conversation: more options. Hourly workers have a lot more choices than before—and not just with traditional hourly jobs. There's a gig economy out there now that's very appealing to many people. During the pandemic, my 17-year-old son got his first job in fast food. Then he turned 18 and started driving for DoorDash and discovered he could make more money *delivering* fast food. He did it whenever he wanted, while playing music, and sometimes with friends in the car. One of those friends made good money putting videos on YouTube. Other former hourly workers have found remote work doing data entry, customer service, language tutoring, or sales.

The pool of workers who once relied on traditional hourly jobs had two years to search their souls and search the internet. They found options that provided more flexibility, better work-life balance, and more money. Those who did go back to the traditional hourly jobs found they had more choices. They chose—and will continue to choose—the best jobs for them.

This isn't about entitlement. It's pure economics. What happened was basic supply and demand. With more opportunities to choose from and fewer workers available, the supply of workers after the pandemic couldn't meet the demands of employers. In conditions like these, workers have leverage. It was as if a spontaneous worker revolution had occurred. The workers took over and demanded more from the employers who wanted them. The competition for employees became as fierce as the competition for customers. Things settled down somewhat in 2023, but the demand for great employees remains—and always will.

Your job, then, is to be *more* competitive. You need to become an employer of choice. And throwing money at the problem isn't enough. Anyone can offer higher starting salaries and signing bonuses. That won't make you stand out, nor is it how you *want* to stand out. Yes, you should pay people well. But there's a lot more to compensation than money. You should strive to create a best-in-class work experience. That's what drives top-performing teams. It's what the great leaders we'll talk about in this book do.

Most bosses won't. They're waiting for things to go back to the way they were. They've spent years calling their workers entitled, yet *they* feel entitled to a full team of loyal employees without any effort on their part. I'm not saying the new system is better or worse than the old one. I'm saying today is today, and tomorrow is coming. Yesterday is gone, and it ain't coming back. We need to look at our workplace through the windshield—not through the rearview mirror.

Because most bosses won't or are taking too long to update their practices, that's your opportunity to pull ahead. And honestly, it's your opportunity to become a better boss for your hourly workers, to bring out their best and help them grow. They want that from you. They *need* that from you. And when you level up and become a better coach, they'll become a better team that will help you run a better organization.

The first step is determining what level you're on now.

CHAPTER 2

What Kind of Manager Are You?

utomotive oil company Valvoline brought me in to present the closing conference keynote for their line of quick-lube stores, Great Canadian Oil Change. One of my messages in the speech was the importance of embracing change, continuously improving, and staying relevant.

Given the audience, I couldn't resist using the metaphor of changing oil. No matter how great the oil is when you first pour it into the engine, over time it gets dirty, becomes less effective, and needs replacement. But you can't add new oil until you drain out the old.

Without formal leadership training, most managers learn leadership from their previous bosses. Those bosses may not have been so great. Or maybe they were great at the time, but the tactics they used may not work today.

Because the workforce changes over time, so must your approach to management. You need to be willing to "change your oil"—to let go of old, outdated methods that may no longer work (or never worked well to begin with) and embrace new ideas that align with today's workers.

Updating Your Management Style

In the early 2000s, I paid big money to attend a marketing workshop for professional speakers. The entire workshop was about a then-exciting new concept known as "search engine optimization." The consultant explained what we could do to our websites to ensure they'd rank high in internet searches. But within a year, search engines changed their algorithms. Then came email blasts. Then social media. Then other ways of marketing a business. Almost nothing I learned during that expensive workshop was useful within a few years.

You may be asking at this point how you can find good employees, but the problem is that the answer is always changing. There are all kinds of factors that influence the number of available workers, where they look to find jobs, and what they want when considering opportunities.

What you really want to know is how to find employees in *any* climate. What are the perspectives and approaches to hiring that have always worked and always will? The same goes for managing and motivating: How can you ensure you'll always be an effective, top-performing, state-of-the-art manager?

The answers lie in a philosophical understanding of what *doesn't* change. Let's go back to the example of marketing. As we discussed, marketing strategies constantly evolve. What never changes is the need to know where people are looking, to make multiple impressions on them, and to make them feel something. Whether you market on the internet, a billboard, or a stone tablet, these are the universal rules of marketing. A great marketing strategy uses fresh ways to deliver on these timeless ideas.

Management works the same way. The labor market changes, but there are universal, timeless truths about workers you need to understand. And once you grasp the *philosophy* of great management, you'll be able to update your approach in the most effective ways. The concepts we're discussing in this book are evergreen. If you've found this book on your grandfather's bookshelf well into the 21st century, I promise it can still help you become a better manager. You'll always be positioned to build and maintain a top-performing team of employees, regardless of labor-force conditions.

Increasing Your Self-Awareness

I'm constantly asked by managers, "How can I get my employees to _____?" Fill in the blank: "work as a team," "step up their performance," "care about their work," etc. The question always focuses on fixing the employee. Rarely am I asked, "How can I improve as a leader?" In most cases, the answer to the second question will also resolve the first.

It starts with more self-awareness. Be willing to reflect on your thoughts and behaviors so you can have more impact on the thoughts and behaviors of your team. Most managers are too busy to reflect. They're so focused on everything that needs to get done that they don't realize how their leadership style may be affecting the process and their people. Or maybe they don't believe they're part of the problem at all. It always feels better to point the finger than to look in the mirror.

Please don't feel defensive. I don't know you or your employees. But I've generally found managers can do more to boost their team's performance. And the truth is, you _want_ employee underperformance to be partially your fault. Because if it is, you can do something about it. Taking responsibility is more empowering than laying blame. And it's easier to change yourself than it is to change others.

Your management technique doesn't have to be problematic to still be limiting. You may have built a functional team that gets the job done. But there may be a way to do even better, to go from functional to exceptional. Our objective isn't to be adequate but to be excellent.

Assessing Your Management Style

Let's begin by evaluating your current management methods. Please take a moment to go through the following assessment, shown in Figure 2.1. Don't think too much about right or wrong answers or about what you're "supposed" to think. Just go with your first instincts.

Figure 2.1. Management Style Assessment

For each belief listed below, circle the number that corresponds with how much you agree:

Belief	Strongly Disagree	Disagree	Neutral	Agree	Strongly Agree
1. Employees should follow orders without questioning them.	1	2	3	4	5
2. Employees should have a say in the decisions that impact their work.	1	2	3	4	5
3. Employees should have the freedom to work in the way that suits them best.	1	2	3	4	5
4. Leaders should inspire and motivate employees to do their best work.	1	2	3	4	5
5. The manager's role is to oversee and direct employees at all times.	1	2	3	4	5

6. The manager's role is to promote open communication and cooperation among employees.	1	2	3	4	5
7. The manager's role is to provide resources and support, but otherwise let employees manage their own work.	1	2	3	4	5
8. The manager's role is to empower employees to take ownership of their work and contribute to the organization's goals.	1	2	3	4	5
9. Employees should be closely monitored to ensure they're meeting expectations.	1	2	3	4	5

10. Employees should be trusted to make good decisions and contribute to the success of the organization.	1	2	3	4	5
11. Employees should be given the flexibility to work in their own way and manage their own schedules.	1	2	3	4	5
12. Employees should be given opportunities to grow and develop their skills and abilities.	1	2	3	4	5
13. The manager's authority should be respected without question.	1	2	3	4	5
14. The manager should be open to feedback and willing to adjust their approach based on input from their team.	1	2	3	4	5

15. The manager should provide guidance, but otherwise let employees manage themselves.	1	2	3	4	5
16. The manager should lead by example and inspire employees to excel.	1	2	3	4	5
17. Discipline is necessary to maintain order and productivity in the workplace.	1	2	3	4	5
18. Collaboration and teamwork are essential for achieving success in the workplace.	1	2	3	4	5
19. Autonomy and self-direction are important for employee satisfaction and productivity.	1	2	3	4	5

	1	2	3	4	5
20. A clear vision and sense of purpose are important for motivating employees to achieve their goals.	1	2	3	4	5
21. The manager is ultimately responsible for the success or failure of the team.	1	2	3	4	5
22. The success of the team is the result of everyone's contributions and collaboration.	1	2	3	4	5
23. The success of the team is largely dependent on each individual's ability to manage their own work.	1	2	3	4	5
24. The success of the team is driven by a shared sense of purpose and commitment to excellence.	1	2	3	4	5

OK, now let's add up your scores to determine your dominant management style/s:

Management Style 1: Add up the responses for Beliefs 1, 5, 9, 13, 17, and 21:   _____

Management Style 2: Add up the responses for Beliefs 2, 6, 10, 14, 18, and 22:   _____

Management Style 3: Add up the responses for Beliefs 3, 7, 11, 15, 19, and 23:   _____

Management Style 4: Add up the responses for Beliefs 4, 8, 12, 16, 20, and 24:   _____

The style with the highest score best represents your primary management method. You may lean heavily toward one style or have a balance of multiple styles. Let's look at each one:

Management Style 1: The Top Dog

This manager prefers to be in control. Communication tends to be one way. They say what to do and expect team members to do it. It's an autocratic approach to leadership that has advantages and disadvantages.

When there's a crisis, or when things need to get done quickly, a take-charge approach to leadership can be very efficient. Sometimes we need a strong general to get us through the battle, or a decisive coach to dictate the next play.

But while Top Dog leadership gets things done, it sometimes comes at the cost of team morale. Often these leaders speak in an urgent tone that doesn't feel too good to hear. They give feedback to employees without considering the impact of their words. They may also miss others' good ideas by failing to listen. Or maybe they just neglect employee welfare altogether because they're so focused on the task at hand.

Our close friends' 16-year-old son left his first job at McDonald's, which he loved, because he felt one of the managers was way too critical. The kid was happy to work *for* a manager but unwilling to get worked *by* a manager. This type of management can easily get too extreme (or be perceived that way), and workers will no longer accept that. For this style of leadership to work, managers need to know how far they can push for results without breaking their employees' spirit.

Top Dog management is best for urgent, high-stakes situations where a quick end result is the biggest priority, provided the manager actually knows what's best and can keep their severity in check.

Management Style 2: The Collaborator

This manager enjoys give-and-take with team members. Communication is two-way, and all ideas are welcome and considered. The additional input yields more perspectives, information, and choices. This style of management, in which decisions are made collectively, is empowering to everyone. People like to have a say, and when they do, they have more ownership in the outcome. Collaborators like to keep their teams happy. Giving employees a voice will do that.

But this style can also be inefficient. Consensus takes time. When things need to be dealt with immediately, this approach won't work. And not all work is suited for groups. There's a saying that "A camel is a horse drawn by committee." On the few occasions I've attempted to help groups write a mission statement, the result is a long, wordy sentence everyone has altered and no one likes. And when the stakes are high and work is stressful, there are a lot more personalities needing to be managed.

Collaborator management is best for brainstorming and making plans when the work is less time-sensitive or urgent, with employees who have lots of experience and knowledge.

Management Style 3: The Chillaxer

Sometimes referred to as a "laissez-faire leader," this manager prefers to hang back a bit ("chill") and let the team do its thing. That doesn't mean they don't care. They just don't want to get in the way. They see their team as smart and capable and want to empower them. They believe people learn best by doing and are willing to let employees make mistakes, knowing they'll learn from them. They also know skilled employees dislike being micromanaged and appreciate being trusted. The added space allows them to spread their wings. In this environment, employees can take risks and be creative. Steve Jobs was known as this kind of manager (when he wasn't top dogging!), famously saying, "It doesn't make sense to hire smart people and then tell them what to do; we hire smart people so they can tell *us* what to do."

But this style of management doesn't work well with unmotivated employees or those lacking proper training, ability, and/or confidence. They need supervision, direction, feedback, and accountability. I remember my son's basketball coach got so fed up with players pushing back on his directions that during one game he decided to give them what they wanted. He sat on the bench and let them play without coaching. Once they fell 26 points behind, the team captain reached out to him for help. The team had realized they didn't want a Chillaxer; they needed a Top Dog! The coach called for a time-out, reengaged in the game, and by the end got the team back within four points. They lost the game but learned some respect.

Chillaxer management is best for proven, skilled employees who have earned their independence and can be trusted to get results.

Management Style 4: The Visionary

While many managers work just to get through a shift, Visionary managers are all about the big picture. Everything they do is about supporting the organization's mission. They inspire their teams by speaking in broader terms, giving meaning and purpose to their work. Every Valentine's Day at Edible Arrangements, I started the day with a pep talk, reminding my employees that each fruit basket they were about to create would be an expression of someone's love. Every order was going to make someone happy and bring couples closer together. They liked having that strong sense of "why." Visionaries also focus a lot on employee growth and constantly facilitate their learning.

Visionaries have a wonderful larger perspective but often miss the important details of day-to-day work. Fulfilling a mission is great, but sometimes you just need to get the pizza sliced, boxed, and out the door. Visionaries aren't as effective with the *small* picture, and that picture matters a lot, too. The temporary help we brought in on Valentine's Day loved knowing they were doing important work. But that wasn't enough. They also needed to be told what to do so they could fulfill that mission.

Visionary management is great when team members need inspiration, purpose, and personal growth.

Now that we've discussed these four management styles, don't get too hung up on them. In spite of the many leadership and personality assessments out there, most people can't be accurately described with just one label. Nor are there just four ways to manage people. Human beings are complex. There's a lot of nuance to who we are and how we behave.

The point of the above exercise is to get you thinking about your management style and how it shapes the way you treat your team. It's easier to adjust when you know which way you lean.

It's also important to understand the difference between how you're inclined to manage and how your employees *need* you to manage. If you were leading a team of highly skilled employees with education, experience, and a salary, a less hands-on approach to management (Collaborator or Chillaxer) might be more appropriate. Scientists researching cures for cancer probably don't need as much close supervision or direction or a reminder of their big-picture mission. In an hourly setting, chances are greater your employees are newer and/or less skilled. You may have to be more engaged and direct (Top Dog) and may need to remind your team more often of their purpose (Visionary). Do this well, and you'll soon be able to lead them more as partners (Collaborator) and delegate to them more confidently (Chillaxer).

Be willing to shift your management style based on your people and the situation. (We'll talk a lot more about this in Part 3.)

TOP-PERFORMANCE SPOTLIGHT

KFC
Western U.S.

Justin Stewart and his brother Todd are second-generation KFC owners. Inspired by their father, the brothers built their own enterprise of 128 restaurants across multiple states in the western U.S., making them the sixth-largest operator in the system. They run

TOP-PERFORMANCE SPOTLIGHT, continued

the top three locations in the United States, and they're within the top 10 franchisees for average unit volume. In addition to ranking restaurants by sales, KFC assigns owners an operational ranking based on a combination of metrics. For seven of the last eight years, they've been the number one large operator (50+ locations) in the system. Last year they won Franchisee of the Year. Justin currently serves as president of the Association of Kentucky Fried Chicken Franchisees and as board chair of the KFC Foundation. I asked him to what he attributes his success.

"Recognizing our team," he said. "They do it all!"

Recognition really is vital to their operation. In fact, Justin correlates the timing of their top rankings with the implementation of their internal recognition program. Every high-level leader within his organization, including his executive team, district managers, and directors, is required to create and give out their own award. Something about that award must be personal to them to ensure it has meaning to the recipient. Each leader puts in a lot of time determining who should receive the recognition to ensure they reinforce the behaviors the company wants to encourage.

New employees start at 110 to 140 percent of local minimum wage. During the height of what Justin called the "war for talent," they out-recruited other quick-service restaurants via higher wages. They conducted local market studies in every region and offered an extra dollar an hour above their competitors to get people through the door.

"This was always meant to be a short-term strategy," said Justin, "and it paid off for us." He pointed out that high wages alone wouldn't solve their labor problems. "There's no use recruiting them if we can't keep them. We knew we had to be an employer of choice."

Every new employee begins by spending an entire day with the store manager. In addition to onboarding and job training, the manager

TOP-PERFORMANCE SPOTLIGHT, continued

introduces the new worker to all employees and works to cultivate a personal connection. "Other employers just want to throw new employees into the job. Taking time to build a relationship with them and bring them into the team has made a huge difference for us," he said. But this only works if managers themselves are well-trained, so new managers are mentored by the top-performing managers in the company. KFC awards "Best of the Best" recognition to the best 40 managers in their system. Last year, nine of the 40 were from Justin and Todd's restaurants.

Managers at every location are given a budget to recognize employees. They inquire during the hiring process about each person's favorite candy and other preferences so they can acknowledge employees in ways they'll appreciate. They also have parties, catered meetings, and company outings.

In addition to general appreciation gifts, employees are offered performance-based incentives. They can earn these through increased sales, lower drive-thru times, and other benchmarks critical to store performance. Employees enjoy meeting the challenges as much as receiving the prizes.

I hear a lot of complaints from those managing fast food employees. Justin is an outlier. "I love my team. They've changed my life in incalculable ways," he said. When we spoke, Justin was wearing a cap from Pebble Beach. He's an avid golfer, and his reliable hourly team enables him to get out on the links. "They've made everything I have possible." He recoiled at my referring to them as "employees." "They don't work for us," he said. "They work *with* us. It's a team, a family, and we all work together."

Justin and Todd have proved that even in the tough world of quick-service restaurants, you can still build a top-performing team, one employee at a time. "In the end," he said, "I'd like them to say we made their lives better because of working with us."

TOP-PERFORMANCE SPOTLIGHT, continued

Top-Performance Takeaways:

⟫ Out-recruit other businesses by offering an extra dollar per hour.

⟫ Retain employees (so you don't have to keep recruiting) by building a strong culture.

⟫ Create personalized awards and be generous with recognition.

⟫ Set aside a budget for tokens of appreciation.

⟫ Spend time with new employees at the beginning to ensure they feel cared about.

⟫ Find out early what employees like so you can use that to reward them.

⟫ Offer incentives based on performance and give employees specific benchmarks to target.

GSD vs. TLC

Many leaders lean toward being either results-oriented or people-oriented. Those focusing on results are what I call *GSD* managers, which stands for "Get Stuff Done." (Feel free to replace "stuff" with another word. I often do!) This is the objective of Top Dog managers. They want to achieve goals and hit their numbers. Employees are their worker bees. What matters most is the honey.

Then there are those who are driven by *TLC*, or "Tender Loving Care." They focus on people. They want to build a culture, they want employees to grow, and they see their role as the facilitator of that growth. Without people, the organization can't exist, and nothing can get done. Collaborators, especially, are very people-oriented, though that's also part of the Chillaxer and Visionary profiles. And while TLC sounds touchy-feely, the "loving" part of TLC includes *tough* love. A strong reprimand can be quite loving if the intent behind it is to help the employee grow. TLC isn't about making people feel good. It's about focusing more on people than on the product.

So which focal point is more effective, GSD or TLC?

John Zenger, CEO of leadership consulting company Zenger Folkman, and his team answered this question through their extensive study of more than 100,000 managers and more than a million of their employees. When they looked at managers who were described by employees as results-oriented but not people-oriented, only 9 percent of that group were perceived as great leaders. Then they looked at the opposite group—the managers who were perceived to be people-oriented but not results-oriented. If you've guessed this group did better, you're wrong. They did *worse*. Only 8 percent ranked among the top managers. It turns out employees don't like someone who's nice but doesn't get things done.

When they looked at those managers whom employees saw as both results-oriented *and* people-oriented, however, 82 percent of that group ranked among the top 10 percent of all managers. The vast majority of great leaders focus equally on results and people. This concept is echoed by a U.S. Army motto: "Mission first, people always."

Here's the rub. Each focal point requires using a different part of the brain. Results are achieved using the frontal lobe, while relationships require using the middle brain. Researchers have found that when one region activates, the other grows quieter, which they refer to as a "neural seesaw." That makes it difficult to focus on social issues while you're thinking analytically, and vice versa.

So you need to be deliberate about working toward results and growing your people. You must conscientiously switch from one focus to the other if you want to be as effective as possible. That's why self-awareness is so important, so you know what you're working on, and where you may need to put in more time.

Top-Performance Managers vs. Typical Managers

Another way to assess your management style is to compare top managers to typical managers. Both work hard and perform the same duties. But their approaches are quite different and lead to different results. Take a look at their contrasting perspectives on the same areas of management in Figure 2.2, and notice which manager your perspectives align with the most.

Figure 2.2. Management Perspectives

Management Perspective	Top Manager	Typical Manager
Primary objective	To facilitate employee growth as work gets done	To facilitate employee behavior so work gets done
Manager/employee relationship	Manager works in service of employees	Employees work in service of manager
Recruiting	Sells position, courts prospective employees, appeals to emotional desires	Runs ad, outlines duties and requirements, appeals to financial desires
Hiring	Builds culture	Fills positions
Interviewing	Keeps biases in check and looks for specific characteristics	Gets quick impressions and goes with gut
Selecting employees	Hires those who fit position and culture, prioritizes attitude	Hires those they like, prioritizes aptitude
Onboarding	Sets goals with employee, establishes healthy manager/employee relationship, explains work culture	Fills out paperwork

Training	Explains and demonstrates each task, confirms task mastery by asking employee questions and watching them perform, continues supervision until task is mastered	Shows employee how to perform each task and asks if they have any questions, puts them to work as soon as possible
Retention	Monitors employee needs, improves the employee experience	Complains about job jumpers, pays more to keep people
Motivation	Feeds a fire within them	Lights a fire under them
Coaching	Monitors employee skill set and mindset separately, addresses low performance, reinforces high performance	Looks for problems, offers occasional praise
Rewarding employees	Focuses on emotional payoff in addition to financial rewards	Focuses on financial payoff

Discipline	Remains level-headed, addresses issues fairly, holds employees accountable for responsibilities and culture, lets go of unfit employees quickly	Rules with iron fist or feathery finger, gives in to emotion, lets things slide, hangs on to unfit employees too long
Time management	Invests most time in developing employees and protecting culture, empowers other managers	Works on floor to fill employee gaps and save on labor, or rarely there and relies on other managers
Employee underperformance	Reflects on management before addressing employee	Blames employee

At first glance, it may seem like top managers are softer and more touchy-feely. They're not. When the situation calls for it, they're as tough as they need to be. They hire slow and fire fast. They hold employees accountable and let them know when they're not stepping up. Top managers defend the customers they're supposed to serve (consumers or other departments) and protect the culture. They don't tolerate underperformance or toxic behavior. But even in these situations, they're deliberate in their words and tone. They keep their emotions in check. They don't see "hard" or "soft" as conflicting management styles. They see them as two different tools they can use, depending on what the moment calls for. They're constantly asking what their team members need most in that situation to become better employees.

Is Management Ability Something You're Born With?

Gallup seems to think so. Their research suggests that only 10 percent of people in management positions have the talent to lead people. This group has the ability to "naturally engage team members and customers, retain top performers, and sustain a culture of high productivity." Some people come into the world already equipped with intelligence, drive, empathy, EQ, curiosity, humility, integrity, etc. If you're born with these traits, you have an advantage.

But even if you weren't, you can still develop them. Gallup also indicates another 20 percent of people have the potential to become strong managers, provided they receive adequate coaching and training. I've seen plenty of people become better managers. They've had to work harder and be more mindful about their thoughts and behaviors. They've had to go against a few instincts, change their thinking, and break some habits. But over time they gained influence and elevated their teams. You may not be among the lucky 10 percent. I don't believe I was. But you can get better. While talent is something you're born with, skill is something you can develop. Don't let the data discourage you from working to improve. As a great pilot once said, "Never tell me the odds!"

If you've hung in with me this far and you're open to improving as a manager, we can now actually start making those improvements. We'll get to helping your employees get better soon. But first, let's try to understand them so you can then start to influence them.

CHAPTER 3

Understanding Your Team and Increasing Your Influence

I n the 1981 movie *On Golden Pond*, Henry Fonda, playing a curmudgeonly old man, tries to build a friendship with a 13-year-old boy, Billy. Here's a memorable conversation they share:

NORMAN: What do you do out there in California? I mean, what does one do for recreation when one is 13 and not in school?

BILLY: We cruise chicks.

NORMAN: Hmm?

BILLY: Cruise chicks. You know, meet 'em. Girls. Try to pick 'em up.

NORMAN: What do you do with 'em when you have 'em?

BILLY: Suck face.

NORMAN: I beg your pardon.

BILLY: You know, kiss. Suck face. You kiss.

In shock, Norman's only response is to instruct the boy to go read *Treasure Island*. While Norman and Billy's generations may overlap in the world, they live in very *different* worlds.

This is also often the case between bosses and employees. Age, nationality, education, socioeconomics—all these factors can shape our views and make it hard to communicate and understand each other.

They also impact your ability to manage your team. Your role as a manager is to inspire employees and promote the behaviors needed by your organization. But to influence what your employees do, you first need to understand how they think. And that starts with understanding how *you* think.

Manager Subjectivity

At the end of the last chapter, I quoted a certain pilot. My fellow Gen Xers will recognize the *Star Wars* reference. Like many who were born between 1964 and 1980, I grew up as a latchkey kid. I was babysat by *Gilligan's Island* reruns and MTV. As my parents' investments grew, so did my mullet. (I'm being vulnerable here—don't judge.) Our generation feared the Soviet Union, sharks (thank you, *Jaws*), and Coke mixed with Pop Rocks. Our president was shot. We were taught manhood by Fonzie, Danny Zuko, and Hawkeye Pierce, and womanhood by Madonna, Oprah, and Molly Ringwald. Major historical events included the hostage crisis in Iran, the explosion of the space shuttle *Challenger*, and the AIDS epidemic. These factors, along with where I grew up and who *brought* me up, made me who I am. When we're in our formative years, the world around us shapes our perspective.

After our formative years, our perspective shapes how we see the world. No longer do we see it as it is; we see it in comparison to how it *used* to be. Society evolves faster than we do as individuals. The older we get, the more we struggle to keep up. The changes can be unsettling.

A lot has changed since I was a kid. Tattoos were once the marks of sailors and bikers. Today they mean you work at the Gap. Sending handwritten thank-you notes used to be standard protocol after receiving a gift or attending a dinner party. Today, even if people have stamps, many don't know how to address an envelope. Books were bought in stores, and Amazon was a river.

The workplace has also changed. No longer do people believe the customer is always right. Remaining with one employer for many years used to demonstrate loyalty. Today it makes you seem stuck. Smoking breaks have been replaced with Instagram checks. Quitting has been replaced by ghosting. Job interviews were once sacred, honored appointments. Today they're optional meetings for which applicants may or may not show up. Workers used to schedule their lives around their work, asking employers for time off to attend personal functions. Today workers increasingly let their bosses know when they'll be coming in.

When I look at today's workplace through my Gen X glasses (if such a thing existed, no doubt they would be Ray-Ban Wayfarers), I have strong feelings about many of these changes. A lot of the expectations and behaviors we see now conflict with my view of what's right, what's appropriate, and how things should be. It makes me angry. Not showing up for an interview? Are you kidding me?

But I've also learned that most suffering in life comes from the tension between our expectations and our reality. As workers change and our expectations don't, our frustration only increases. Even if the old ways of doing things really were more civilized and efficient, those days are over. And let's not forget those days came with their own problems, such as discrimination, sexual harassment, verbal abuse, and other stresses tolerated by earlier generations but not by the current one.

If your intention is to manage people today (and most certainly tomorrow), you need to check your belief system about how things *should* be and look at how things *are*, as objectively as you can.

Overcoming the "Kids These Days" Effect

When I turned 13, my dad let me start working at our family ice cream store in San Diego. The business was managed by my grandfather, Pop, a retired army pilot who flew bombing missions in World War II. (OK, maybe Han Solo was my *second* favorite pilot.) Likely inspired by his time in the service, Pop had a very top-down approach to leading employees. He told people what to do and expected them to do it. He leaned heavily toward Top Dog management.

This style worked well with his flight crew, but with young hourly workers, not so much. They never seemed to respond the way people did in the army. This was a source of deep frustration for him.

"I don't get it," he'd complain. "I'm not holding out on their paychecks. Why do they hold out on their effort?"

Pop's argument seemed logical—both parties should fully commit to their responsibilities. But anyone who's led hourly workers knows that's not realistic. Paying employees doesn't necessarily motivate them. That reality has led to a complaint that's been propagated as long as hired labor has existed: younger generations are worse than their predecessors. You've heard the comments and have probably said them. I know I have.

"Kids these days."

"It wasn't like this when I was young."

"These people are so entitled!"

"Back in my day . . ."

The employers making these comments forget these very things were once said about *them*. In 2013, *Time* magazine published a cover story called "The Me Me Me Generation," describing Millennials as "lazy, entitled narcissists who still live with their parents." More than three decades earlier, *New York* magazine ran a famous cover story by Tom Wolfe called "The 'Me' Decade," which discussed baby boomers' new focus on individual well-being rather than broader social concerns. In this case, the decade it referenced was the 1970s. Fifty years before *that*, in a piece called "The Conduct of Young People," *Hull Daily Mail* printed, "We defy anyone who goes about with his eyes open to deny that there is, as never before, an attitude on the part of young folk which is best described as grossly thoughtless, rude, and utterly selfish." And finally, "They [young people] are high-minded, for they have not yet been humbled by life nor have they experienced the force of necessity . . . And they think they know everything, and confidently affirm it, and this is the cause of their excess in everything." That was from Aristotle's *Rhetoric*, written in the 4th century BCE. The old have been hating on the young for millennia. It's likely that Aristotle's parents even complained about *him*. ("What's with this lazy kid? All he ever does is sit around and think!")

There's some interesting research from 2019 that explores the dynamic between generations. Social scientists from the University of California, Santa Barbara interviewed older subjects to get their take on younger people. They observed biases based on the older person's level of confidence in a given area and their idealized memories of their younger selves. According to the study's abstract, "Two mechanisms contribute to humanity's perennial tendency to denigrate kids: a person-specific tendency to notice the limitations of others where one excels and a memory bias projecting one's current qualities onto the youth of the past. When observing current children, we compare our biased memory to the present and a decline appears. This may explain why the 'kids these days' effect has been happening for millennia."

Scientific studies are great, but I pay a lot more attention to my mom. I recently complained to her about my son's lack of common sense. She responded by rattling off stories of my college years when I behaved with equal cluelessness. I couldn't argue with the evidence. Apparently I wasn't the smart, responsible kid I remember being. Further reflection made me wonder if, back then, I wasn't the reliable, hardworking employee I thought I was, either. Maybe I contributed to my grandfather's frustration.

Since *Time*'s cover story in 2013, Millennials have managed to advance their careers, start families, and mature just as well as every generation before them. Despite their participation trophies and screen addictions (which older generations love to criticize), today they run corporations, perform surgeries, and even govern countries. They've become important, independent contributors to society. But they're also aging. Listen closely, and you'll start to hear them complain about Generation Z.

Are today's workers really as lazy and entitled as many of us believe them to be? We're asking the wrong question. What we should be asking is what we need to do on our end to earn their devotion and grow them into the team we want them to be. If we're not willing to do that, then maybe it's not our employees who are entitled.

Replacing Judgment with Curiosity

Consumer behavior has evolved considerably over the years. The Industrial Revolution enabled the mass production of affordable goods, triggering an increase in consumerism. A century and a half later, the internet made shopping from home faster and easier. The global financial crisis in 2008 made people cut back on their spending and look for bargains. COVID-19 got a lot more people to order just about everything delivered.

Businesses have always adapted to these changes in consumer preference and behavior. They don't judge their customers or complain about what they want. They just notice and accommodate it.

The same shift is needed in hourly employee management. You need to set aside your opinions about workers and instead seek to understand them. Let go of how you think they *should* be and learn more about how they *are*.

Closing Generation Gaps

Let's go back to my family's ice cream store. My grandfather was part of the Greatest Generation, people born between 1901 and 1924. At our store, he led a team from Generation X, born decades later. There are huge differences between these generations that manifest in the workplace. Pop grew up at a time when job security was a top priority. Many workers spent their careers in one place. It was virtuous to be a "company man." My peers and I grew up watching the economic ups and downs of our Baby Boomer parents, making us more cynical about employers, and certainly less loyal. Pop grew up with more respect for authority. He and his peers were less likely to question their boss. They valued social protocol and professionalism. Imagine their horror when their Boomer kids grew their hair long, pushed for civil rights, and quit their jobs mid-career to go somewhere else. With that as our role model, we Gen Xers are even more likely to push back on employers and leave for something better.

These differences in values and expectations make it difficult for one generation to lead another, especially if management is two or three generations older than employees. It also makes it challenging to lead teams made up of multiple generations. I had one older male worker at Edible Arrangements who playfully handed a younger female employee a heart-shaped pineapple wedge. She took it as a sexual advance. I met with both employees separately to discuss the matter. The older man insisted he meant nothing by it. He reminded me of my father, who's always loved to put on the charm without any ill intent. But the younger woman felt very uncomfortable, believing he intended something more. It's possible the man really was making a pass. It's also possible he was an older guy attempting to express friendship to a woman in a way that was once acceptable in the workplace. I had no way of knowing for sure, but I took the younger woman's feelings seriously and issued him a written warning. Ultimately, every generation is accountable for meeting present-day norms. And when it comes to making people feel safe, there can be no gray areas.

Still, management needs to be empathetic and understanding. You need to see the workplace through the eyes of everyone who's in it. Knowing how every generation you employ thinks will help you interpret their behaviors and influence them to demonstrate the best conduct.

There's a whole industry offering insights into each generation. I'm not going to get into the specifics of these age groups in this book, as that information can easily be found elsewhere. You're only about 10 online minutes away from quickly learning about the values and needs of every working-age group.

What's more important is to appreciate that there are differences you must understand. And not just among generations—gender, nationality, religion, and other factors also impact how individuals think. You can't be an expert in all of them, but you should at least be aware of them.

You're probably associated with an organization that does market research. They learn enough about your customers to accommodate them. As a manager, get in the habit of doing *labor market research*. Be curious about the people you want to employ and those you already do, and do so with more curiosity and less judgment.

Reframing Your Observations About Employees

One way to shift your perspective is to reframe your subjective opinions into objective observations, or at least into alternative opinions that are less judgmental and more useful. For example, you may feel that your employees never want to work. Try restating that same idea, but without making assumptions or casting any negative judgment. You could say instead:

"My employees have limited availability."

"My employees have a lot of other responsibilities."

"My employees need more flexible schedules."

Another approach is to make the statement about you. For example:

"I don't know why my employees aren't more available."

"I need to seek out employees who are able to work more shifts."

None of these statements changes the facts. But they may change your perspective or your feelings about the situation. They may sound like excuses. They might also be *reasons*. This exercise really isn't about your employees. It's about you and your perceptions of their behavior. I'm not suggesting you enable unprofessionalism. Nor am I asking you to be more forgiving or even more positive. I just want you to be more constructive, to see their behavior in a way that reduces your frustration and increases your interest in coaching your team and finding solutions.

Let's spend a little time identifying and reframing your observations. On the left side of the table in Figure 3.1 below, list all the observations you've made about workers and how they challenge you. Next to each one, in the right-hand column, list some alternative thoughts and perspectives that may also be true. I'll get you started with a few examples:

Figure 3.1. Reframing Observations

Observations About Your Employees	Reframed Observations
My employees seem so unmotivated.	• My employees are working more slowly than I need them to. • Our work environment isn't bringing out the best in our team. • I'm not sure how to motivate my team. • I need to talk to my employees to understand how they're feeling and what might light their fire.

Job applicants aren't showing up for interviews.	· Job applicants aren't getting excited about coming to interviews. · We're still not selling the job well when people call to inquire. · We need to create a more personal connection to job candidates when they inquire about the job. · We need to improve our process for scheduling and confirming interviews.
My employees are so thin-skinned.	· My employees are more sensitive. · My employees are very in tune with their feelings. · My employees need a softer touch. · I need to be more empathetic. · I need to advocate for my employees' well-being. · I need to ensure we maintain a healthy work environment.

Hopefully this exercise is encouraging you to shift your perspective from complaining about your workers to better understanding them and to considering what you might do to help them. As I said earlier, I don't want to excuse them; I want to empower *you*.

TOP-PERFORMANCE SPOTLIGHT

INDUSTRIAL PACKAGING
Webster, Massachusetts

Industrial Packaging's stated purpose is "Protecting people, products, and brands throughout the supply chain." They do this with a team of hourly factory workers who provide packaging for a variety of well-known manufacturers in food, electronics, and other industries. On average they have around 100 workers on the production line, but their daily production needs vary significantly. To build more flexibility into their scheduling, 80 percent of their hourly workers are temporary help provided by an outside staffing agency. While that gives them the freedom to use only the help they need, it also allows workers whose needs aren't met to go elsewhere.

That hasn't stopped the company from building a unified, reliable team. In this case, "temporary" is more of a technical job status than a limitation on time. Half of their regular contracted help has worked with the company long term, many for more than 20 years. And you wouldn't know which employees on a shift are temporary and which are permanent. No one comes onto the plant floor without being trained in the company mission, values, and culture, and no one comes back unless they embody it. The company invests in training their temporary help and puts them on a path to higher wages and possible permanent employment. The workers love how they're treated and consistently request that the employment agency send them back for more shifts at market-rate wages (about 130 percent of the local

TOP-PERFORMANCE SPOTLIGHT, continued

minimum wage). The plant is never short-staffed, even when the staffing agency struggles to find workers for other clients.

The company works hard to keep everyone in the building happy. Their plant and production managers spend little time in the office, preferring to walk the floor and engage with workers. They keep the mood light and fun while ensuring everyone gets what they need to hit their targets.

Once a week, the company sponsors "Thankful Thursday," where employees are treated to coffee, ice cream, pizza, or other edible tokens of gratitude. For Thanksgiving, workers are given turkeys to enjoy with their families. The company also hosts cookouts and other social events, both on- and off-site. And since many of their team are Spanish speakers, the company sponsors English as a second language (ESL) classes on weekends. I asked Industrial Packaging president Ed Cote if that's only offered to permanent employees and long-term temps. "We extend it to anyone who raises their hand," he said. Permanent hourly workers also get an extensive benefits package that includes all the usual insurance along with 401(k) matching, student loan payoff, and even pet insurance.

Employee satisfaction is measured weekly among all workers. When they come in, there's a tablet where they can tap an emoji that corresponds to how they're feeling about their work environment, allowing the company to easily calculate their "employee net promoter score," or eNPS (discussed in Chapter 13). On a scale of -100 to +100, Industrial Packaging's eNPS consistently hovers around +72. To put this in context, the average eNPS in the manufacturing sector is +9. Employees can also add comments and suggestions anonymously, allowing them to provide candid feedback. The company uses this information to find ways to improve the employee experience.

TOP-PERFORMANCE SPOTLIGHT, continued

Team members report they love working for Industrial Packaging because:

"The team spirit. It's present. It's clear every day. It's from the top to the bottom."

"The positive environment."

"A unified team that's always got your back."

"It's a company that recognizes and rewards good work. It's a place where your voice is heard, and everyone is respected."

"You really feel valued as an employee. They're continuously offering you opportunities to grow and learn."

It's almost a cliché for employers to say their team works as a family. In the case of Industrial Packaging, some even feel it's a great place *for* their family. As one team member said, "Every day I go home to my wife and talk about it. I love this company. It has helped me grow. This is the first job that I actually enjoy. Maybe one day my sons can come work for this company!"

Top-Performance Takeaways:

> ◊ Consider using an outside staffing service. Then become an employer of choice for whom workers will request shifts.
> ◊ Train everyone who works for you in your company culture, regardless of their job status.
> ◊ Keep your shifts efficient but fun.
> ◊ Make employee appreciation a ritual.
> ◊ Measure employee satisfaction regularly.
> ◊ Consistently solicit feedback from your team on how to improve the work environment.

Increasing Your Influence

This book is about what you can do to influence your employees' behavior. Thus far, we've talked about how you need to think to be influential. Now let's spend a little time looking at how you need to *be*.

In Aristotle's *Rhetoric*, in which the philosopher rags on young people, he also describes three modes of persuasion. The first mode he calls *logos*, which means "logic." People need data, information, and reason to understand an argument. As a manager, you need to understand the inner workings of your operation and be able to communicate them to your team. In Part 3 of this book, we'll talk more about training and how to boost your employees' skill sets.

He also discusses *pathos*, or emotion. If you can get people to feel something, you can persuade them to do something. Much of this book is about understanding the emotional needs of your employees and creating a work environment where they feel safe, engaged, and motivated. It's easier to get them to do their best work when those needs are met.

Aristotle's third mode of persuasion is *ethos*, which translates to "character." It means behaving in a way that gives you credibility. If I trust you, I'll listen more closely to what you have to say. It's why consumers pay attention to online reviews and word-of-mouth. It's why athletes listen to winning coaches who've taken time to build a relationship with them. It's also why employees prefer bosses who are people-oriented *and* results-oriented. Their track record makes them credible.

Previous generations gave employers respect based on their job titles. That was enough to establish ethos. Not anymore. These days, authority must be earned. You need to behave in ways employees like and respect to get them to behave in ways *you* like. And that's something *I* like. No one is entitled to anything, including respect. If younger generations are forcing bosses to up their game, that's a good thing. We all need to be held accountable.

So how can you increase your credibility and up your game? It comes down to three things: character, connection, and competence (see Figure 3.2).

Figure 3.2. The Credibility Triangle

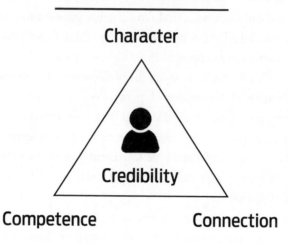

Character

Credibility

Competence · · · Connection

Let's look at each one in turn.

Character

Who you are and *how* you are matters to your employees. No one likes a boss who cuts corners, breaks rules, or preys on customers. They don't want to work for someone who belittles their employees or gossips. Workers want a role model. Employees are watching the way you act, the way you work, and the way you *live*. But true character is about how you behave even when *no one* is watching. When you always do the right thing, you never have to worry about getting caught.

Character is easy to understand conceptually. The hard part is practicing it, especially when there's temptation. The wrong way of doing things is often easier, more profitable, or more fun. When I was a teenager, a group of us were invited into a movie theater for free by a friend who was taking tickets at the door. One member of our group was home on spring break from West Point. Instead of walking in with the rest of us, he bought a ticket. Why? Because of the West Point honor code. I never forgot that. Seeing his higher standard of behavior made me much more self-conscious of my own. That's what being a good role model does.

In an hourly work environment, you can demonstrate character in a few small ways that make a big impression. Follow the company rules, systems, and protocols. Be in uniform and show up on time. Speak respectfully, not just to people but *about* people. That includes customers, other managers (and upper management), and most certainly employees. Always tell the truth and follow through on your promises. When you make a mistake, be willing to admit it. These are all the things you want your employees to do. Show them how to be the person you want them to be.

Legendary UCLA basketball coach John Wooden once said, "Be more concerned with your character than your reputation, because your character is what you really are, while your reputation is merely what others think you are." Living this way didn't just win Wooden the respect of his players. It also won him 10 national championships in 12 years.

Competence

If character is who you are, competence is what you *do*. Doing it well is important to being influential. Winning 10 national championships commands respect. So does winning awards, driving sales, and hitting company goals. Employees want to work for a winner, for someone who gets things done. That's why it's important for you to be great at your job. Your technical skills will go a long way toward making your workers want to listen to you.

According to a 2016 article in the *Harvard Business Review*, "Modern evidence demonstrates, for example, that hospitals may do better if led by doctors rather than by general managers, that U.S. basketball teams do better when led by a former All-Star basketball player, that Formula One racing teams do better if led by successful former racing drivers, and that universities do better when led by top researchers rather than talented administrators." The authors of the article studied 35,000 randomly selected employees in the U.S. and the UK. They determined that "the benefit of having a highly competent boss is easily the largest positive influence on a typical worker's level of job satisfaction." Among the American workers they studied, the impact of a technically competent boss was even more significant on employee satisfaction than a high salary.

Work to improve yourself as much as you work to improve your organization. (Embracing the ideas in this book will help.)

Connection

People relate to each other in one of two ways: by *what* they are or by *whom* they are. Throughout the day we interact with people based on what they are. If you buy a bottle of wine at the store, you bring the bottle to the register, where the cashier rings it up and tells you the price. You pay and receive a receipt. You thank the cashier, who wishes you a good day. Both of you are relating to each other based on *what* you are: a customer and a cashier. The encounter may have been friendly, but you're not friends.

That evening, you bring the wine to a dinner party. There are handshakes and hugs. You ask about each other's lives. You share stories and laugh, and you get to know everyone a little better. At certain points there's some vulnerability and reveal of emotion. It's a nice evening that brings everyone closer together and an experience everyone wants to *re*experience sometime soon. You've related to each other based on *who* you are. You have no feelings about the cashier who sold you the wine. But for these friends with whom you drank it, you'd do anything.

Many bosses see their employees only as what they are: as personnel, not people. They may say please and thank you, they may offer some praise or even politely ask about their personal lives, but they don't acknowledge their individuality. They don't consider their employees' desires, fears, or humanity. They don't make their employees feel seen or cared about. And that disconnect is typically reciprocated—all the employees see is a manager, not a person who happens to be managing.

People who make us feel seen will more easily earn our trust. They matter when we matter. In the introduction, I mocked the platitude, "Nobody cares what you know until they know that you care." But we really do respond to people we feel are invested in our growth.

You can't be friends with your employees, nor can you remember every detail about them. But whatever you can do, whatever moments you can share with them will go a long way. When you hire and onboard an employee, sit down with them and have a conversation. Find out a little about them and share a little about yourself. Ask about their life goals and how this job might help move them a little closer to those goals. Find a way to relate as people, appropriately but warmly. Continue having those conversations. Look for moments to *re*connect whenever you can.

Many hourly workers lead some pretty tough lives. Your workplace might be the *best* place where they spend time. Maintain boundaries, but be real, be compassionate, and be kind. Shuckin' Shack Oyster Bar CEO Jonathan Weathington put it quite simply to me: "Just be nice to people. If you can just offer an ounce of being a pleasant person, they'll run through a wall for you."

These first three chapters have been all about you and your impact on your work environment. It's that important. *You're* that important. Who you are matters as much as what your employees do, because you might be the reason they're doing it (or not doing it). If you can accept that responsibility and continuously work to be the best manager you can, you're ready to create the best team you can.

We begin by designing your ideal team culture.

PART 2

BUILDING YOUR TOP-PERFORMING TEAM

CHAPTER 4

Designing Your Ideal Culture

In December of 2022, I took my family to Paris. For five days we immersed ourselves in the French lifestyle (at least from the tourist's perspective!). We strolled along the Seine. We sipped coffee. We scarfed baguettes. We savored the rich food and admired the chic fashion. But of all the things we experienced, nothing distinguished French culture more than what we witnessed while we were there: the FIFA World Cup finals between France and Argentina.

With the Eiffel Tower looming in the background, every café and bar in Paris was packed wall to wall with people. Outside, crowds three persons deep peered through the windows, eyes glued to the TV. For more than two hours, millions of Frenchmen collectively cheered, groaned, and bit their nails.

We were watching through a café window ourselves late in the game when French forward Kylian Mbappé scored the third goal against Argentina to tie the match. Every soul in Paris lost their minds. Cheers, victory fists, car horns—it was total mayhem. The entire crowd in the café stood on their chairs and sang a celebratory anthem my family had never heard before.

While it was a beautiful moment to watch, it was not our moment to experience. This celebration was *theirs*. These people got to watch *their* people bring hope and pride to their country. The coolest thing in the world to be at that moment was French. The kicking of a ball into a goal 3,000 miles away united this country in a way we American tourists could only admire as outsiders. Ultimately Argentina won the match on penalty kicks. The collective joy shared by the French became collective heartbreak. It was disappointing but no less unifying. The entire country had come together as one. That night, the most French thing about France wasn't the food; it was the fellowship.

While I didn't get to participate in that particular sense of unity, I've experienced it in other groups. I've felt it at UCLA basketball games (Go Bruins!). I've felt it at rock concerts. I've felt it on Thanksgiving with my family and on the Fourth of July with my neighbors. And in my later years as a business owner, I experienced it many times with my employees. There are few things more meaningful than feeling bonded to those around you. If you've played sports, practiced a religion, or served in the military, you know how powerful a connected community can be.

You've probably also experienced the opposite. Maybe you've been in a dysfunctional group or toxic work environment. Perhaps you've feuded with a neighbor. You know what it's like to coexist with people you *don't* like. Every group of two or more people has a culture, a way of being together that either unites and elevates its members or divides and diminishes them.

Building a cohesive culture is one of the most powerful ways to turn your hourly workers into a top-performing team. Employees who only work for money won't do it for long, and won't do it well. Those who work for each other and are engaged in collective efforts are the ones who thrive and last. Culture and engagement are not the same things, but they're correlated. According to Gallup, a strong workplace culture leads to a 50-point increase in employee engagement over three years and an 85 percent increase in net profit over five years. Culture really matters.

Bad work cultures exist because they're allowed to. It's one thing to have one or two bad employees slip through the hiring process. But when a team doesn't function well, that's on management. Culture depends on *you*.

What Is "Culture"?

Let's start with what culture *isn't*. It's not compensation. It's not benefits. It's not perks, privileges, or anything else your company gives employees. In researching this book, I conducted numerous searches for the best companies to work for. The internet is full of lists. But when you look at them and see the basis for the rankings, often they're rated solely on what employees get. That means those workplaces offering the most money and perks have literally bought themselves a place at the top of these lists. Compensation is important, true, but it's not the same thing as culture— and it's not the only thing that matters to employees.

Culture is a group's unique way of functioning together (good or bad). It's their social norms. It's their combined thoughts and collective interactions. Culture is how multiple people behave as a unit. It's their combined identity.

Every group has a culture. The best exist by design. Most emerge by default. One summer in college, I was one of the original bellhops hired to start at a new resort. My school schedule prevented me from starting for a week, and that's all it took for a new culture to form among the bellhops. It became a competition to see who would greet guests pulling up in luxury cars (who were presumably bigger tippers). Newer bellhops had to carry all the luggage during training, and more experienced ones would keep the tips. My trainer started only a week before me and explained to me, "That's how it's done." Management never defined a culture for us, so we created one ourselves. It wasn't a positive one.

Everyone pays lip service to the idea of building culture, but few prioritize it. It's not as tangible as sales, marketing, or inventory. It doesn't feel like you're getting things done. In a stressful, fast-paced environment, who has time to discuss mission, values, and relationships? There's too much to do. "Order up!"

Even among those who really do want a great culture, many don't know how to create one. "I just don't understand!" complained one restaurant owner to me. "I do so much for them but they just don't seem to care." She listed all the ways she's nice to employees, such as buying them food, paying them compliments, and rewarding them with gift cards. She believed, like many others do, that commitment comes from kindness.

But culture isn't something you can earn through good deeds, like someone in a fairy tale. It's something you build. Like a physical structure, it needs to be well-designed, carefully created, and scrupulously maintained.

Team Building vs. Culture Building

"Team building" is the gathering and uniting of people into a cohesive group. "Culture building" is designing how these people—regardless of who they are—will interact. A team recognizes its unique members and plays to each person's abilities. A culture, on the other hand, isn't about the individuals but about what goes on between them, even as some people leave and new ones arrive to take their place.

My nephew joined a fraternity at UCLA that in my day was known as a party house. Decades later, in my nephew's time, that was still the case. The members have come and gone, but the traditions, the handshake, the welcome rituals (i.e., hazing) are the same. For better or for worse, cultures outlast their members.

It's easier to build a team in a salaried environment because the workforce is more reliable. Talented people are paid salaries because of their unique, essential skill sets. They stick around for a while, so you can create ways of doing things based on what each person has to offer.

Hourly workers tend not to last as long. As we discussed earlier, they turn over three times as much as those on salary. With that much coming and going, it's risky to build an operation that relies on specific people. Even with better retention rates, your door will be constantly revolving. That means your team is constantly *evolving*.

Both salaried and hourly environments need strong cultures, but without being able to offer higher wages or long-term career opportunities, hourly environments must rely on culture more. Your people will change, so you need a strong, stable culture to sustain performance.

Building Healthy Cultures

You have a culture among your team right now, although it may or may not be the one you want. Your most important responsibility as a leader is to clarify how you want your culture to be and do the work to promote it. It must be created and maintained on three different fronts:

1. **In the Head:** Employees must understand their culture intellectually.
2. **In the Heart:** Employees must feel their culture emotionally.
3. **On the Floor:** Employees must experience their culture through what's actually happening on the job.

When all three things happen purposefully and consistently, your culture will drive employees to perform at a higher level. When they don't, your culture will limit what your team can do.

Let's examine the difference between a healthy work culture and an unhealthy one. Take a look at Figure 4.1 below:

Figure 4.1. Healthy vs. Unhealthy Work Cultures

Workplace Elements	Healthy Culture	Unhealthy Culture
Focus	"We" focus	"Me" focus
Mission	"We're going to achieve our goals."	"I'm going to achieve my goals."
Accountability	Employees hold each other accountable.	Employees mind their own business.
Communication	Information flows to whoever needs it.	Ideas and information are withheld.
Interaction	Co-workers demonstrate trust and respect with entire team.	Team is splintered.

Collaboration	Employees do their part to support others' work.	Employees focus solely on their own work.
Employee growth	Emphasis on employee development and work excellence	Emphasis on tasks and work completion
Employees' perception of management	Respected, appreciated, seen as mentors	Disrespected, feared, seen as authorities
Management's perception of employees	Believes in them, feels grateful and encouraged	Expects little of them, feels frustrated and cynical
Feedback	Employees receive consistent praise and redirection.	Employees wonder how they're doing.
Relationships	Strong social bonds, care for one another, compassion, family	Disconnection, indifference, animosity, dysfunctional family
Beneficiaries	Organization, employees, and customers all benefit from the work being done.	Some benefit at the expense of others.
Compensation	Focus on what employees get and how they feel.	Focus only on what employees get.
Work environment	Challenging, energizing	Toxic, draining

Work ethic	Employees exert maximum effort.	"Quiet quitting"
Service	Employees serve customers.	Employees serve themselves and/or management.
Employee satisfaction	High ratings and eNPS (see Chapter 13), positive online posts	Low ratings and eNPS, negative online posts

Many workplaces have an unhealthy culture. Most are a mixture of healthy and unhealthy. Our goal is to make your workplace resemble the healthy culture as much as possible. But that won't just happen. You must make it happen.

The Two Elements of Culture

Culture is made up of two distinct elements: how your team *thinks*, and how it *behaves*. Their collective thoughts and behaviors define them as a group. See Figure 4.2 below:

Figure 4.2. Two Elements of Culture

Culture

Thoughts

- Purpose
- Mission
- Focus
- Beliefs
- Values

Behaviors

- Ethics
- Customs
- Rituals
- Interaction
- Communication

Great organizations build their culture by formally taking control of both elements. Earlier in the chapter, I referenced sports teams, religion, and the military. These institutions excel at building cohesive groups. They accomplish this by establishing ways of thinking and behaving that are unique to that culture. They define their beliefs and values and establish practices that align with them. When they do this well, their members are passionate and unified.

These dynamics are also found in cults, gangs, and other *un*healthy environments where people seek a sense of belonging. These groups, too, have shared beliefs and rituals that promote passion and unity. Ultimately they are destructive, but they excel at meeting (and exploiting) needs their members aren't getting fulfilled elsewhere. People will latch onto community wherever they can get it and embrace the norms of the group to remain part of it. That's the power of culture—and of cults. There's a reason the two words are so closely related, etymologically speaking.

But you don't want a cult in your workplace. Your goal is to build a healthy, constructive culture that benefits everyone it touches. We're going to show you how to do that by establishing the specific thoughts and behaviors that will define (or redefine) your workplace.

TOP-PERFORMANCE SPOTLIGHT

WALFINCH INDEPENDENT HOME LIVING
Wantage, England

The senior in-home care industry is one of the biggest employers of hourly workers. Given how much care is needed for the large aging population, companies providing homecare have no problem finding clients. Their problem is finding enough caregivers. This is especially true in affluent areas such as Oxfordshire, England.

Still, Walfinch Independent Home Living managing director Amrit Dhaliwal has found a way to attract and retain care workers at a much higher rate than industry averages. Most companies in home health care can only hang onto 35 percent of their workers annually. Amrit's retention rate is 85 to 90 percent, and that's with paying typical

TOP-PERFORMANCE SPOTLIGHT, continued

industry wages, which are approximately 25 percent over the local minimum wage.

Amrit has found that applicants who are referred by current team members are more likely to last on the job than those who come through external sources. He and his managers strive to create a work experience worthy of those referrals.

It begins with the interview. Amrit and his management team go out of their way to make all applicants feel special, especially compared to the other workplaces they're considering. When the applicant arrives, they find a parking space reserved for them with a sign welcoming them by name. The personalized welcome is repeated inside on a video monitor. Then the interviewing manager offers the applicant a hot beverage. "We've run A-B tests and have found applicants are much more likely to accept the position if offered a coffee or tea," Amrit said.

As difficult as it is to find care workers, Amrit still holds applicants to the highest standards. He'd rather turn away new clients than hire unfit caregivers. "If I wouldn't trust them to look after my own mum," he said, "I won't trust them to look after someone else's." A full-time care worker is worth tens of thousands of pounds per year to his business, so he would rather invest his time training and supporting the right people than constantly replacing the wrong ones. "You can stop the recruiting and retention problem by hiring the right people," he said. The "right" people don't all have a caregiving background, but they do have the right mindset.

He also invests a lot in training his management team, especially in soft skills. And because their workforce is out in the field, they stay in contact with them via weekly phone calls and site visits. Part of this is supervision, but equally important is giving their team of 50 to 60 care workers a feeling of connection and belonging to the company.

TOP-PERFORMANCE SPOTLIGHT, continued

Additionally, they celebrate workers' birthdays, send handwritten notes of praise and recognition, and plan quarterly social events.

"We also clarify their availability upon hiring them and never ask them to work outside of that time," he said. "We want them to know we respect their lives outside of work."

Care workers love working for Walfinch, saying:

"The management are open and honest with you, listen to you, have good communication skills, and show that they value you as a team member."

"The reason I stay here is simple ... This is the only care company where I have felt appreciated and valued."

"I don't feel like I'm only a number."

"I really feel at home with Walfinch and go to the team about any issues."

"I share the same values. I am really listened to, and we bounce around ideas to ensure we achieve our goals."

In addition to personally owning the Oxfordshire branch, Amrit has franchised the business and is scaling the operation and its culture across the United Kingdom. The company has received multiple awards, nominations, and recognition from the Homecare Association and other professional organizations. "It's all about the people," Amrit said. "That's the heart of what we do."

Walfinch are specialists in care. Applying their mission to their workers as well as their clients has made them an employer of choice and a top-shelf care provider for lots of UK "mums."

Top-Performance Takeaways:

⟫ Make every job applicant feel special. Treat them as a valued guest.

⟫ Maintain high standards, even when short-staffed.

TOP-PERFORMANCE SPOTLIGHT, continued

》 Train your managers on how to lead people, not just the operation.

》 Hire for mindset more than for skill set.

》 Send your employees regular, handwritten notes with praise and recognition.

》 Keep your employees connected to the company and to each other, even if they don't work together.

》 Offer applicants coffee and tea!

Defining Your "Why"

I'm sure you can appreciate the differences between a vision, purpose, and mission statement, but your hourly workers probably don't. Mine didn't. When I tried to explain my vision for what we can be a part of, the reason why we exist, and the great things I wanted us to achieve, they weren't particularly moved. The concepts were too abstract.

That's the problem with all the pageantry around organizational "statements." Too often these declarations of mission and purpose are written at 30,000 feet and are totally inaccessible to those doing the work on the ground. When I ask my audiences how many of them even know their organization's mission statement, I rarely see many hands go up.

Mission statements are often broadcast to the world but aren't instilled in employees. They're worded beautifully but communicated poorly. Sometimes they sound more like marketing jargon written to impress customers and/or investors rather than to inspire and guide employees. And some are so grand that hourly workers dismiss them altogether. If the Bill & Melinda Gates Foundation declares, "Our mission is to create a world where every person has the opportunity to live a healthy, productive life," I believe them. They're doing that kind of work and operating on a global scale. When a small frozen custard business states it wants to change the world, I don't see how it can, and neither will its hourly employees. The mission statement is out of proportion to the work being done. Delighting a customer with a frozen treat is wonderful. It's even important. But it's not going to change the world. Speaking in those terms may lose you credibility with your team—and prevent you from legitimately inspiring them with the work they actually do.

I coached a couple in Australia whose mission statement was "to empower people to go out and do extraordinary things." So how did they do this? That's the problem. The statement revealed nothing about what they actually did. It was overly broad, vague, and interchangeable with any organization. And it wasn't aligned with how their employees spent their time.

As it happened, the couple was opening a skin care clinic. In their own unique way, they wanted to empower people, but their mission statement didn't specify how. I advised them to incorporate their unique approach into their statement. They eventually changed it to "We boost people's confidence by providing high-quality skin care." The new statement still has an aspirational element to it—boosting confidence. It's important to communicate the *why* behind what they do. It reminds employees they're doing more than applying skin treatments. But it's also grounded in their tangible work. That's the real function of a mission statement—to connect the work being done with a higher purpose. Help your employees be proud of what they do without pretending they're doing more.

I personally like mission statements, but you don't actually need one to give your employees purpose. The language is less important than the idea. I never had an explicit mission statement at Edible Arrangements, but my team understood that we were creating beautiful fruit baskets to help people celebrate special occasions. They knew this because we constantly talked about it. We always discussed the emotional needs of the people who placed orders and the reactions of the people who received them. It was obvious we were trying to create a certain feeling. We always talked about the occasions people were celebrating and how we contributed. When our team made people happier, we praised them. When they just sold fruit baskets, we reminded them that wasn't good enough.

If you're going to write an official statement for your hourly team, keep the language simple and the conversation ongoing. A beautifully written mission statement will die if left to linger on a poster. Keep the spirit of your mission alive through constant discussion and reinforcement. If you're part of a larger organization, there's probably already an official mission statement. Be sure that anything you create aligns with your parent company's objectives.

Defining Your "How"

Clearly communicating your mission creates a singular focus for your team. It gets everyone working toward the same goal. But *how* they do that work also matters.

While it's unnecessary to write a formal mission statement, I do think it's important to codify your values. Values are the principles that inform your behavior. They're the things you prioritize above all else.

Each of us has our own value system that has been instilled in us by our upbringing, environment, and experiences. That value system determines how we live and work. If what you value most is profit, you'll focus on making money. If you value human connection, you'll sacrifice other things to maintain those personal bonds.

Your value system isn't just a list of things you care about—the order in which you rank them is also important. We might both value ambition and health highly, but if we rank the two differently, it will influence our choices. One of us might wake up early to get a head start on our work, while the other heads to the gym.

That brings us to the problem of conflicting values. It's harder for people to collaborate when they're driven by different values. If you value adventure and your spouse values relaxation, it's going to be harder to plan a vacation. My son once played in a basketball championship. With only two minutes left and a close score, one of his teammates hadn't been put into the game. The coach had to make a decision. Should he sub in players based on what was best for the team, or should he make sure every kid gets to participate? The coach was a good man who valued both winning and inclusion. But which did he value *more*? Which did the team value more? They had discussed this possibility before the game and collectively agreed what mattered most was winning. So the kid stayed on the bench, better players were put in, and the team won the championship. In the victory photo, all the players had medals in their hands. The kid who didn't get to play also had tears in his eyes. The team's value system didn't mesh with his, and he ultimately left the team. When individual and group values don't align, someone suffers.

Your employees won't coalesce the way you want them to if they're driven only by their individual values. Some will want to socialize while others just want to work and leave. One person will pursue recognition while another pursues advancement. Some will work on behalf of the team while others care only about themselves. Buying them pizza or paying them more won't change that. Neither will hanging up a poster that says, "There's no 'I' in team."

It also won't work to ignore the values of your individual employees. If someone values family more than anything, you can't expect them to skip their sister's wedding to cover a shift. As with any healthy relationship, you must find a way to balance everyone's needs. There must be some reasonable give-and-take.

The idea behind culture building is to enroll everyone in the same value system and get them working toward the same goal in the same way. The process entails three steps:

1. Identifying job candidates who already have the same or similar values that you want in your workplace (We'll discuss this more in Chapter 7.)
2. Teaching and instilling these values
3. Reminding, reinforcing, and living these values

But you can't do any of these things until you determine what your values are. Once again, if you're part of a larger organization, they may already be established, in which case you need to make sure your local work environment honors those values. If they don't exist, then you need to decide what matters most in your workplace.

Some companies express their values in single words. For example, The Coffee Bean & Tea Leaf states their values as Friendliness, Respect, Ownership, Teamwork, and Honesty (expressed as the acronym "FROTH"). Others, such as Chick-fil-A, use phrases: "We're here to serve," "We're better together," "We are purpose-driven," and "We pursue what's next."

Like mission statements, values are easily declared and just as easily ignored. They only matter if you're going to infuse them into your daily operations. Chick-fil-A leans heavily on the above four values in their recruiting and employee evaluation process. Ritz-Carlton requires team members to carry their "credo card" on their person, outlining what they call their "Gold Standards." They review these standards in a daily lineup meeting. Great organizations wrap everything they do around their values.

All this may seem very touchy-feely. But remember, something is driving your employees. If you can influence their drivers, you can change their performance.

Deepening the Meaning of Your Values

It's important to avoid abstraction. Do your employees really know what you mean by "integrity" or "compassion"? Explain what it means to honor each of your values. What does "integrity" look like in the workplace? What does a lack of "compassion" look like?

I was once hired by a restaurant group in Texas to revamp their culture. They already had a solid list of values, which included things like "respect," "excellence," and "teamwork." They discussed these concepts a lot with employees.

The problem was that their discussions were vague, almost academic. They would say during meetings, "Remember, we stand for respect and excellence. These are important to who we are." Employees would nod their heads. But what wasn't clear was specifically how they were supposed to demonstrate respect and excellence in their work and how they would be held accountable.

So I had them go deeper with each value by listing four to six bullets for each one, explaining the dos and don'ts behind them. For "respect," they said things like:

"We only speak kindly to one another."

"We accept each other's differences."

"We disagree without being disagreeable."

They did this for each of their seven values, resulting in several dozen specific behaviors they clearly understood and agreed with. The exercise made their values more accessible, and the specificity made it easier to hold employees accountable.

The more clarity you can bring to your expectations, the more likely it is that your hourly workers will meet them. Take your values off the pedestal and put them on the floor where your people are.

Clarifying your mission and values will help your team work toward the same goals in the same way. They are the foundation for building culture—but they're not enough. You also need to influence behaviors that reflect this thinking.

CHAPTER 5

Living Your Culture

A while back I was brought in to deliver a motivational presentation to workers at a manufacturing plant. The company website proudly described its strong culture and explained how its dedicated "family of employees" was the foundation for its success. It claimed it was totally committed to being a "people first" organization.

So why were they bringing me in? Because they were about to shut down the plant and outsource production overseas, so they wanted me to offer some encouraging words as they prepared to lay everyone off. The only reason the workers didn't feel the company violated their values was that they had no idea what those values were. The organizational principles existed in the "About Us" section of its website—and pretty much nowhere else.

Every organization is free to decide who and how its going to be. There's nothing wrong with a *profit first* value system—unless the organization claims to be something else. Companies whose practices contradict its stated values breed mistrust within its organizations.

In the introduction, I described a young man working the pizza counter at the mall food court. As he repeatedly mumbled, "Next in line," his co-workers pushed out trays. "Order number 56!" Meanwhile, a poster on the wall listed the company's top core value as "Delighting Customers."

Plenty of organizations map out their culture on paper, and that's where it stays. They post their mission and values on their website or on the wall but don't act on them.

Healthy, deliberate culture only succeeds when it's infused into your operation. For it to mean something to your hourly team, it must transcend abstraction and become tangible. That means highlighting it, referring to it, and living it in visible ways. It must influence every policy and practice. It should reflect what you're trying to do (your mission) and be executed in a way that honors who you are (your values).

Remember that every group has a culture. If you don't set out to create one, it'll develop on its own. And that one will probably cost you time and inhibit your operation. A culture that you design and create from scratch will *save* you time by reducing your problems. Your team will perform at a higher level—and they'll do it together. Your workplace will be healthier, more attractive, more retentive, and a lot more productive. Employees will feel more joyful and pass that feeling on to customers.

So many of the great leaders I interviewed for this book said the same thing when I asked how they build culture: "It starts with the top down." They walk the talk. They don't outsource culture to posters. They demonstrate it and celebrate it. More important, they use it to manage their teams.

In this chapter, we're going to look at specific ways to incorporate culture into your daily operation to ensure it boosts performance. Many of these ideas may seem like kowtowing to employees, as if being extra nice will make them work harder. That's not what this is about. We're not trying to make them feel happy. We're making them feel loyal, connected, and committed, which is different. Even if you have the budget to pay them well, these feelings can't be bought. They must be *earned*. That requires creating specific conditions proven to engage hourly teams.

You're going to operationalize your culture through two approaches: rituals and practices.

Rituals and Practices

Rituals are a series of repeated actions rooted in tradition and social agreement. They're associated with religions and ancient civilizations, but we participate in common rituals every day. Blowing out birthday candles, saying "bless you" to someone who sneezes, and clinking glasses in a toast are all rituals. There's no legal requirement to do this stuff. But willing participation in these traditions keeps us civil and connected.

Practices are formal, predetermined ways of doing things, likely rooted in rules and official procedures. Things like yielding to pedestrians, waiting in line, and making/taking reservations are accepted ways of interacting so we all understand what's expected of us. They help society function more smoothly.

Often rituals and practices overlap in the same setting. Think of an evening at the theater. The actors remain backstage prior to performance. Superstition dictates they never utter the name "Macbeth," lest they risk giving a disastrous performance. Nor (in the U.S., at least) does anyone say "good luck," as the traditional wish for a good performance is "break a leg." When the lights go down, the audience knows to stop talking. They remain quiet (hopefully) unless there's a joke to laugh at or a song to applaud. At the end of the show, the actors take a bow and the audience applauds. If the performance went particularly well, the audience stands up while applauding. These are all rituals that are part of live theater: widely understood behaviors that help create the experience.

But there are also common practices that *regulate* the experience. Audience members buy tickets and go to assigned seats. Programs are distributed. Refreshments are sold in the lobby. Blinking lights and chimes indicate the show is about to start. Smoking isn't permitted and cellphones are requested to be silenced. No one is allowed backstage. These procedures keep the evening functional for everyone.

In a business or other organization, rituals are rooted in team protocol, and procedures are rooted in the operation. Both must be optimized to achieve top performance. A great culture won't last long if it's not part of your daily operation. And your daily operation will hit a low performance ceiling if the culture isn't there to elevate it.

What follows are a number of rituals and practices you can implement (or modify) to elevate your organization. Some of them may not appeal to you, while others won't apply to your workplace. All of them are in use somewhere. Hopefully, you'll find a nugget or two you can adopt or adapt for your business.

Welcome Customs

New employees have probably applied for other jobs and may still be communicating with those employers when they start with you. You need to make a good first impression so they mentally commit to *staying* with you. You also want to set them up for success.

It's nerve-racking to start a new job—not just because they're having to learn how to do new tasks, but also because they're joining a new team. People worry about how they're going to fit in, what their social role will be, how to remember who everyone is, and how people get along. A first day at work is like your first day at a new school. Remember, we create culture on three fronts—in the head, in the heart, and on the floor. Your first priority is the heart, which means easing those first-day feelings.

Begin with a memorable, warm reception. Hang a sign with their name and perhaps some festive decorations to welcome them to their new family. Have co-workers greet them at the door with a round of applause. Give them a welcome basket or bag of goodies. You'll never get another opportunity to create this moment, so give them something to tell their friends and family about.

Rituals like this also communicate something to the rest of your team— that new people are important and should be treated with kindness. Your team is probably wondering how this new person will impact the work environment. A good welcome ritual cuts through that initial iciness and promotes camaraderie.

I met one business owner who sends new employees home with a small gift for their family and a note thanking them for sharing their loved one. He commits to protecting their well-being and invites the family to visit the workplace sometime. This may seem a bit over-the-top, but it's an interesting way to win over an employee's family and stand out from other employers. As the owner told me, "You can never have too many people telling your employees how lucky they are to work for you!"

Be sure to take photos of your welcome customs. Share them with the new team member and post them on social media. Let the world see your hospitality toward your employees and see how you should be the employer of *their* choice.

Farewell Customs

How employees depart is just as important as how they arrive. Even if you're glad the person is leaving, publicly thanking them for their contribution sends a message to the remaining team that everyone matters. In Chapter 3, we talked about recognizing people for who they are, not just what they are. A good farewell lets your entire team know you see them as people, not just as workers.

Perhaps give the outgoing employee a parting gift and/or a card signed by team members. Get them a cake. Obviously, if they're leaving on bad terms, this may have to change. But do your best to wish everyone well. Every time someone joins or departs, it affects the social dynamic of your workplace. Use these moments to reinforce your culture and remind everyone that they're valued. The farewell ritual is really about those who are staying. And if employees appreciate these customs, they're more likely to give you proper notice when their time comes to leave rather than ghost you.

Try to conduct an exit interview, too. Find out what they liked and didn't like about their work experience. Ask what could have been done to improve things. This might be the most honest conversation they ever have with you. Try to learn from it.

Employee Onboarding

You may be eager to get new recruits working as soon as possible, but you also want them to stay. Before you train them on the job, train them in your culture. Don't just tell them what your mission and values are. Discuss them. At In-N-Out Burger, no one puts on the red apron until they've watched a series of videos explaining their culture and ways of doing things. A lot of great hourly workplaces use videos, information packets, and even quizzes to confirm new employees understand the culture they're joining. Make sure new employees appreciate who you are as an organization, not just what you do. Share stories of your culture so they can understand how your workplace is different. Even better, have other employees explain the culture. It'll be more credible if it comes from co-workers.

This is also a good time to assign them a mentor—perhaps the same co-worker who explained the culture. Mentors (sometimes called "coaches," "big brothers/sisters," or "buddies") can offer guidance without eliciting the anxiety new employees sometimes feel around their boss. Co-worker mentorships promote a more collaborative atmosphere and get your team invested in one another's success.

Also use this time to establish your relationship with the new employee. Explain your management style. Inquire about their goals, how they'd like to grow, and what kind of management they respond to. Find out what they like (which you can use later for rewards and incentives). Explain your approach to providing feedback. Let them know you'll be checking in with them from time to time, and what to expect from those conversations. Help them see you as an advocate for their growth, not just an authority figure.

Never underestimate the emotional rawness of starting a new job. The faster you build their confidence, the faster you can train them for competence.

Honoring Uniforms

Clothing creates community. Sports jerseys and caps, college sweatshirts, military battle dress, and other uniform attire don't just identify people's affiliations—they promote them. But the power of clothing doesn't lie in what people are wearing. It's in their relationship to it. There's a pride that comes with visual affiliation. It feels good to be part of an institution with other members. Clothing is a way of saying to the world, "I'm part of *this* group."

That's how you want your employees to relate to the clothing you provide them. Whether it's Walmart's blue vest, UPS' browns, or anything with McDonald's golden arches, the smart use of uniforms can create a sense of belonging.

One of the best examples I've ever seen is the bright, crazy costume worn at Hot Dog on a Stick. Employees wear shirts striped in what they call "red, white, and blue with a splash of lemonade." The matching mod beehive caps are so coveted by customers that employees are required to keep them in the store. Most people wouldn't be caught dead dressing this way. But Hot Dog on a Stick doesn't employ "most people." Their "hotdoggers" are bubbly brand ambassadors who wear their stripes with pride. A few years back, the company brought me in to spend half a day training store managers. The off-site event was at a nice hotel, but every manager arrived dressed from head to toe in red, white, and blue with a splash of lemonade. (And yes, I absolutely snapped a pic with them!) Outwardly the uniform promotes the Hot Dog on a Stick brand. Inwardly, it promotes the Hot Dog on a Stick *spirit*. Jenn Johnston, CMO of parent company FAT Brands, shared with me the impact of their iconic outfits:

"The uniform is so recognizable it has catapulted the brand into a cultural phenomenon," she says. "It captures perfectly the sunny, entertaining spirit of Hot Dog on a Stick. When you have well-known celebrities calling your headquarters to request uniforms as Halloween costumes, you know the brand has arrived. Our hotdoggers love that, and it deepens their pride in the company. *They* are Hot Dog on a Stick, and the uniform reinforces that."

Make a fuss over your company clothing. Don't "issue uniforms." Instead, give them "swag." Put the uniform in a gift bag, perhaps the one you give them on their first day. Or consider starting them with a low-key (i.e., cheaper) shirt or hat and let them earn the official gear once they complete training. Make it a moment when they earn their stripes. Offer additional branded clothing as prizes and incentives.

Presentation matters, and so do rituals. Honor your colors. Let employees feel lucky to receive a uniform, rather than burdened to wear one.

Badges, Stickers, and Symbols

In addition to providing uniforms, acknowledge team members with visual tokens of achievement. The military issues chevrons and bars. Ohio

State University presents football players with helmet stickers after each winning game. Some organizations recognize exceptional performance with custom challenge coins. The meaning of these keepsake symbols often exceeds the value of consumable gift cards. (And they may be more tax-deductible. Ask your accountant.)

Starbucks recognizes their "coffee masters," employees who complete a course of study at their Coffee Academy, with their prestigious black apron. Disney Resorts housekeepers who complete their training period "earn their ears"—customized Mickey ears and a Disney-themed graduation ceremony. McDonald's team members earn star pins as they progress through four areas of training: quality, service, cleanliness, and operational excellence. Home Depot employees earn "Homer Awards" for excellent job performance; multiple Homer Awards can eventually add up to bronze, silver, gold, platinum, and diamond Homer Awards.

Sometimes the best thing to give employees is a positive feeling, and a small token of appreciation can have a big effect.

Daily Huddles

Many of the businesses I've encountered have daily discussions, not only to review the day but also to reinforce the company philosophy. Some require employees to share one way they've furthered the company mission or demonstrated one of their values. These conversations can break employees out of the automatic habit of working without thinking.

Ritz-Carlton famously has every employee at every property participate in a daily lineup meeting to review the day's events and discuss culture. Mendocino Farms, with locations in California, Texas, and Washington state, holds huddles that include identifying a "customer of the day," chosen from among their regular guests to receive a welcome message on the counter chalkboard and a free lunch. Their intent is less about marketing and more about reminding their team to focus on guests. They also have a "value of the week," and each team member must share how they intend to live that value in their position that day. Their co-founder, Mario Del Pero (with whom I created 30-Second Leadership), who's been involved in several restaurant concepts, loves to include two minutes of peer-to-peer appreciations in his huddles, reinforcing the care and respect employees have for one another. Throughout this book, you'll read about other employers of hourly workers who use daily huddles to boost morale, strengthen culture, and engage their team.

There's no one ideal way to facilitate a daily huddle, but here are a few tips to keep them productive:

⟩ **Keep your huddles short (10 to 15 minutes).**

⟩ **Consider having employees lead the huddle, the same way sports team captains might get players pumped up before a game.** This reminds them that the culture belongs to them.

⟩ **Stand, don't sit, to keep people focused and alert.**

⟩ **Always start on time.**

⟩ **Standardize the format.** This is a ritual, so it should be consistent and predictable. You may have to experiment at first to figure out the ideal agenda. Just remember it needs to be informative and inspirational.

⟩ **Clarify what topics are appropriate for discussion.** This is not the time for brainstorming or problem solving. The objective is to set a tone for the shift, share important information, and pump up the team.

⟩ **Keep the huddle interactive.** It shouldn't be 15 minutes of you talking and them listening. Instead, make it a discussion.

⟩ **Include staff from multiple stations and departments to keep your team united and not siloed.**

⟩ **Ask each person to share one goal or promise for the day.**

⟩ **Reference both what needs to get done and something related to culture so the team is reminded that the two elements are connected and hold equal weight.**

⟩ **Keep the huddle positive.** Acknowledge individual and group accomplishments. Share positive reviews from customers. Use this time to elevate your team's feelings. The huddle should be something they look forward to, and it should boost their spirits.

Don't underestimate the power of a huddle. It's a short time investment that will yield many long-term benefits.

One-on-One Meetings

Many workers only receive attention from the boss when there's a problem, so they're intimidated by the idea of talking to you. But they shouldn't be. You don't have to be scary to boost your team's performance. They'll still respect you when they see you as their advocate, the same way an athlete respects a coach. Players see their coach as someone who's there to facilitate their growth and hold them accountable. That's how you want your team to see you. And a great way to promote this kind of relationship is through regular one-on-one meetings.

One-on-ones are not performance reviews or reprimands. Those are also important conversations to have, but not during one-on-ones. These serve a different purpose. They are frequent conversational check-ins to discuss and refine their performance. They're an opportunity to strengthen your relationship with employees and help them improve—and a way to communicate that you care about their success. If they're done well, employees will look forward to them. Here are some ideas for doing that:

> » **Schedule them on a regular basis.** You'll need to determine what's practical for your business. The data shows that most employees want more frequent and more immediate feedback. According to a 2022 article from Gallup, "When employees strongly agree they received 'meaningful feedback' in the past week, they are almost four times more likely than other employees to be engaged." It may be tough to do one-on-ones weekly, but even a quick, spontaneous compliment or suggestion will remind them you're invested in their success.

> » **Keep the conversation two-way.** The worker should be doing at least 50 percent of the talking. One-on-ones aren't about teaching— they're about facilitating learning, which is different. Listen with an open mind and ask questions. What they realize on their own (perhaps with a little prompting from you) will have more impact than what you tell them. Keep in mind that questions like "Do you think you'd benefit from more practice?" aren't really questions. They're statements pretending to be questions. You're better off asking open-ended questions, like "What could you do to improve

your skills?" If they don't get there on their own, then you can make suggestions.

⟫ **Start with a personal check-in.** In other words, begin by relating as people. That reminds the employee you see who they are, not just what they are. Ask about their lives and show genuine interest. Obviously you should remain professional and maintain appropriate boundaries.

⟫ **Follow that with a work check-in.** Ask how they're feeling about work, what they're doing well, and where they'd like to improve. Often they'll point out issues on their own so you don't have to. Offer suggestions and ask how you can be of help.

⟫ **Address any other issues they didn't bring up.** Be sure to offer constructive advice and not just criticism. The one-on-one is not an intervention. It's a collaborative performance discussion. The employee should leave the meeting feeling informed and encouraged. Save the reprimands for other conversations as needed. (We'll discuss these in Chapter 11.)

⟫ **Offer praise.** Most people get a lot less praise than they need. Use this time to acknowledge what they're doing right to make sure they keep doing it. (We'll talk about this in Chapter 10.)

⟫ **Discuss their future goals.** These should be identified during onboarding and should be part of your ongoing conversations to remind them their job is part of their larger path forward.

⟫ **Ask for any ideas they have for improving things.** They'll appreciate having a voice.

Promote Gratitude

Acknowledgment makes employees feel good. What might feel even better is helping them acknowledge *others*. Neuroscientists have shown that there's a release of dopamine and serotonin, which help create a sense of happiness and well-being, when a person either gives or receives thanks. So instead of always giving employees a thank-you gift, provide a gift they can give to someone else. Ask team members to identify someone in their life who makes a difference for them and pay for flowers, a gift card, or another token of appreciation on their behalf.

Also get your team to start acknowledging one another. One of the most powerful team-building practices we used at my stores was a simple validation exercise. We went around a circle, focusing for a few minutes on each person. During that time, team members told that co-worker what they appreciated about them. For two to three minutes, each person heard nothing but love and praise, which many of them weren't getting anywhere else in their lives. My team *loved* this exercise. Be sure to keep plenty of tissues around.

Social Time

The majority of employers profiled in this book plan occasional social events for their teams. Most of these experiences aren't rewards for performance but simply time devoted to helping their employees interact as people, which strengthens their bonds.

Social events can be on-site or off-site. I had success with both. My teams enjoyed having weekend picnics at a park. We also had potlucks at the stores. I often bought them food. But when employees prepared and shared their own food, the gatherings felt more personal. There's a difference between consuming a meal and contributing to one. The act of sharing is powerful.

One Qdoba franchisee has found success with Wednesday "Family Night," also a potluck. Their employees love the weekly ritual, and it's given them better retention rates than other restaurants in the chain. An owner of a Mighty Auto Parts franchise told me that when his delivery drivers return their vehicles to the garage and shut everything down, they'll usually hang out together for an additional hour. He keeps them on the clock and insists that that hour of fellowship is the best labor dollars he spends. It creates team bonds among employees who otherwise work alone. Payroll services company Paychex organizes "mystery coffees" that randomly connect two team members from within the company for 15-minute virtual coffee chats. (They also maintain a team of "Culture Champions" who volunteer to act as role models and promote their organizational values.) Socializing doesn't have to be formal to promote camaraderie.

Having said that, formal social events can be effective if done well. Any team can get a pizza party. That's not special. (As my Gen Z nephew told me, "Young people see a pizza party as a cheap way to say sorry for screwing them over. It comes off as disingenuous. We're not in third grade.") Pizzas feed people—they don't bond them. You want to be more thoughtful about how you facilitate social connection. Your events should get people talking. It's not enough to share a meal or have fun. You want them to get to know one another better and forge closer relationships. Seeing a movie is fine. Talking about a movie is better. Even at casual parties and meetings, you might want to take them through sharing exercises that help them learn more about each other. We played games like Public Interview and Two Truths and a Lie, and our team loved it.

Team building exercises are enjoyable, but they won't have much effect unless they're followed by a debriefing discussion. Solving a problem or completing an obstacle course together might lead to lots of high fives and temporary euphoria. But the long-term value comes from discussing what they did, what they learned, and how those takeaways can promote more collaboration at work. Practical application is what really matters.

Social time is highly productive. Keep your team engaged with one another, and they'll be more engaged in their work.

Community Service

The "cause marketing" movement has inspired many organizations to become more active in their communities. Not only is this a great way to keep your name out there, but it's also a powerful way to unite your team and boost morale. According to a 2016 survey by consulting company Deloitte, "Millennials who frequently participate in workplace volunteer activities are more likely to be proud, loyal, and satisfied employees, as compared to those who rarely or never volunteer. These and other findings suggest a link between volunteerism and several drivers of employee perceptions of positive corporate culture."

Volunteering brings out the best in people. It's a chance for your team to do some good and interact in a less stressful environment. Many organizations put a lot of emphasis on this, creating "teams" that do charity walks, community projects, and fundraising events. Often they'll create special shirts for their teams to wear, tapping into the unifying power of uniforms.

The course for AIDS Walk Los Angeles passed in front of one of my stores. My team handed out free strawberries and pineapple slices to walkers and loved participating in the day. They always offered to do it unpaid. I paid them anyway to demonstrate my commitment to the cause (and to avoid any potential labor issues). Lots of walkers were volunteer teams representing their own companies. Like my employees, these groups were talking, laughing, and sharing a powerful experience.

Home Depot's volunteer force, "Team Depot," has donated millions of volunteer hours helping to improve the lives and homes of veterans and those impacted by natural disasters. Lowe's partners with a number of national organizations to do similar work through their "Lowe's Heroes" volunteer program. Retailer Kohl's combines volunteering with financial donations through the Kohl's Volunteer Program. For every hour associates volunteer for eligible charities, Kohl's donates $25 to those organizations.

Many companies hold fundraisers, give away a percentage of their profits, or have counter jars to collect change for charities. These donations can make a big difference to their communities. But don't mistake giving for volunteering. For the purposes of this discussion, we're trying to get your employees to actively put in time collaborating on behalf of a cause. Their service will have as much impact on their own team as it will on those they serve.

Social Media Postings

Social media is a big part of modern living, and many people look for a sense of community there. Use that to reinforce your culture. Make your social media pages fun places for employees to engage. Encourage them to post comments. Ask them to share photos and videos. Use your pages to celebrate wins, acknowledge birthdays and milestones, and honor the humanity of your team. You want your employees to put down deep roots in their job, so give them a place to experience their work community and feel a sense of belonging. This is also a great way to market your workplace for potential new hires. Let them see how positive and dynamic your work environment is. Monitor your pages closely to ensure all posts reflect your organization well.

Monitoring and Measuring

Measurement is important for any initiative. You need to verify whether your efforts are having the desired effect. We'll talk about how to evaluate and quantify culture in Chapter 14. Just be prepared to monitor it as you would sales, costs, and productivity.

Hopefully by this point you've found a few ideas that might work for you. What's more important is the theory behind these ideas. Tactics can change, but there are some universal themes here that are timeless. The purpose of creating your culture is to promote employee loyalty and pride. When you appeal to employees at that level, you're more likely to retain your team and boost their performance. Your efforts must be ongoing. A culture isn't just something you talk about and build once. It's something you live and maintain.

TOP-PERFORMANCE SPOTLIGHT

STEAMER CLEANERS
Sherman Oaks, California

If you've seen me present live anytime over the past 20 years, it's likely you've seen me wearing clothing that's been cleaned by Steamer Cleaners. Founded by Shawn Basseri and his wife, Nicole, more than 30 years ago, this neighborhood dry cleaner is a fixture in the Los Angeles suburb of Sherman Oaks. Their website boasts, "Steamer Cleaners is the proud winner of Best of LA, *Los Angeles* magazine, SOS Go Green Club Community Recognition Award, Reader's Choice Award by *LA Daily News*, and My Fox LA for Best Dry Cleaner in Los Angeles." CINET, a global professional textile care organization, named them the number four dry cleaner in the entire world.

More important than any of this, my wife really likes them. I'm not picky when it comes to my dry cleaning, but customer service means a lot to me. Shawn and Nicole's team of 24 employees consistently provides my family and thousands of others with the exact kind of warm, friendly, fast attention you want from a business. I've seen the same faces there for years. They have counter workers who've been there for 8 to 10 years, pressers who've been with them for 17 to 18

TOP-PERFORMANCE SPOTLIGHT, continued

years, and a manager who's been there for 25. Shawn told me that he spends more time in the business with the team than he does at home, so his work family is a top priority. His wife and two daughters are also actively involved, so this truly is a family business in every sense.

Shawn explained that dry-cleaning work has an image problem. "It's not fun, happy work like at Edible Arrangements," he said. (He clearly has never worked at one.) "Dry cleaning is perceived as steamy and dirty, like a sweatshop."

That makes staffing one difficult. He advertises when short-staffed and hires based on "fit." I asked how he makes this determination. "I look for people who reflect our business," he said. During their two weeks of probation, he watches to see if they smile. Do they look customers in the eye when they walk in? Do they seem genuine when they welcome them with the signature greeting: "Hello, welcome to Steamer Cleaners!"?

"There's a feeling you get during the first few weeks," he said. "If I don't feel they reflect who we are, I let them know this may not be the best job for them. They typically don't last."

Shawn would rather put his time into retention than recruiting. Employees start at 107 percent of the minimum wage and receive their first $1 raise after the two-week probation period ends. They also receive bonuses for providing enhanced customer service, such as parking lot trunk delivery, collecting email addresses from customers, and keeping customer credit cards on file. Employees receive a 50 percent discount on their own dry cleaning, but all orders must be entered into the system by another team member.

Shawn checks in with each employee daily and makes a point of using their name when he greets them. He pays attention to what they share about their personal lives and always asks how things are going. "Be close to them," he told me. "Talk to them and let them see that you care."

TOP-PERFORMANCE SPOTLIGHT, continued

Shawn can be a bit flexible when it comes to employees clocking in before getting into uniform or attending to personal matters on company time. If someone overdoes it, he gently reminds them what's expected. "It's about mutual respect," he said. But he's not flexible when it comes to performance. Every position has standards, and he tracks them closely. He showed me the reports on his desk. Counter service workers have benchmarks for order accuracy. Spotters (those doing the cleaning) must have a limited number of "rejects" (unacceptable cleanings). Pressers must also have minimal rejects and press a certain number of pieces per hour. He watches these numbers closely and holds his employees accountable. He also has team members who focus entirely on quality control. His employees know what's expected of them and work to hit their numbers.

I dislike running errands, but I'm always happy to pick up the dry cleaning. Delivery is available, or I could stay in my car and request trunk service. But the hourly workers at Steamer Cleaners provide such a pleasant experience that I look forward to coming inside. Anyone can clean my shirts. Steamer Cleaners brightens my day.

Top-Performance Takeaways:

> Treat your team like family. Build a personal relationship with them.
> Hire people who fit your culture and reflect your brand.
> Start new employees on a probationary period.
> Pay attention to how your employees interact with customers and make sure their warmth is genuine.
> Greet your employees by name.
> Give your employees clear performance standards and measure them closely.

Changing Existing Cultures

There's a good chance you're already managing a team. In that case, instead of building a culture from scratch, you may need to rebuild an existing culture. That entails undoing some of the current ways of your workplace, which can be tough. Trust takes time to earn, and habits are hard to break. Your team will have strong feelings if you try to introduce new ways of doing things.

Unlike teams, cultures don't depend on specific people. They're about the ongoing norms of a group. So if you have a current culture that isn't working well, you might need to change your team. Specifically, you might need to let go of the people who are preventing the culture from becoming what it needs to be. That's easy for me to say because I'm not the one who's trying to run your organization. I'm not feeling your staffing pressures or the stress of losing someone who has an important skill set. But I have felt those things when I was running my own business. Looking back, my biggest regret is hanging onto the wrong people for too long.

Culture is aspirational, and re-creating it might take some time. Do what you need to do in the short term, but you should always be working toward creating the culture you want.

Starting the Conversation

Begin with a discussion. Gather your team and ask how they feel about the current culture. You may have to define what culture is in the workplace. Be sure to distinguish between a culture and a team, and make sure they understand this isn't a conversation about specific people. This isn't the time to name names or assign blame. This is about how everyone can think and behave to enhance their work environment.

Ask them to describe their ideal workplace, and have them brainstorm the characteristics of a great team. Ask them what thoughts and behaviors might be preventing them from having an ideal workplace. (Again, stick to generalizations without finger-pointing.) Consider conducting a blind survey to get additional feedback. They'll appreciate you asking the questions.

Emphasize that culture belongs to everyone. Each team member impacts your culture, positively or negatively. Explain that at your workplace, everyone is expected to make it better. Everyone must protect it.

It's not enough for employees to do good work. They must also demonstrate good *team*work.

If you already have a formal mission statement and values, now is the time to revisit them. If not, now's the time to introduce them. Many leaders like to include employees in defining their whats and hows. I don't. I find these conversations counterproductive. It's often hard to reach consensus, and hourly workers may find the exercise too abstract. It's better if leadership—after collecting feedback from the team—explains what the organization's culture should be and why it's important.

Explain your intention to make this a better workplace and let them know there will be some new initiatives that will strengthen their culture. As you introduce new rituals and practices, explain their purpose. Ask the team to stay open-minded. Assure them you welcome their feedback, but you expect their buy-in.

Expect some pushback. Employees are used to doing things a certain way, and some will have a hard time with the changes. Others will question the motives behind them. Some might not be a good fit for the new culture you intend to create. This is where you may have to make some hard decisions.

Changing the Team

I've learned from experience that everyone is replaceable. I had some team members in my business who seemed essential. They had amazing skills and a strong work ethic. Some of them were also a great addition to our culture. Then new opportunities came their way. Great people deserve as much as they can get, and if I did my job, they should outgrow their position. If I couldn't offer them a new one, it made sense for them to move on. Each time one of these folks gave notice, it caused me great anxiety.

But we always survived. New people came along who were also great. Shifts got covered, and work was completed. A lot of people moved through our company over the years. The more we focused on culture, the better our team became, even as individual team members came and went.

A great culture can afford to lose a few great people. What it can't afford is to hang onto some not-so-great people. One bad employee can significantly weaken your team and drive away promising applicants.

There's often a tension between an employee's operational contribution and their cultural impact. It's hard to let go of someone with integral abilities, even when their behavior is toxic for your workplace. Employers often overrate how critical an individual is to their operation and underrate how costly they are to their team. You may have someone on your staff you believe you can't live without. Just remember that every other top-performing team out there is doing fine without them.

Changing your culture will require patience and discipline and entail a lot of adjustments, possibly including replacing some personnel. But if there's one consistent characteristic I've seen across all top-performing teams, it's the loyalty management has to their culture. Have faith that whatever you do in service of your team, it'll be the best thing you can do for your organization. Let culture be your North Star.

Now that we've built your culture, it's time to build your team.

CHAPTER 6

Staffing Part 1: Attracting Top Performers

had big plans for my first team at Edible Arrangements. I figured I'd have many employees over the years, but only one team would be the *first*. Only one original group of individuals would get to pose in that opening day photo I envisioned hanging in the office.

My plan was to recruit the very best Los Angeles had to offer. We hung a help wanted sign out front while we were still under construction. I casually mentioned job openings to employees I'd met at nearby businesses. I placed an ad in the *Los Angeles Times* announcing our application open house on Tuesday. Between 10 a.m. and 2 p.m., all were welcome to come in and apply.

To my delight, a number of people did! Some were younger, some were older. Some had grown up in the area, and others had just moved to town. One applicant had recently left the Banana Republic at the mall across the street. Another was a transplant from Maine looking for a new adventure out west. One gentleman had delivery experience back in Australia. He was well-spoken and outgoing, perfect for delivering our fruit baskets—until he asked if his checks could be made out to his cousin.

Several were aspiring actors and musicians—not unusual in LA. One was a successful guitarist from a band I had loved in high school. He'd been working at a nearby Whole Foods and now wanted something new. I wasn't sure why someone with his past success was seeking hourly work, but how cool would it be to have him on staff?!

Many made good first impressions, making it easy to see them as part of my team. Others were shy or nervous. Some already knew the brand and were excited to be part of it. Others just needed a job. One woman readily admitted she was serving time for embezzlement and was part of a program that allowed her to work during the day and return to the correctional facility after her shift.

From that group of applicants, I built my first team of 12 people. I imagined them being with me the moment the health inspector signed off and we were free to open. I had a cold bottle of Martinelli's and a dozen plastic champagne flutes ready.

Our corporate office suggested I hire 30 percent more people than I actually needed, which I thought was ridiculous. I know people. I can recognize talent. I know how to connect with and inspire my employees. If I can get 'em to come, I'll get 'em to stay.

Or so I thought.

Two of my original hires didn't show up for the first day of training. Another didn't come back after the first break. One finished the first day and said the job just wasn't for her. By my third day with the team, before we had officially opened, I was already short-staffed. I hadn't sold a single fruit basket and was already having staffing problems. I never did take that photo.

All that happened in a market where people were looking for work. At other times, we advertised extensively for new hires and got no responses. In those cases, it was a delicate balancing act to see how far we could push my team to compensate for our lack of staff while we continued our hunt. When we did find new people, we trained them with our fingers crossed and hoped they'd keep showing up. Building a team was *much* harder than I'd anticipated.

When we discuss staffing in my live workshops, it can quickly devolve into a venting session. So many employers struggle to find the workers they need that they can become cynical and bitter about the labor force in general:

"No one wants to work!"

"They'd rather live with their parents than get a job."

"They come in with no experience, expecting to make big money."

"I pay higher than ever to attract employees. Then they leave a week later to work somewhere else for an extra buck an hour."

Management involves many pain points. Staffing seems to be an *agony* point. I've felt that agony myself. But the pain eased when I made some changes to our approach. I learned a lot over time, mostly through trial and error. I eventually did take a photo of my spectacular team, but they weren't the first group—they were the *last*.

I meet many employers in a variety of industries who consistently build and maintain top-performing hourly teams. Many of them are profiled throughout this book. They, too, find themselves understaffed at times, and each has their own way of rebuilding. What they share is a common philosophy about staffing—an attitude that informs their perspective and their actions.

Maintaining an Attractive Attitude

Frustration is natural. It's human. It's normal to become cynical when people don't behave the way you want them to—the way *you* would behave in the same conditions. When you offer fair wages and good opportunities, and no one responds, you're bound to have some feelings about it. You're also likely to draw certain conclusions about those who aren't responding. Your frustration may be heightened by your desperate need for help. These feelings are natural.

But they're not helpful. The employers I meet doing great things with hourly teams face the same challenges as the rest of us. But I've noticed an empowered mindset among them. They're persistent. They're focused.

They keep their frustration in check and their minds open. They're less judgmental and more curious about the workforce. That self-regulation, combined with an aggressive outreach, allows them to approach staffing constructively. Honestly, every solid employer profiled in this book has a calm, positive outlook about the hourly workforce that helps them out-recruit the competition. Their attitude helps them attract.

Achieving top performance in anything always starts with a look in the mirror. What are your thoughts and feelings, and how might they be impacting your ability to recruit? We tend to see what we expect to see. If you see hourly workers as lazy, entitled, or broken, you'll find plenty of examples to confirm that. But if you believe there are plenty of great people out there, you'll spot them more quickly.

I don't want to diminish your staffing challenges, and I'm not suggesting you "visualize" your way to a full team. But I'd be remiss if I didn't point out the common denominator I've observed among those who consistently attract and retain solid hourly employees. Their attitude is part of their profile. It's not enough to do what they do. You must also think as they think. You're more likely to duplicate their results when you replicate their mindset.

Maintaining an Attractive Workplace

If you've done everything we've discussed up to this point, hourly workers will want to work for you. Word will get out. Your team will let their friends and family know. Your social media will broadcast your culture. (So will theirs.) Your customers will take note, ask for applications, and mention it to others. That's what happens when you're an employer of choice.

But you'll still need to do outreach. You want as many candidates to apply as possible so you can be choosy. That entails recruiting competitively. In the same way you need to out-market other organizations for customers, you must also out-market them for employees.

Where Should I Look for Good Talent?

In a word, everywhere.

I've been asking this question for years. I asked when I was an employer and I've asked as I worked with other employers. I posed the question to everyone I interviewed for the book. I was really hoping to give you a treasure map toward staffing salvation. Unfortunately, there is no one treasure trove. There's no secret fishing hole. These organizations cast a wide net. They advertise in publications, on websites, and in the window out front. They reach out to high schools and colleges. They have booths at job fairs. They offer bonuses to employees who bring in friends. They poach from other organizations. They do all the things you may already be doing.

But many of them do it better, the same way a skilled angler will catch more fish than others with bait in the same stream. They use better bait, and they know how to set the hook. That sounds a little predatory, but staffing really is like hunting or fishing.

And even the best fishermen have bad days. Sometimes the fish just aren't biting. A lot of great managers tell me staffing still challenges them. The labor market is constantly in flux, and when there are employee shortages, sometimes you have to lower your standards. (I know, they say you should never settle when hiring. But not being able to serve customers because you're understaffed is also a form of settling.) As someone who's been both a motivational speaker and an employer, I've come to appreciate the need for balance. We maintain our aspirations while also living in reality. We do the best we can.

Hopefully the tools you're acquiring here will help you get better performance out of anyone you hire. But you may still achieve better performance in your recruiting so you can maintain the best possible standards of candidate quality. Let's start by looking at what hourly workers *really* want in a job.

Hard Needs vs. Soft Needs

In a tight labor market, most employers double down on what I call *hard needs*. These are the *things* employees get from their jobs. The primary hard need is money, but there are others like benefits, flexibility, and even job titles (see Figure 6.1 below). When employers want to motivate people to apply for a job or do better at their job, most focus on hard needs—in other words, they throw money at the problem. It's become common in hourly work environments for employers to offer higher starting salaries and signing bonuses to attract employees.

Some of this is by necessity. Employers will never be immune to the basic rules of economics, especially rule number one: supply and demand. When the demand for labor exceeds the supply of workers, organizations must pay employees more. That's not a management issue—it's an economic one. In the same way businesses compete for market share by discounting prices, they also try to gain *labor market* share by increasing wages. That one-upmanship continues until the economics are no longer sustainable or until the labor market levels out.

But even when wages increase, if they don't go up proportionally to inflation, workers' hard needs may go unmet. In those conditions, workers need more money just to maintain their lifestyle, so higher wages have less buying power. They may not be trying to gouge employers. They may just be trying to keep their apartment.

And money isn't the only hard need. For many, flexibility is just as important, if not more so. Younger workers may be juggling school, sports, and other activities. Others may have child-care responsibilities and other jobs. Scheduling around these things may be more important than a high paycheck. Flexible scheduling can give you a competitive advantage.

That's what Jim and Debbie Cochonour, owners of the Camp Bow Wow doggy daycare in South Chicago, discovered. They pay typical wages for their region but have still found great staffing success by allowing employees to determine when they'd like to work each week. They hire enough part-time workers to ensure all shifts can be covered, and team members collaborate to trade shifts when needed.

"Younger generations see employment differently," Jim tells me. "They can drive for Uber or DoorDash and end their shift whenever they want with one click on their phone. We adapted our scheduling process by giving them more control over when they work. It's a different approach than when we were young, but it works well for us. It's led to higher morale and increased retention."

The market will determine what wages you need to pay. All things being equal, employees will go where they'll get paid the most. Fortunately, all things don't have to be equal. You can compensate by meeting other hard needs.

But what most employers fail to appreciate is that hourly workers also have *soft needs*. These are the feelings they get from a job (see Figure 6.1), such as a sense of belonging, or a feeling of purpose. As more recent generations have become increasingly attuned to their emotions (some older people might say "softer," "weaker," or "thin-skinned"), these things matter more than ever. They'll come for money, but they won't stay for it. No one wants to feel bad at work. They want to be somewhere that's healthy and inspiring.

Figure 6.1. Hard Needs vs. Soft Needs

Needs

HARD Needs
(Things They Get)

- Money
- Benefits
- Perks
- Flexibility
- Titles

SOFT Needs
(Things They Feel)

- Belonging
- Respect
- Purpose
- Praise
- Well-being
- Compassion
- Stability

Employees want a certain kind of work experience, just like consumers want a certain kind of customer experience. When you provide a better customer experience, people will pay more money for it. When you provide a better employee experience—one that feels good—workers will accept *less* pay for it, assuming their hard needs are still being met overall.

Don't get me wrong. I believe in paying people well. But you'll get more return on your labor investment when your employees also receive more soft compensation. They'll work harder, stay longer, and provide better service. They might even sell better. People excel when they feel good.

Everything we're discussing here will improve your team's work experience. Hopefully you've realized that meeting soft needs entails more than just being nice. You need to build a relationship with your team members and create working conditions that meet their specific emotional requirements. Just because you say "please," "thank you," and "good job" and ask about their families doesn't mean you're giving them a sense of purpose or connection to the team. They'll appreciate a gift card or a pizza, but it won't make them feel stable or inspired.

We'll talk more in Chapter 13 about how motivating your team based on their internal needs may be more effective than dangling more money in front of them. You don't have to pay the highest wages to inspire top performance. Employers who neglect soft needs do. Let them cut into their profit margins while recruiting workers who only care about money. You're trying to create a top-performing team of people who come and stay for the right reasons. There are many of them out there, and we're going to find them. We'll do this by helping them find *you*.

TOP-PERFORMANCE SPOTLIGHT

MAINE COURSE HOSPITALITY GROUP
New England

From working in the hospitality business, I've learned that the guest experience can be influenced as much by the people as by the property. Nowhere is that more on display than the Maine Course Hospitality Group. The company owns and operates 24 highly profitable hotels across multiple states in New England. Most are Marriott- and Hilton-branded and rank among the top 25 percent in both brands for operations and guest satisfaction.

President and CEO Sean Riley has been in the business for 40 years. It's clear when you talk to him that he's less an innkeeper and more a *people* keeper. "Nothing matters more than our people," he told me.

Sean regularly visits properties more to connect than to inspect. He leaves operations to his highly trained leaders. His focus is on ensuring the company's 650 associates feel cared about. "Culture

TOP-PERFORMANCE SPOTLIGHT, continued

can't happen without all of us, especially me, participating," he said. He personally writes out birthday cards for every associate, and many reach out thanking him for the acknowledgment. On Thanksgiving and Christmas, he calls every hotel on every shift to wish them well and thank them. It's not uncommon for him to check in with night auditors at 4 a.m.

Sean and his leadership team are also known for "pop drops," delivering popsicles to associates on hot days. Unlike gift cards, the popsicles need to be eaten right away, so the joy is felt in the moment. It's a small, inexpensive gesture that makes a big impression. Each property is also given a budget for food, treats, and activities that honor their value of "Fun."

He believes culture starts at the top, but he wants associates to feel it at every level of the organization. His gestures reflect a larger company feeling. He doesn't seek personal adoration—he wants associates to love the entirety of Maine Course Hospitality Group. The company works hard to train leaders and give them autonomy. As long as they meet brand standards and honor the four company values (integrity, respect, fun, and family), they're free to operate as they see fit. Each has their own way of doing things, but all provide the same high-level experience for both associates and guests.

Supervisors are urged to personally call every new associate the day they start (or the day before or after) to welcome them to the company. They're also encouraged to send handwritten "welcome to the family" cards to new employees immediately upon hiring them. "They may not start for a few weeks, and a lot can happen in that time," Sean told me. "The personalized note makes them feel good and helps maintain their commitment to join our team." He does this himself for new leaders.

TOP-PERFORMANCE SPOTLIGHT, continued

Given their location in New England, their business is highly seasonal, which creates staffing challenges. Their commitment to the employee experience has built a solid core group they can depend on each year.

Many of their properties reinforce their culture with a daily huddle. One has created their own culture committee made up mostly of associates, which brainstorms new practices and events to celebrate their values and promote unity. The company also publishes the *Maine Course Courier*, a quarterly newsletter that honors associates, publishes positive guest feedback, and highlights community impact. The newsletter is distributed internally for team members but posted publicly online to share with potential new hires.

Maine Course has a three strikes policy and uses all the standard documentation to address personnel issues when necessary, but they rely much more on coaching and counseling than on discipline. "Many of our hourly associates come from challenging circumstances," Sean said. "We need to meet them where they're at and get them where they need to be. The legal options are there if we need them, but we always begin with caring and coaching."

New employees start at 110 to 120 percent of local minimum wage. While Maine Course relies on competitive pay to recruit, they believe what keeps employees is love. "Employees are not going to leave someone they love," Sean said. "If they leave a job for another dollar an hour somewhere else, the love wasn't there."

The primary messaging on the Maine Course Hospitality Group website focuses not on what they do but on what they stand for. The banner at the top of the site shares three ideas: "We're about team. We're about service. We're about fun." Putting those words into action is the secret to their decades of success. As Sean states on their

TOP-PERFORMANCE SPOTLIGHT, continued

website: "The culture at Maine Course is what separates us from other companies. Every one of us has to respect each other and embrace the culture. Our purpose, values, and mission have evolved over time. But our core values are who we are and what we stand for."

Top-Performance Takeaways:

- ❯ Use small gestures to show your appreciation.
- ❯ Create fun moments for employees that generate on-the-spot joy.
- ❯ Convey your appreciation during especially tough shifts.
- ❯ Formally welcome new team members as soon as possible to make them feel part of the family.
- ❯ Empower well-trained managers with autonomy.
- ❯ Help employees love the culture more than any one leader.
- ❯ Celebrate and reinforce culture with huddles, committees, and communications.
- ❯ Rely more on caring and coaching than discipline.

Writing Powerful Help Wanted Ads

Visit any staffing website and read through the listings for the jobs you also need to fill. Now go back and take a second look at the posts you *didn't* notice. In other words, which ones get lost in the mix? Which ones did you skim? What do they have in common? What are they lacking? What are the feelings they're *not* generating? For most organizations, the problem isn't that they've posted a bad help wanted ad. It's that they've posted a forgettable one.

We've already discussed many elements of management that most people neglect because they're too busy being busy. The wording of your help wanted ad is another of those important factors that doesn't get enough attention. That's good—it's one more way you can pull ahead of other employers. Let's look at a few ways to do this that work well for finding hourly employees.

Use Simple Language

Write in a style that appeals to the employees you're targeting. Hourly workers are different from salaried workers. All that grandiose corporate speak so many companies put in their posts might turn off the kind of people you want.

If I have an MBA and I'm looking for an organization where I can have a future, I want an in-depth job posting. I want a comprehensive breakdown of the job requirements and benefits package, as well as how that position interfaces with other verticals in the company's portfolio. And I want to learn about the company: its rich history, its future aspirations, corporate leadership, current mission, and how the position I'm considering contributes to that greater purpose.

But if I'm looking for a part-time job to save up for prom, I just want to know what I'll be doing, what it's going to be like on a day-to-day basis, and how much I'll get paid. I don't want a lot of business jargon, and I'm not going to spend much time reading about the job, either. The listing shouldn't take longer to get through than the application. If you want me to finish reading your ad, you had better get my attention quickly and make the post interesting.

Write for your audience. You wouldn't use the same language in a marketing piece for teens that you would for senior citizens. Help wanted posts are no different. Consider whom you want to hire, and write the post for them. You may want to create a few different posts and run them past your current team members to see what resonates.

Get Help from Aristotle!

In Chapter 3, we discussed the Greek philosopher's three modes of persuasion: *logos* (logic, data, information), *ethos* (character, credibility), and *pathos* (emotion). Incorporate all three into your help wanted listings.

Everyone shares the "whats" (or *logos*) about the position, such as job requirements, duties, hours, and salary. That's basic information.

Better posts don't just focus on the job, however. They sell the organization (*ethos*) and explain why it's a great place to work. Boast about your ratings and reviews. Share testimonials from current employees. Paint a picture of who you are and why you're a great employer to work for. Lots of retail stores need stockers, so tell them why they should want to be a stocker at *your* store.

The best posts also tap into people's feelings (*pathos*) by getting applicants excited, tempting them with the promise of an emotional experience they know employees want, even if they're not actively pursuing it. This is done by focusing on *soft needs*. Sell your culture and the fun. Sell your humanity and your appreciation of theirs. Describe an environment that would make them feel great.

Let's look at two examples based on real help wanted listings I found posted on the same website. I've taken some liberties with the content and length, but both capture the spirit of the original posts, which were seeking a new dishwasher.

Listing #1:

FULL-TIME DISHWASHER WANTED

MUST BE ABLE TO WORK NIGHTS UNTIL 12 a.m. ON WEEKENDS AND UNTIL 11 p.m. ON WEEKNIGHTS.

MUST HAVE OWN TRANSPORTATION.

MUST HAVE PRIOR DISHWASHING EXPERIENCE!!!!!

PLEASE DO NOT SUBMIT APPLICATION IF YOU CAN'T MEET THESE REQUIREMENTS.

You will be required to use the dishwashing machine to ensure all dishes are properly washed. Afterward you must put all the dishes away. At closing you will scrub all grills and hot cooking surfaces.
Starting pay is $X per hour.

$X signing bonus given after working three months.

I have a few thoughts on this listing. First, the top half is in all caps, so they're yelling at us. That doesn't feel good (pathos). The word "must" appears four times. And do they really need a veteran in the dishwashing arts? They used five exclamation marks after that sentence, so I guess so. Dishwashing is usually a great entry-level position, so requiring experience will limit the number of applications they get. When jobs are scarce, that might be OK. In a labor shortage, it's risky.

There is plenty of logos in this listing. It provides the facts about the job. It doesn't provide much ethos—information about the workplace—although the repeated use of the word "must" certainly gives an impression. Is there much pathos—emotion? To me, there's quite a bit of emotion that comes across in this ad. Fear! Writing in all caps, listing such strict requirements-- this place seems tough! It's cold. It's unfriendly. It's all about hard needs with no mention of soft needs. The actual workplace may be great, but the workplace, as described in this ad, doesn't reflect that.

Many employers purposely emphasize the difficult parts of the job to weed out those who can't handle it. Your listing should be transparent about the requirements of the job. But failing to address any soft needs will also scare away some great applicants.

Let's look at another listing for the same job at a different restaurant:

Listing #2:

Wanted: Restaurant Family Member (to help with dishes!)

Why We're Here

We seek to make people's lives better. We need your help to improve the lives of guests, co-workers, owners, and our community. Your work here has meaning.

Our restaurant family will celebrate you—the lively, rebellious, genuine you—with your diverse background, abilities, and plucky personality. We know that when people can be themselves at work, they shine. That leads to a work environment that's a little quirky, irreverent, exciting, uncommon, empowering, and downright exceptional. Guests feel it, and you will, too.

How You'll Help

Ensure guests get clean and spotless dishes, silverware, and glassware. Provide co-workers with support and assistance. Keep all areas clean, dry, and safe while providing outstanding service to our guests along the way.

Prior experience and Food Handler Certification are preferred (but we can talk!). We also need a little schedule flexibility, especially during evenings, weekends, and holidays.

Starting Pay: $X per hour

Apply today—we'd love to meet you!

Be Yourself. Lead Yourself. Make It Count.

Among the many "what's" shared in this listing is what working there will feel like. It seems like it would feel great. Clearly this dishwasher has a job to do. But they get to do it somewhere that acknowledges soft needs.

When I share these two examples with my audiences, everyone agrees they'd much rather work for the second employer. Most say they'd accept a dollar less per hour to work in that kind of environment. That's what's great about soft needs: When you do a good job selling and providing them, there's less pressure to overcompensate with hard needs. It's important to pay people well, but it's more important to treat them well.

Consider the type of employee that thrives in your workplace. What soft needs matter to *them*? Address those needs along with the hard needs, and you'll attract more applicants than those employers just sharing the "whats" of the job.

We'll talk more about appealing to soft needs in Chapter 13. For now, add this bait to your hook.

Get Someone (or Something) Else to Write Your Posts

You might be a good manager but not the best writer. That's OK, but you want your posts to use the best writing, just as you would in any marketing piece. It may be worth spending a few dollars getting someone else to generate your help wanted copy.

Alternatively, use artificial intelligence. With some good prompting, an AI platform can instantly crank out some decent copy. Be sure to feed it all the information you need. Instruct it to use simple language, to target hourly workers, and to use elements of logos, ethos, and pathos. It'll know what that means. You may need to give it some feedback for the first few attempts and ultimately make some changes on your own, but it's an excellent tool that can make writing much easier. Keep in mind that lots of others are already using AI for writing help wanted ads (and other things). So stay on top of this to ensure you do it better.

Be aggressive with your recruiting. Depending on the labor market, it may take a little persistence to get the applicants you need. Don't stop looking. It's worth the extra time, effort, and expense to bring in as many possible employees as you can. If you know what you're looking for, you'll be that much closer to top performance and a team photo to hang on your wall.

Let's look more closely at how to do that.

CHAPTER 7

Staffing Part 2: Identifying the Top Performers

'␣ve heard employers compare staffing to looking for a needle in a haystack. I don't think it's the best metaphor, because at least a needle and a stalk of hay look different. In hiring, good candidates and bad candidates all look and talk the same. They're all trying to convince you they're the best person for the job. It's like trying to find the best stalk of hay in a haystack.

That first team I hired at Edible Arrangements was made up of good people, but they were the *wrong* people. They weren't the right fit for the job. Those who left early did me a favor by weeding themselves out so quickly. At the time I complained about how flaky they were. In retrospect,

I realize it was my fault for not having a better selection process. It took a few years for us to develop one, but when we did, building and sustaining a top-performing team became considerably easier.

There's no way to avoid an occasional mis-hire, but you can improve your batting average. You just need to be more deliberate about evaluating candidates and use selection practices that focus on what matters most.

What to Look For

If your outreach has worked, you now have some candidates. But whom do you choose? What are you looking for as you review their applications and conduct interviews? Later in this chapter, we'll discuss a few ways to test for the characteristics you want. For now, let's consider what those characteristics should be.

Skill Set vs. Mindset

Most hourly jobs require fewer skills than salaried positions. With good training and a little time, your employees will become competent. Previous experience, therefore, is less important. Some of the best employees I ever had came with little or no experience. If you need a licensed or credentialed employee such as a massage therapist, stylist, or aesthetician, obviously their skill set matters more.

Regardless of the position you're filling, what really matters is the applicant's mindset. They should be enthusiastic, positive, and willing to learn. They shouldn't just want *a* job; they should want *this* job. When it comes to hourly employees, attitude is usually much more important than aptitude. It's easier to improve the latter. Having the wrong mindset is a nonstarter.

Cultural Fit

If you've done the work to define your culture, look for those who gel with it. New employees should be able to support your mission and live your values. They should bring out the best in their co-workers. They might have a lot of talent or experience, but that won't help if they can't align with the team. It may be a good idea to involve team members in the hiring process to help determine if the applicant is a good fit.

Personality Type

You might find you need diverse types of people to round out your team, or you may have some positions that work well for certain kinds of people. Personality profiles such as the DiSC and Myers-Briggs have been around for years, helping employers better understand what type of people they have and what type they need. We should be careful about assigning labels, but there's value in understanding a person's disposition and where they're most likely to thrive.

In a salaried work environment that requires abstract thinking, understanding the nuances of team members' personalities can be extremely helpful for managing them. With hourly employees, it may not be practical, so we need to simplify the process. In my workshops, I discuss my own system of four personality types. There's no need to administer an assessment—when I describe these types, most people quickly self-identify with one (sometimes with leanings toward another). The four personality types are *Doers*, *Thinkers*, *Feelers*, and *Connectors*. Each type is suited for certain kinds of work.

Doers are task-oriented. They want to get to work and get things done. In some ways, they resemble Top Dog managers. They, too, can be dismissive of others and can be a bit impulsive. But when work needs to be finished, they make it happen.

Thinkers like to collect information and analyze things. They're good at problem solving, but they can take a while. If they lack all the information, they may hesitate to act. Given time and adequate data, however, they'll come up with great ideas.

Feelers are more emotionally aware. They're sensitive and naturally empathetic, which makes them very helpful to others. But emotions can be distracting in the workplace, so they may need a gentle touch. In return, they're good at meeting others' soft needs.

Connectors are social. They love to talk, network, and bring people together. They're "people people." That's great, but sometimes socializing can lower productivity. They might struggle in solitude or on an assembly line. In settings where human connection is important, however, no one does it better.

During my workshops, I ask participants to sort themselves into groups based on their dominant personality type. Each group brainstorms and then shares their strengths, weaknesses, and needs. As you might expect, the Doers always complete the assignment first and the Thinkers take the longest! Then I give the groups a puzzle to solve, and often the opposite is true. Everyone has their superpowers and their kryptonite.

You can probably think of people you know and quickly determine what group they belong to. Most of us are a combination but lean toward one dominant trait, and those tendencies inform our behavior.

I had some employees at Edible Arrangements who were very social. That was great when they were serving customers. But when they were in the kitchen preparing fruit baskets, they tended to talk and get distracted. I also had some very heads-down, results-oriented employees who could efficiently crank out fruit baskets. Put them in front of customers, however, and they struggled to create the warm, friendly connections I wanted.

What are the positions you need to fill, and what kinds of people do you need to fill them? Understanding these personality types may be useful for hiring and assigning employees the positions for which they're best-suited. Figure 7.1 below shows some examples:

Figure 7.1. Best Positions for Personalities

Personality Type	Best Positions
Doers	• Warehouse associate • Production line worker • Food-service worker • Groundskeeper • Retail stocker
Thinkers	• Data entry operator • Paralegal • Billing specialist • Shipping and receiving clerk • Research assistant

Feelers	• Child-care provider • Customer service rep • Home health aide • Animal care attendant • Special education assistant
Connectors	• Retail sales associate • Food-service host • Amusement park attendant • Tour guide • Movie theater usher

I'll be the first to acknowledge this isn't very scientific, especially compared to the complex, research-based profiles out there. But you may not have the time or the budget for those. The idea is to just be a bit more thoughtful about what personality types might do better in certain roles.

However, I'd advise against ruling someone out just because their apparent personality type doesn't directly align with the job, especially if they have other good qualities. People are multilayered. Labels and "types" have some use, but they don't tell the entire story. You need to look at people in their entirety.

Hiring Bias

Once you know what you're looking for, you need to be able to identify it in a candidate. That's the purpose of the hiring process, to find the right people and weed out the wrong people.

But candidate evaluation can be tricky. In addition to the dishonesty sometimes involved when people are trying to sell themselves, a lot can happen on *your* end that might cause you to hire the wrong people and weed out the right ones.

When you meet a job candidate, you're not just gathering information about them. You're interpreting it and forming an opinion. You're measuring them against your hopes for who you want them to be and your expectation of how you need them to be.

The conclusions you draw may also be informed by unconscious biases. Without realizing it, you may have thought processes happening on your end that alter your impressions of people, including:

> **Halo Effect:** Something makes a positive impression on you early in the conversation, causing you to dismiss your concerns.

> **Horn Effect:** Something makes a negative impression on you early in the conversation, causing you to dismiss their positive qualities.

> **Affinity Bias:** You form a positive impression because you and the candidate have something in common.

> **Confirmation Bias:** You draw a conclusion about the candidate and start asking questions and interpreting answers in a way that confirms what you already believe.

> **Attraction Bias:** Physical attraction or personal chemistry causes you to like them as a job candidate, regardless of their qualifications.

> **Contrast Effect:** Rather than judging the candidate on their own merits, you judge them based on how they measure up to another candidate.

> **Illusory Correlation:** Incorrectly assuming one certain thing about the candidate means they can or cannot do the job.

> **Interview Fatigue:** You're so tired from conducting interviews that you just want to get them over with. Later candidates may not get fair consideration when your brain is fried.

> **Hiring Urgency:** The stress of needing to fill the position causes you to mentally commit to the current candidate, simply because they showed up.

> **Mood:** The weather, your hunger, outside issues—all may impact how you feel in general and, therefore, how you feel about the candidate.

In the worst cases, interviewers may also be swayed by racism, sexism, ageism, and other "isms" that are illegal, immoral, and ultimately unhelpful. They'll cause you to miss out on great candidates. People should be judged by who they are, not what they are.

Going with Your Gut

Your gut isn't reliable. Too often your gut goes with people you like. But you're not looking for a friend—you're looking for someone who'll contribute to your culture and excel at a job.

Recently I was with my daughter at a smoothie store when she asked an employee if they were hiring. They had a pleasant conversation, and the young lady said to her, "I hope you get the job. You seem really nice!" Both my daughter and I appreciated the compliment. But does being "nice" really mean she's qualified? Nice is, well, nice. But it doesn't mean she can solve problems, communicate well, or follow through on commitments. Hopefully the manager probes a little deeper in formal interviews. But a lot of managers don't. They hire people they like, only to find later a lot they *don't* like.

It's normal to have bias—but it's not beneficial to your business. The more you can keep your subjectivity in check, the clearer your decisions will be.

Evaluation Software and Preemployment Assessments

There are many companies that provide software or AI that you can use to evaluate job candidates via online assessments. If you're part of a larger organization, you're probably already using these tools to prequalify candidates. When used properly, these tests can provide valuable information about applicants' abilities, skills, and fit for the job. Some can go quite deep. McDonald's, Walmart, and Amazon are known for their in-depth personality and psychometric testing.

The accuracy and trustworthiness of these tests can vary, however, depending both on the test and on how it's administered. One potential issue with preemployment tests is that applicants may choose the answers they think you want to make themselves seem more employable. This is known as *response distortion*, and it can be a problem with any type of self-reporting measurement, including personality tests and job knowledge tests. For many large companies (such as those mentioned above), the internet is filled with tutorials and test primers that offer tips on how to respond to their assessments. However, many of these tests are designed to detect response distortion and flag suspicious results.

My son did really well at his first job at In-N-Out Burger. He got that job after another fast-food company's assessment eliminated him as a candidate before even meeting him. He would have thrived there. (That's not me being a proud parent. There are many things I'd rather brag about than my son thriving in fast food!) These assessments aren't perfect. Of course, neither are job interviews.

Undoubtedly, technology will play an increasingly large role in hiring. These tools can be very helpful, but they should be used in conjunction with other sources of information, such as resumes, references, and interviews—however imperfect they may be. Even with the best technology at your disposal, you still need to meet people.

Interview Ghosting

Interview no-shows are one of the most common rants I hear from employers in my workshops. It's such a hot-button topic, let me just come out and acknowledge it: Ghosting sucks.

Ghosting—breaking off communication without an explanation—triggers my Gen X sensibilities about what's professional. It's rude and inconsiderate, and it leaves us to speculate as to why the person has disappeared. It's not cool. Ghosting has made society worse.

Now that we've gotten that out of the way, let's have a constructive conversation about it. Social protocol has changed, and ghosting has become increasingly common with each generation—and not just in the workplace. According to a 2023 study published in the *Journal of Social and Personal Relationships*, two-thirds of people surveyed have ghosted their way out of a romantic relationship—and have been ghosted themselves. It's a form of conflict avoidance.

The act of ghosting in the hiring process is less important than the reasons for it. Blowing off a job interview is a reaction to something that's always existed—people's desire to exit a relationship, which includes the applicant-employer relationship. Something happens between the initial contact and the interview that causes the applicant to want to stop the process.

In some cases, more information comes out that wasn't revealed in the job posting. Maybe the pay is lower than they want. Maybe the hours aren't ideal. Maybe the person who scheduled the interview made them uncomfortable. Maybe they received another job offer in the meantime. Or maybe after some thought they realized the job just wasn't for them.

"OK, well, why not just come out and say so?"

Hourly workers may not have the confidence or communication skills to speak up. They may be too uncomfortable to express their change of heart. It's less considerate but easier just to disappear. And honestly, they may not even understand that blowing off an interview is unprofessional. You don't know their background, and what they were or weren't taught growing up. I'm not excusing the behavior; I'm just trying to go a little deeper than labeling them a flake.

When people don't show up for interviews, it's tempting to immediately disqualify them. Don't be so quick to write them off. There might be a legitimate reason. If that's the case, they may feel too embarrassed to call or feel it's too late to recover.

Reach out to them and see if you can find out what happened. Chances are you won't connect with them, but on a few occasions you might. Ask if they're OK. If you're leaving a message, invite them to contact you if they're still interested in the job. In most cases, you won't hear back. That's all right. You're reaching out for two reasons. The first is to give someone with a good explanation another chance. The second is to find out why they didn't come. The intent isn't to make them defensive. You just want to know what happened so you can learn. Was there something on your end you could have done to prevent the no-show? Was there something misleading about the job listing or something off-putting about your initial contact? Hopefully you'll learn a thing or two that will help you moving forward. Thank them for the information and wish them well.

Interview no-shows are just part of doing business in the 21st century, so try not to get too frustrated. Instead, look at your interview show-up rate as another metric and work to improve your numbers.

Chapter 7 / Staffing Part 2: Identifying the Top Performers

Scheduling Interviews

As with everything else in a top-performing work environment, the better employers I've met get ghosted less. In addition to attracting more and better applicants, they also have a few best practices they insist make a difference. Here are a few tips they've shared:

Offer Applicants Multiple Times to Come In

There may be certain hours that are most convenient for you. But job applicants have their own schedules, transportation issues, child-care issues, and even other jobs. The more time slot options you offer, the easier it will be for them to make it, so be flexible. Work with their schedules now, and they'll work with yours later.

Confirm Your Interviews

Unless you've talked to the applicant within the past 24 hours, call or text to remind them of the appointment. Tell them you're looking forward to meeting them. Also invite them to reschedule if they need to. Remember, compared with employees on salary, hourly workers' lives are more likely to be in flux and they may be juggling multiple responsibilities. Sure, you want your employees to see the job as a priority. But they don't have the job yet and might need some flexibility. Being cool about rescheduling might preserve them as a candidate, and they'll appreciate the understanding on your part.

Build a Preinterview Connection with Them

As much as they must sell themselves to you, you must sell yourself to them. During your preinterview conversation, work to start building a relationship. Ask a few questions to get a sense of who they are. Share a little something about yourself. Be friendly. When you confirm the interview, refer to something you discussed in this first conversation. Multiple managers have told me that when they take the time to do this, more applicants show up.

TOP-PERFORMANCE SPOTLIGHT

CONSERVA IRRIGATION AND MOSQUITO SQUAD
Northeast Florida

Vanesa Ellis runs two thriving businesses "in a man's world." Conserva Irrigation provides commercial and residential irrigation services, and Mosquito Squad provides pest control. In both cases, she oversees two all-male teams who are out in the field doing manual labor. "As a woman, I feel I have to be that much more deliberate about earning their respect," she said, although she added she's not sure if that's really true or just a fear she has. Either way, it's not a problem. She's built two teams of hourly employees whom she describes as "hardworking, committed, and loyal."

That loyalty has been important for employee retention. She's owned her irrigation business for three years and her pest control business for six years. In both cases, most of her employees have been with her since she opened. But hiring is still an important part of her operation so she can grow and serve more clients. New technicians start at between 145 and 170 percent of local minimum wage, plus commissions that can bump their pay up to 225 percent. Though they have opportunities to make more money elsewhere, what her crews appreciate most about her businesses is the team environment. Just before we spoke, she had hired a technician who was making a dollar an hour more for a competitor but wanted to work with the kind of team he heard Vanesa had created.

Vanesa emigrated from Argentina to the U.S. when she was 12 and appreciates the opportunities her adopted country has provided her family. She's set out to create a business that would appeal to the kind of employees who also hunger for a better life. She told me about a team member who had to share a car with his wife. Vanesa sat down with him and developed a plan for him to earn enough to buy

TOP-PERFORMANCE SPOTLIGHT, continued

another vehicle. Knowing that her business allowed him to accomplish that goal is deeply meaningful to her. "We're growing this company not just for my family, but for theirs as well," she said. "We're growing together."

Togetherness is a major part of her operation. In both businesses, technicians work in the field. Vanesa's gone out of her way to give them a sense of camaraderie to ensure everyone feels supported and feels they are part of something larger. Each day before heading out to their job sites, technicians meet for a huddle up at the warehouse. They share personal updates, discuss the day, and exchange ideas on that day's jobs. If there's enough time at the end of the day, they meet back at the warehouse and play basketball on the hoop Vanesa had installed. Often they're still on the clock when they play. Vanesa sees this time as crucial to maintaining team spirit. They also have a more formal company meeting every Wednesday. Occasionally the company will bring crew members pizza on site or a manager will take them to lunch. "Our main tactic is to care," Vanesa told me. "Sometimes we express that just by saying thank you or asking about their sick child."

And because her employees feel cared about, they, in turn, care about clients. "We train our technicians to always do right by our clients," she said. "Sales and commissions should always come second to what's in our clients' best interests." The technicians appreciate this more wholesome approach to business growth, and it hasn't slowed them down: Vanesa is the first female owner in the Conserva network to hit $1 million in annual gross sales.

Top-Performance Takeaways:

- ▷ Build in extra financial incentives for employees.
- ▷ Help employees work toward their own goals, rather than just focusing on them working toward yours.

Welcoming Applicants

It's great if they show up for the interview, but it'll be a waste of time if you offer them the job and they don't accept. As I said, you're still selling. *Court* them. Demonstrate your great culture and your support of soft needs. Just as you want to pique their interest with your help wanted listing, you now want to capture their interest in person. They've probably applied for other jobs, too. You want this job to stand out. You want to be their employer of choice.

Greet them warmly and treat them as a guest. Show them around. Make them comfortable. Offer them a beverage or a snack. Train your employees to be equally welcoming. Increasing their comfort level will help them be themselves. That's the person you want to meet during the interview.

The best candidates will have choices. You want them to choose you.

Conducting Interviews

Your conversations with candidates are only as good as your questions. The standard ones don't reveal a whole lot:

"Tell me a little bit about yourself."

"Why do you want to work here?"

"What's your biggest weakness?"

It's likely they've heard these questions before and have prepared answers. It would be great if there really were as many "perfectionists" as there are people who claim to be one when asked about their biggest weakness.

Having said that, these questions can still be useful, depending on what you're listening for. "Tell me a little about yourself" is a good icebreaker. In the same way that first throwaway pancake primes the griddle, this question is about easing candidates into the conversation while letting them calm down. If they're too nervous, it might hide their strengths. You want them as comfortable as possible.

"Why do you want to work here?" I'm interested in the "here" part of the question. Are they interested in something unique about us, or are we one of many places that could meet their needs? If something about us is special to them, hopefully they'll come to work with a little more enthusiasm. That's better than someone willing to work anywhere. As Cheap Trick once sang, "I want you to want *me*."

As far as the weakness question goes, I don't trust their specific answer. What I'm listening for is humility and commitment to improvement.

What you really want is to test for the position's key criteria. Teachers know the answers they're looking for on a test, and so should you. A job interview shouldn't be a casual conversation. It's a critical part of the evaluation process. Know going in what you're looking for and measure each candidate based on those specific traits.

Using a Hiring Matrix

A great way to limit your biases and focus on what matters most is to use a formal evaluation process during job interviews. This allows you to measure potential employees against a predetermined set of criteria and ask questions to determine how well they embody each one. An easy way to select the criteria for the matrix is to look at the best employees you've had for each position and name the most important characteristics they share.

At Edible Arrangements, I had customer service workers, production workers, and delivery drivers. Everyone was cross trained, but most excelled in one of the three jobs. My best customer service workers were personable, good writers (to quickly take down gift messages), and good at selling. My best production workers had flexible schedules (our shifts were based on the number of orders coming in), were good with their hands, and had a strong work ethic. My best drivers were problem solvers, friendly, and had clean driving records. While there were overlapping qualities among all my best people, such as a sense of responsibility and a good cultural fit, each position had its own unique profile.

Once we knew the ideal requirements for each position, we could evaluate candidates based on those characteristics, rather than on how we "felt" about them. We couldn't eliminate all subjectivity, but we could at least focus on what mattered most and treat all candidates equally. For each key characteristic, we rated the applicant from zero to five and then calculated a total score. The candidates with the highest scores were considered most qualified for the job.

Let's look at an example of how this might work:

Say you're running a large retail store and need a new cashier. After placing an ad and collecting resumes, you invite two candidates for an interview, Susie and Sloane.

Susie greets you with a firm handshake and warm smile. You ask how the traffic was, and she shares a funny story about a recent flat tire she had on Easter. She's great with small talk, and it's easy to envision her chatting with customers. You ask her to share a little about herself, and you learn about her large family, her hobbies, and her unapologetic love of anime.

Throughout the interview, she maintains eye contact, nods attentively, and demonstrates strong communication skills. Her resume lists cashier positions at multiple stores since high school. You ask about her last job, and she's diplomatic about describing an obviously unhealthy environment. She says she's heard great things about your store and is available to start right away, any shift. You test her ability to make change.

"OK, Susie. A customer's order total is $6.67. The customer gives you $10.92. How much change do you give back?"

"No problem," she replies, taking out her phone. "I take this mini cash register with me wherever I go!" she jokes before quickly calculating the correct answer. This one's a charmer.

Had you not already scheduled another interview, you'd hire her on the spot.

You look at the clock and realize you're running late for your interview with Sloane. As you walk Susie out, she thanks you for your time and assures you she has a spare tire in her trunk, ready to go in case you need her next Easter. The joke makes you smile.

Chapter 7 / Staffing Part 2: Identifying the Top Performers

Sloane is waiting in the hallway outside your office. You apologize for the wait and shake her hand. Her grip is a little soft. She follows you into the office and sits quietly, waiting for you to kick things off. She seems uncomfortable, rubbing her fingers together.

Sloane answers questions politely but doesn't elaborate on her responses. Her resume shows she's worked at the same fast-food restaurant for the past three years. She didn't get much time at the counter, she explains, but she's spent the past year working the drive-thru window. She's really enjoyed her work there, but she's going back to school and needs something closer to campus. Her classes will be on Tuesday and Thursday evenings, so she won't be available for those shifts. She also does occasional volunteer work on Sundays, but that's flexible. If hired, however, she'll need two weeks so she can give her current employer adequate notice.

As the interview progresses, she loosens up a bit. She tells you about the volunteer work she does with her church. She also shares a story about how she managed the drive-thru one lunch hour when the point-of-sale system went down, requiring her to take orders by hand. She personally checked each order to ensure it was accurate and apologized to every car for the delay. She tells the story with confidence and pride. You compliment her on surviving the shift, and she responds with a large, embarrassed grin.

You then ask her the same money calculation question you asked Susie. Sloane seems taken aback, not expecting a sudden math test. She quickly composes herself and then pinches her lip as she thinks.

"Uh, $4.25?"

"That's correct. Nice job." She nods.

"Sorry for the hesitation. Just had to shift my brain for a second."

After a few more questions, your conversation ends, and you thank her for coming by. She shakes your hand.

"Thank you for your time," she says. "I know you're talking to other people, but I really appreciate you considering me. I'd love to work here." It took her a little while, but she definitely warmed up.

Alone in your office, you recall Susie's Easter spare tire joke, and it makes you smile again. You were good friends with someone like her in high school. You return to your desk and prepare to call her to offer her the job.

But something stops you. You've felt this way before about job applicants, only to have them disappoint you. You decide to take a moment to reevaluate your two candidates.

Thinking of the best cashiers you've ever hired, you make a list of the important characteristics they've shared. You determine they all:

> Had lots of availability
> Worked well in fast-paced environments
> Were responsible
> Had strong social skills
> Provided great customer service

You decide to measure Susie and Sloane against these criteria. As you consider the important characteristics, you determine that customer service is especially important for your clientele. You'll assign that twice the weight and will double that score. Your matrix looks like the one in Figure 7.2 below:

Figure 7.2. Susie/Sloane Hiring Matrix

	Susie	Sloane
Availability		
Fast-Paced		
Responsibility		
Social Skills		
Customer Service (x2)		
TOTAL:		

Now it's time to fill in the numbers. You start with Availability. Susie can work anytime, starting immediately. She gets an easy 5. Sloane has some conflicts and can't start right away. She gets a 3.

Chapter 7 / Staffing Part 2: Identifying the Top Performers

Next is their ability to work in a Fast-Paced environment. You haven't seen Susie work, but something tells you her cashier experience, combined with her quick wit, implies she can think fast. You give her a 5. Sloan's worked three years in fast food, including one year at the drive-thru. That's not easy. She also gets a 5.

Then there's Responsibility. Susie made a great impression on you personally, but something bothers you about her having multiple jobs over just a few years. There could be a good reason, but you can't deny it's a red flag. It was great that she thought to calculate change on her phone, but can she dispense it properly from the drawer? Better give her a 3. Sloan has stayed in one job in an industry known for high turnover, she's willing to work, and she wants to give proper notice to her boss. You don't like having to wait two weeks for her to start, but you admire her loyalty to her current employer. And she calculated the change in her head pretty quickly. She gets a 5.

Then there's Social Skills. Susie has the gift of gab and is an easy 5. Sloane was awkward at first, but definitely warmed up. She wasn't unfriendly. Admittedly, she's not the personality type you'd socialize with. She might be a little more of a Thinker than a Connector. But would she be friendly *enough*? Does she really need to have long conversations with customers? They like friendly, but they also appreciate speed, which Sloane can provide. You give her a 4.

But that makes you reconsider your score for Susie. She's friendly, but she's also *talkative*. You enjoyed that (which is why the interview ran long), but it's not ideal for a cashier. You decide to lower her score to a 4.

For Customer Service, Susie has experience, and she communicates well. You probably could have asked more questions in this area, but you suspect she'd be pretty good. You give her a 4, which is doubled to 8. Sloane's handling of the drive-thru crisis revealed a lot about how she sees her role and the importance of taking care of customers. You also like that she volunteers. That suggests she thinks of others. She gets a 5, which is doubled to 10.

Your hiring matrix now looks like the one in Figure 7.3:

Figure 7.3. Completed Susie/Sloane Hiring Matrix

	Susie	Sloane
Availability	5	3
Fast-Paced	5	5
Responsibility	3	5
Social Skills	4	4
Customer Service (x2)	8	10
TOTAL:	25	27

Your gut told you to go with Susie, and it could be correct. You might want to speak with her again to get a better sense of her customer service skills and find out why she's changed jobs so many times.

But the hiring matrix favored Sloane. Statistically, based on the criteria you decided were important, she's more qualified for the job. You don't have to hire her, but you'd be smart to give her serious consideration.

The point of this tool is to manage and reduce (you'll never eliminate) your biases. Susie may be more likable, but that doesn't mean she's more qualified, unless "likability" is one of your criteria. Too often this factor overshadows more important qualities. Remember, this process is about finding the best worker, not a best friend.

Another advantage of using this matrix is that you can invite others into the hiring process and get them to evaluate candidates using the same matrix. You can then compare or even combine your scores.

And no matter which characteristics you test for, always be sure to consider whether the candidate is a good fit for your culture. You may want to include that among the criteria you score.

Ask Powerful Questions

Every question you ask should serve a specific purpose. The best questions shed light on the characteristics that matter most. However, the interview should still feel conversational, not scripted. Feel free to ask follow-up questions and be spontaneous. But always bring the discussion back to your predetermined criteria.

Be sure to take notes. You don't want to assign a score in front of the applicant. Until they've answered the last question and left the room, you're just listening and collecting information. Let the candidate know in advance you'll be taking notes so you can remember their responses later. Assure them it doesn't mean they've said something wrong.

Ask Close-Ended Questions to Prequalify Them

These are yes-or-no questions for non-negotiable requirements. "Do you have a work permit?" "Do you already have food handler certification?" "Can you work nights?" Ask these early, perhaps even before you schedule an interview. There's no need to continue if you can immediately disqualify them.

Ask Open-Ended Questions to Evaluate Them

These questions often begin with "What," "Why," or "How." They require the candidate to talk and explain. A nervous or less articulate candidate might struggle answering these questions, especially at the beginning of the interview. Be patient and listen. Unless high confidence and being well-spoken are important for the position, don't let a shaky performance throw you. Pay attention to the answers themselves.

Ask Behavioral Questions to Give You Insight

These are open-ended questions that require candidates to describe real situations they've been in and how they handled them. They prompt the candidate with phrases like "Tell me about a time when . . ." or "Explain a situation where you . . ." Examples might be:

"Tell me about a time when you were asked to do something you knew was wrong."

"Explain a situation where you had two people asking you to do something, and you could only choose one."

"Tell me about the most stressful day you've ever had on a job."

These aren't hypothetical questions, where you're asking what they *would* do. You're asking about something that actually happened. Maybe they made a mistake, but perhaps they learned from it. You're listening to learn their values, their drivers, and anything else that might give you some insight into their character. Another nice thing about using a hiring matrix is that you can come up with questions that specifically test for your criteria. Let's go back to our retail store example and look at how you might do this:

To see how well they do in a fast-paced environment, you could ask:

"Give me an example of a time you had to work quickly to get the job done."

"What have you done to stay calm when lots of work was coming at you all at once?"

"Tell me about your experience in fast-paced work environments."

For responsibility, you might ask:

"Describe the biggest setback you've dealt with. How did you handle it?"

"Tell me about a time when people relied on you."

"Talk about the biggest thing you've accomplished without supervision."

You get the idea. The internet is full of lists of behavioral interview questions that test for almost any characteristic you can imagine. Prepare a list of questions that correspond to whatever qualities you're looking for. Be sure to give them time to answer. They probably weren't expecting these questions and might need a few seconds to come up with the best answers.

In the end, there's no way to be certain how well people will perform on the job, but a more thoughtful evaluation process will improve your odds of hiring a good fit. Take as much time as you can afford to make careful selections. It'll strengthen your culture, improve your retention, and boost your team's performance.

What it *won't* do is eliminate all problems, and it definitely won't stop you from having to manage. Even the best people don't always do their best, and the best teams don't always work as a team. Employees need feedback and encouragement, and they need your leadership.

Now that you've assembled a team of top performers, it's time to talk about how to coach them for top performance.

PART 3

COACHING FOR TOP PERFORMANCE

CHAPTER 8

30-Second
Leadership™

Imagine you're in a crowded hospital emergency room packed with people suffering from a variety of ailments. A man in construction clothes complains of chest pains. An elderly woman has an uncontrollable cough. A teenage girl in a soccer uniform has her leg propped up with an ice pack on her knee. Everyone waits quietly, listening for their name to be called.

Suddenly, a doctor in a long lab coat bursts through the double doors. He approaches the man with chest pain, writes him a prescription for penicillin, and sends him home. He sees the woman with the cough, writes her a prescription for penicillin, and sends her home. He moves on to the teenager with the injured knee and—you guessed it—writes her a prescription for penicillin and sends her home. The ER is super busy tonight, so the doctor quickly moves from patient to patient, prescribing everyone the same treatment. Once he's cleared the waiting room, he returns through the double doors to continue his work.

There's a name for this kind of medicine: malpractice. The doctor sees each patient's symptoms. But without taking the time to conduct a proper examination, he can't possibly diagnose their problems. And without a proper diagnosis, he certainly can't offer the right treatment.

Managerial Malpractice

Most frontline bosses are guilty of *managerial malpractice*. They're so busy overseeing everything that they fail to properly diagnose the reasons for employee underperformance. They observe behaviors they don't like but make assumptions about the reasons behind them. Consequently, they apply ineffective management that fails to address the real problem and often makes it worse.

That busyness also prevents them from acknowledging the behaviors they *do* like. They don't reinforce high performance, causing skilled, motivated workers to grow bored or feel unappreciated. Their needs aren't being met, either.

I've discussed this issue at length with a good friend of mine, Mario Del Pero. Mario and his wife, Ellen Chen, have run several businesses and cofounded the Mendocino Farms restaurant chain. Mario and I have both employed many hourly workers and have spent the better part of our careers studying management. During our many early morning hikes, we've talked about the latest books we've read and leadership conferences we've attended. We used to speak often about how easy it is for busy managers to "downcoach" their team members by failing to properly assess their needs. Those conversations led to a few brainstorming sessions that ultimately inspired what we now call 30-Second Leadership™.

30-Second Leadership is a coaching methodology designed to prevent managerial malpractice. It involves a quick and simple process for diagnosing employee performance and then prescribing the best corresponding coaching to promote excellence. We like the word "coaching" because it suggests that both the manager (coach) and the employee want the same thing, and that the coach is on the employee's side. Coaches are authority figures but are also seen as advocates. That's what we want from managers: to advocate for employees and set them up for success.

We originally tested 30-Second Leadership in Mario's restaurants. Since then, I've trained thousands of managers and business owners in many industries on it, and it's become one of my most requested programs.

The beauty of this tool is its simplicity. There are other frameworks out there for assessing employee performance and choosing management styles, but most are a bit esoteric. The world doesn't need yet another complicated leadership model to study. We wanted to create something people would *use*. It needed to be something that could easily be understood and adopted by a 19-year-old assistant manager running a frozen yogurt shop. And because hourly workplaces are fast-paced, it needed to be something that wouldn't take more than 30 seconds.

Diagnosing for Specific Tasks

Better doctors than the one we mentioned earlier don't typically give patients an overall health grade. They examine multiple bodily systems—the heart, the lungs, the eyes, the ears, etc. —and evaluate each system separately. They may determine that your lungs, eyes, and ears are fine, but your blood pressure is high. Then they prescribe a treatment plan and provide help where needed. They may also offer advice to maintain good health and perhaps a few tips to prevent problems. Only by looking at your body and focusing on its major systems separately can doctors be of help.

The same is true in education. A student's GPA is useful for evaluating their overall performance, and it may determine if they'll graduate and where they'll matriculate, but it's not helpful for the process of education itself. That requires looking at a student's performance in each subject separately. In chemistry, they might need a tutor. In Spanish, they might be able to *be* a tutor. We all have strengths and weaknesses. Both need to be identified and given different kinds of attention.

Chances are your team members perform a variety of duties. An hourly factory worker might be responsible for safety protocols, packaging, and machine maintenance. A retail team member might be responsible for stocking, customer service, and ringing up sales. A busser might need to know cleaning procedures and tableware placement, and how to assist with beverage service. You know the positions specific to your workplace, and you can probably come up with eight to 12 of the main duties associated with each one.

If you evaluate your employees for each of these responsibilities individually, you'll likely find their performance varies depending on the task. Few employees get straight As. Most managers tell me that even their superstar employees are lacking in some areas.

But those seen as "superstars" often don't get coached in areas where they're lacking. Their needs are often overlooked. The opposite is also true: Employees who struggle with a number of tasks don't always get praise and reinforcement in those areas where they do excel.

In Chapter 7, we discussed personality profiles. There's value in these, especially if they promote appreciation for different types of people. But labels are tricky. It's tempting to make generalized assumptions about employees based on our broad perceptions of them. When you think of someone as an "S" (DiSC), an "ISTJ" (Myers-Briggs), or a "Connector" (me), you may only see them in that bucket and not as an individual. The same thing goes for "superstars," "underperformers," or worse, "idiots." Labels reduce people to two dimensions. It's a lazy way to look at them.

Personalities don't change much, but behavior and performance do. So that's where you need to focus your coaching—not on what they are, but on what they're doing. Everyone does many things differently, so assess their performance of each major task separately and coach them accordingly.

We'll begin by setting a baseline for your coaching instincts. Below in Figure 8.1 are 12 situations an employer might find themselves in with team members. For each one, circle the letter next to the answer that best describes how you'd respond. Go with your first instincts, as you probably would in the middle of a shift.

Figure 8.1. Coaching Quiz

Situation	Your Response
1. A new automotive service tech is struggling to understand the shop's safety protocols. He's eager to learn and motivated to improve.	a. Provide positive reinforcement for his enthusiasm and suggest he continue learning the protocols as time allows. b. Schedule a one-on-one training session with a more experienced tech to teach him the system. c. Explain the importance of paying more attention during training and ask him to learn it as he goes. d. Empower him with some time and space to learn the protocols as he works.
2. An employee came to work today with a rumpled uniform and bloodshot eyes. His customer service is worse than usual and not up to standard.	a. Write him up and send him home with a warning. b. Keep an eye on him and give him some time to work it out. c. Acknowledge his customer service skills and express concern for his appearance and his drop in performance. d. Keep the conversation focused on work and offer additional training on customer service.
3. You just promoted one of your custodial staff to night manager. She's thrilled about the new position.	a. Congratulate her and tell her to come to you with any questions. b. Encourage her to spend some time learning about management. c. Buy her some books on leadership. d. Assign her some shifts shadowing a night manager at another facility.

4. A new line cook isn't keeping up with the speed and complexity of the kitchen during peak hours. He's feeling overwhelmed and discouraged.	a. Assign him another role in the restaurant. b. Offer encouragement and remind him of his potential. c. Spend a few shifts retraining him and offer encouragement. d. Restate your expectations and give him a set period of time to get up to speed.
5. You just received another complaint about one of your experienced bank tellers from a co-worker you trust, who's accused her of gossiping about a new employee.	a. Stay out of it and let the team work it out among themselves. b. Solicit feedback from the experienced employee about the new one to see if there's any truth to the gossip you may need to respond to. c. Ask the co-worker who complained to speak directly with the experienced teller about her concerns. d. Confront the experienced teller to remind her of your culture and issue her a warning.
6. Your caregiver with the most tenure continues to enjoy her job and just got another stellar review from a client.	a. Buy her a gift card. b. Acknowledge her and ask in what ways she'd like to grow and get even better. c. Keep her humbled and empowered by keeping some distance. d. Share the review with your other caregivers and explain this is what you expect from all of them.

7. A seasoned factory worker is asked to learn a new machine. He's not excited about it and feels uneasy about the change.	a. Praise his previous success and remind him that this is an opportunity to learn a new skill. b. Respect his feelings and allow him to return to his previous role, where he feels more comfortable. c. Explain your need for him to switch machines with a better attitude. d. Acknowledge his concerns and ask a supervisor to work with him until he's comfortable.
8. Your lead hotel housekeeper has some initial resistance to new procedures for sanitizing rooms. Once she's got them down, she's enthusiastic about contributing to a safer guest experience.	a. She's doing well with the new procedures, so allow her to continue working without interruption. b. Let her know there will always be improvements to the system, and you need her to lean into them without pushback. c. Thank her for her open mind and ask if she has any ideas to refine the procedures. d. Continue training her on the new procedures and offer feedback on other cleaning practices to ensure she continues to improve.
9. You recently lost your temper at one of your bussers who broke a glass. He's experienced and should know better.	a. Ask him why he thinks you lost your temper and what he could have done to prevent that from happening. b. Apologize, but remind him it costs the restaurant money when dishes are broken. c. Compose yourself and continue managing him with a more professional demeanor. d. Apologize for your outburst.

10. A loyal employee informs you that one of the team members who leads the closing shift took home a tub of ice cream without paying for it.

   a. Confront the employee who took the ice cream and explain that you're going to take the cost of the ice cream out of their next check. Tell them to pay in advance next time.

   b. Fire the employee.

   c. Write up a warning and explain that as a shift lead, you expect more from them.

   d. Gather your staff for a meeting to discuss the incident and reprimand the employee publicly so everyone can learn from what happened and hold their co-workers accountable.

11. One of your top delivery drivers seems down lately. His work is getting done, but he's not demonstrating his usual enthusiasm.

   a. Check in with him to see if he's OK and ask if there's anything he needs.

   b. As long as work is being completed to standards, leave him alone.

   c. Before things worsen, explain that attitude matters and you need him to step up.

   d. Surprise him with tickets to a sporting event.

12. A manager who's been working for you for 10 years has been struggling for the past two. She seems to be totally disengaged from her job, and you've spoken with her about it multiple times. She agrees things aren't going as well as they used to, but she can't explain why.

   a. Thank her for her service and let her go.

   b. Write up a warning, restating your expectations.

   c. Give her more time in hopes she can break out of her funk.

   d. Promote her to a new role to light a fire under her.

The above 12 examples are just a tiny fraction of the employee situations managers navigate through daily. There's no one way to handle them all. Our 30-Second Leadership method isn't a solution for all employee issues, but it's a great tool for narrowing down the possibilities.

We'll revisit these situations later and see if something you've learned here might change how you approach them. For now, let's jump into the methodology.

TOP-PERFORMANCE SPOTLIGHT

TROPICAL SMOOTHIE CAFE
Florida

Ray Howell and his son Andrew haven't just built a top-performing hourly team—they've built 19 of them. The father-and-son pair operate 19 Tropical Smoothie Cafes throughout Florida, all of which rely on local hourly help, whom they start at just over minimum wage. Since they need close to 400 team members to run the combined enterprise, their company has a great deal of experience with the challenges of recruiting and maintaining an hourly workforce.

I originally met Ray when I interviewed him prior to my keynote for the Tropical Smoothie Cafe franchise convention. Many operators of fast casual restaurants struggle to find, retain, and manage employees. But their restaurants thrive with a team they love and trust. I asked Ray how they maintain such a strong workforce. He said without hesitation, "We're all about family."

I hear that a lot from business owners, but Ray takes it to a whole new level. He told me stories of helping team members find housing, purchase cars, and even work through immigration issues. In one case he continued paying an employee who was recovering from a gunshot wound, without knowing if they would ever come back to work: "It was just the right thing to do." Employees feel that they're cared about as

TOP-PERFORMANCE SPOTLIGHT, continued

people and reward the company with loyalty. Some of the restaurants have mothers and daughters working side by side.

Ray is known for repeating a few nuggets of wisdom to both his team and his sons:

"Aces in their places."

"When you get the answer you want, stop talking."

"Doing the right thing is always the answer—even over money."

While Ray and Andrew focus on the big picture, they empower their management team to oversee day-to-day operations. I also met two of his district managers at the convention. When I asked what their titles were, they hesitated. "We really don't focus too much on titles," one of them finally responded. "We all sort of know our roles and what we're trying to accomplish." And they accomplish a lot. Their 19 stores are fully staffed and highly profitable.

Ray and Andrew's leadership team runs tight processes, but their priority is people. Each store's general manager is given $50 per week for employee incentives and culture building. It can be used to buy food, prizes, or anything else to keep them feeling happy and appreciated. Rather than guessing what these things should be, they ask employees directly what will motivate them. They also engage employees in operational problem solving, using the Collaborator management style we discussed in Chapter 2. "They appreciate having a voice in what goes on," Ray told me.

But as we also talked about, Collaborator management only works with reliable employees who know their jobs. Ray and Andrew's managers have a clear philosophy about how to build a team worthy of being heard: "Hire right, train 'em right, treat 'em right."

They also reinforce employee performance with constant praise. Managers are trained to catch each employee doing something right every shift and provide specific praise so they know exactly where

TOP-PERFORMANCE SPOTLIGHT, continued

they excelled. "It's not enough to say 'good job,'" one of the district managers told me. "Employees need to know precisely what they did well, so they do it again."

One story both managers shared was about a general manager who decorated for a company Christmas party by hanging up stockings for all the employees. Frontline team members had their stockings hung the highest, management was beneath them, and Ray and Andrew's stockings were at the bottom. The manager explained he wanted it to represent the levels of support, rather than the levels of power. The idea of "flipping the pyramid" is not novel in the corporate world, but for this manager, it was an organic expression of how he felt the company genuinely operated. Without using the phrase, he understood the meaning of *servant leadership*.

It's fair to say that when it comes to running a thriving multiunit restaurant business, culture starts at the bottom.

Top-Performance Takeaways:

- ▷ Be there for your team when they really need you.
- ▷ Invest in small acts of appreciation. Ask your team what those acts should be.
- ▷ Give proven employees a voice.
- ▷ Hire carefully, train thoroughly, and manage lovingly.
- ▷ Offer praise daily and keep it specific.
- ▷ See yourself as a servant leader whose primary role is to push support upward through your managers, then to your workers, and ultimately to those at the top: customers.

Diagnosing Performance

In 30-Second Leadership, coaching encounters begin with your diagnosis. After determining the eight to 12 most important tasks an employee is responsible for and considering their performance for each, decide which task most requires your attention. Evaluate the employee for that task by looking at two things: their *skill set* and their *mindset*.

You'll recall we discussed these two traits during the hiring process. An employee's skill set is their mastery of the necessary hard skills. It's their ability to perform the task to company standards. Hourly workers need your help to acquire these skills. You test for their mastery of each skill by asking two questions:

1. Can the employee *state* the necessary steps to complete the task correctly?
2. Can the employee *demonstrate* the necessary steps to complete the task correctly?

If the answer is yes to both questions, their skill set is High. If the answer is no to one or both questions, their skill set is Low. High and Low are the only options you need. There's no reason to make it any more complicated than that. We want to keep this simple so you'll actually do it.

Don't check for mastery by asking the employee if they understand or if they've "got it." During training, many workers—especially new hires—are reluctant to admit when they're confused and worried about what you'll think of them. They'll say they've got it when they don't—they just intend to figure it out later. The only way you can tell whether they've got it is by asking those two questions.

Next, we look at the employee's mindset, or their mastery of the necessary soft skills. We measure this by assessing two things:

1. Their level of confidence—in other words, their belief they can perform the task well
2. Their enthusiasm—i.e., their willingness to perform the task well

Mindset is a bit more subjective than skill set, but if you're paying attention, you can probably get a pretty good read on it. When we observe an employee performing the task and they seem both confident and enthusiastic, we say their mindset is High. If either or both are lacking, we say their mindset is Low.

The distinction between skill set (hard skills) and mindset (soft skills) is critical when diagnosing employee performance. Skill set is what they know, while mindset is how they feel. These are two distinct factors that impact performance, and each must be assessed and managed separately.

With these two factors measured as either High or Low, there are four possible diagnoses, as illustrated in Figure 8.2 below.

Figure 8.2. 30-Second Leadership Model

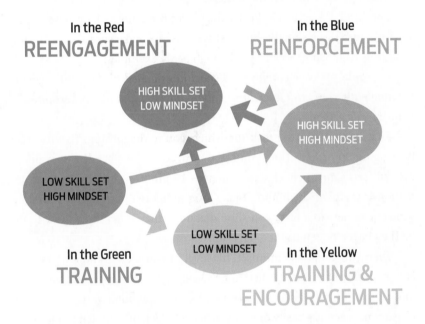

An employee with a **high skill set** and **low mindset** for a task is "in the Red."

An employee with a **high skill set** and **high mindset** for a task is "in the Blue."

An employee with a **low skill set** and **high mindset** for a task is "in the Green."

An employee with a **low skill set** and **low mindset** for a task is "in the Yellow."

It's important to use the phrase "in the . . ." when discussing employee performance. It reminds us that employees are constantly moving in and out of these states due to a myriad of factors, some personal and some work-related. Remember, labels are sticky. Our focus is on their behavior, not on their identity. Resist the urge to describe an employee as "Red" or "a Red." Refer to them as "*in* the Red."

It's also important to understand that these four states aren't sequential. Employees don't move forward in stages. They jump around. Even when they've mastered a skill set, their mindset fluctuates, sometimes daily. Your job, no matter where they are, is to "upcoach" them into the Blue and continue coaching to keep them there.

Figure 8.2 above also indicates the prescription for each of these stages. We'll discuss these shortly. But first we need to make sure *you're* "in the Blue" for diagnosing. So let's go through some examples:

Example #1: *New employee Michael has nodded his head throughout training but secretly still feels unsure about how to input new orders into the point-of-sale system.*

First, you clarify the task for which you're diagnosing. In this case, it's ringing up orders. Then you ask the two questions needed to evaluate his skill set. Can Michael state the steps to input an order? And can he demonstrate them? It shouldn't take long to figure out if he can. Anytime someone is new to a task, you should assume they don't know how to do it. They haven't been trained. His skill set is low.

Then you gauge his mindset, his level of confidence and enthusiasm. He's nodding, acknowledging that he's hearing the training. But that nod is misleading. It's hiding the fact that he feels unsure about inputting orders. A busy manager might easily overlook Michael's lack of confidence and press forward with more information. That keeps the attention on Michael's skill set as his mindset worsens.

Good managers watch closely and ask questions. They check for understanding by asking the employee to repeat what they've heard and demonstrate what they've seen. But they also check for confidence. They really want to know how employees are feeling during training. If they discover Michael is feeling unsure, they know there's a mindset issue and take steps to help him.

So, with a low skill set and a low mindset for inputting orders, you conclude Michael is in the Yellow right now. Hopefully, with a bit more training and encouragement, he can move into the Blue.

Example #2: *The only thing Lynn loves more than mixing drinks for customers is teaching new bartenders how to make signature cocktails.*

The task you're diagnosing is mixing drinks. If you've asked Lynn to train others, you know she has the skills. Lynn has a high skill set. You also know she loves this work, which tells you she also has a high mindset. So for mixing drinks, Lynn is in the Blue.

Example #3: *One of Lynn's co-workers, a server named Megan, has complained that Lynn has been going home after close while the floor in the bar area is still dirty. You stay late that night and confirm what Megan has reported: Lynn is leaving the floor for others to mop. The next day you point out to Lynn what you've observed and ask her about it. She explains that she feels unappreciated by the waitstaff. They ring up orders incorrectly and then blame her when customers complain. She's expected to accommodate them while also taking care of the patrons at the bar. She loves mixing drinks, but after a long shift, mopping the floor is the last thing she wants to do. The waitstaff is getting tips for drinks she's making. There's no reason they can't help with cleaning.*

There's a bit to unpack here. Multiple employees need coaching. (But situations like this are what keep managers employed!) First, focus on the task at hand: mopping the floor. Can Lynn state the steps for correctly mopping the floor? Can she demonstrate them? You've seen her do it many times, so there's no need to discuss it. You know she has the skill set. The problem is her mindset. She *can* clean the floor, but she doesn't want to. With a high skill set and low mindset, Lynn, who's in the Blue for mixing drinks, is in the Red for mopping the floor. After you coach her to boost her mindset around this task (we'll explore how to do this later), meet with your waitstaff to diagnose their taking of drink orders and clarify for everyone your expectations around cleaning. Is the problem what they know (skill set)? How they feel (mindset)? A bit of both? Getting the right answers is critical for helping your entire team work in harmony.

Example #4: *Greg has been fantastic at making pizzas for two years and is psyched to have been promoted to assistant manager.*

Clearly Greg is an expert at making pizzas. You also know he has a terrific attitude and lots of enthusiasm. Promoting him to manager is a great way to keep him engaged. So what's his diagnosis? Well, it depends on the task. For making pizzas, both skill set and mindset are high, so he's in the Blue. But management is a very different role. He's never managed before. He'll be leading employees, scheduling, and taking on new responsibilities. He's excited for the opportunity, so his mindset is high, but because management is new to him, his skill set is low. He's in the Green for management.

It's very common for top-performing employees to be put in leadership positions. The expectation is that if they are good at the job, they'll be good at leading others in the job. There are two problems with this assumption. The first is the belief that great employees make great managers. Often this is not the case, because management requires a completely different skill set. Just because Greg is good at making pizzas doesn't mean he'll be good at training, motivating employees, building culture, etc.

The second problem is that even if Greg does have it in him to be a great manager, he needs training—just like he needed to be trained to make pizzas. But as we discussed earlier, employees rarely get adequate management training when they're promoted. Everyone's busy (often because the previous manager is gone), and they need to step in and start managing immediately. So they get thrown into the deep end, usually without swimming lessons.

Right now Greg is in the Green for management. The proper way to coach him for success would be to identify the main tasks he'll be responsible for as assistant manager. His supervisor should then diagnose him for each of these tasks separately and upcoach him to boost his skill set and mindset in all areas.

Example #5: *Thanksgiving is approaching, so you explain to your grocery store team that the Wednesday before is your busiest day of the year. It's all hands on deck, and everyone needs to be prepared to work. Wednesday morning, Alexis, one of your top baggers, calls in sick. That leaves you short-staffed and makes the day significantly more difficult for everyone working that shift.*

OK, let's diagnose Alexis for bagging. Your goal is always to determine if the issue is what the employee knows (skill set), how they feel (mindset), or both. Does Alexis have the skill set for bagging? She's one of your top baggers, so presumably she does. But what about her mindset? Is she confident? Enthusiastic? Normally she is. But in this instance, many bosses would say she has a low mindset. She called in sick on the busiest day of the year. She's not stepping up, not being a team player. She lacks commitment. Assuming her mindset is low, they treat her as if she's in the Red.

But that approach to managing Alexis is likely to make her mindset worse and possibly drive her to quit. Alexis doesn't have a low commitment. She just got sick! Her skill set and mindset are both high. She's in the Blue for bagging. But she's human, and things happen. She doesn't need to be disciplined; she needs rest. If this were a chronic problem, you might diagnose her differently. But when a great team member suddenly faces unforeseen circumstances, a good manager shows empathy. Alexis is in the Blue, and your job is to treat her in a way that keeps her there. Save the lecture and send her some soup.

To summarize the process for making a correct diagnosis, you first clarify the specific task you're assessing. You distinguish between skill set and mindset, measuring each as either high or low. Then you determine which color the employee is in and prepare to apply the proper coaching, which we'll discuss in the next chapters. Get in the habit of determining if the issue is what they *know* (skill set) or how they *feel* (mindset). Once you start thinking in these terms, diagnosis will come naturally and quickly.

Honestly, if you were to put the book down now and just start noticing the difference between your employees' knowledge and feelings, you'd already be way ahead of most bosses. You'd have a much better sense of what an employee needs and would be able to respond accordingly.

But our goal isn't just to coach a little better. We're trying to build top-performing teams. So let's look now at how to prescribe the right coaching so you can elevate your employees to the top and keep them there.

CHAPTER 9

Coaching in the Green and Yellow

E arly in my 20s, a friend got me a one-day gig helping on a movie set. I had a very specific responsibility that day—to operate a karaoke machine being used in the shoot. It was mindless work, but it got me into the production. As I'd hoped, I was invited to return the next day as a full-fledged production assistant. I was psyched!

But upon arrival the next morning, the second assistant director chewed me out.

"Why are you late?!"

"I am? I came at 8:00 a.m., just like yesterday."

"The call sheet says PAs are to arrive at 7:00 a.m."

"The call sheet? I'm sorry, I didn't know there was one. I just thought I was supposed to come the same as yesterday."

"Well, if you're going to do this job, we need to know you can be responsible. Now go help lay down those boards."

Not only did I not know there was a call sheet, I didn't know what a call sheet was! No one told me.

Later that morning I was ordered to find an extension cord. I saw a truck with equipment, so I climbed inside and started looking around.

"Hey, what are you doing in there?!" It was the head grip (the person in charge of lighting setup).

"Pete told me to find an extension cord."

"Not in there. If you're not on the grip crew, stay out of our truck."

That's how the day went. They kept barking out things for me to do without explanation, and I stumbled through my work, learning what I could by doing everything wrong. A few times I saw crew members shake their heads at my incompetence.

I started out excited. I was actually working on a Hollywood movie set! I was willing to pay my dues and help any way they'd allow me. My mindset was high, but my skill set was low. I didn't need a lecture about being on time or a reprimand for going into the wrong truck. I needed guidance. They must have known I'd never done this before, but they didn't care—or maybe they didn't think about it. They just wanted to finish production and go home.

By the time the second day ended, I had learned very little about how to be a good production assistant. The experience bummed me out. It killed my enthusiasm and lowered my mindset, and my skill set didn't improve much. When they passed out the call sheet for day three, I told them I didn't need one. I wouldn't be returning.

It's common for harried managers to expect new employees to just know things. They're too busy to train them properly, so they just want to put them to work as soon as possible. The unspoken philosophy is "Get to work and figure it out." But that's a great way to set employees up for bad habits, and it's how you prevent them from achieving top performance. It's how you pull people who are in the Green into the Yellow. It might also be how you push them out the door.

No matter what state an employee is in, the goal is always to coach them into the Blue and keep them there. Poorly coaching an employee in the Green wrecks their mindset—and that makes it harder to get them into the Blue.

In the Green vs. in the Yellow

In the Green and in the Yellow are very different states. Both have low skill sets, but what distinguishes them is the emotional state of the worker for a task—their mindset. If it's high, meaning the employee is feeling confident and enthusiastic, the employee is in the Green. As indicated in the model in Figure 8.2 in Chapter 8, they need training. If it's low, they're in the Yellow. This employee needs training and encouragement. In both cases, the employee needs help developing their skills.

Characteristics of Someone in the Green

The color green is associated with newness. Anyone new to a task is in the Green for that task. That might be a new employee. It could also be a veteran employee who's learning something new. Even if they have lots of other skills, they may not have *these* skills. Until they learn them, their skill set is low, and they should be coached accordingly. Often, experienced employees don't get adequate training for new tasks. They're thought of as highly competent, so skill sets are taken for granted.

This happens a lot when a top-performing worker is promoted to management, as we discussed in Chapter 8. The assumption is that because they can work well, they can lead well, but often this just isn't the case. If they've never managed before, they're in the Green for management and need training.

Hourly workers often come with few skills. They're in the Green for a lot of tasks many employers take for granted. During an office internship I had in college, I was asked to do some filing, so I happily placed the papers directly into the hanging folders, not knowing I was supposed to put them in a file folder first and then drop the file into the hanging folder. My boss laughed when she saw what I was doing. She showed me once, and from that moment on, I knew how to file documents properly. It wasn't difficult. Training took about 15 seconds. But unless I'm told, I won't know.

I had a similar moment when I was a teenager working at our family ice cream store. I thought the glass on the ice cream cabinets needed cleaning, so I decided to wipe them from the inside—with a wet rag. The water quickly smeared the glass.

"Scotty, what did you do?" my grandfather asked. I explained I was just trying to clean the glass. "With a wet rag?" he chuckled.

Again, I began the task with good intentions and a lack of knowledge. I was in the Green. I needed training.

As a boss, you can't anticipate everything your employees don't know. They're going to make lots of mistakes performing simple tasks. But simple mistakes are *high* stakes for the employees. Every small failure puts their mindset at risk. They're self-conscious in these moments and worried about what you think. If you scold them or laugh about something you assumed they should know, you risk pushing them into the Yellow. Training someone in the Green is a race. You're trying to boost their skill set before they lose their mindset, so it's critical to create a safe space for them to learn.

This is especially true for hourly workers. Salaried workers are more likely to have experience and the confidence that goes along with it. Hourly workers may be smart, fast learners, but until they've been taught, you must be gentler with them. I've already shared several stories of bad experiences I've had with new jobs. It's not that I had a lot of bad bosses or that I was a bad employee. But when I was young and new, I had a lot to learn. I wasn't an "idiot." I was just in the Green. I wanted to do well, but I needed instructions.

Employees are vulnerable when they're new. They're worried about messing up or looking bad and doubting whether they'll ever master the new skill. They're worried about what you and their team members think. They'll remember how you treat them during those moments, so if you neglect them or laugh at them, it's going to make an impression. I remember these moments as if they happened yesterday, and so will your employees.

Looking back, I realize that my bosses, even my grandfather, may not have fully understood how vulnerable new employees are. They weren't jerks any more than I was an idiot. The problem wasn't with what they felt—it was with what they knew. As managers, they were probably still in the Green or Yellow and could have benefited from more training of their own.

Employees in the Green appreciate the new opportunity and are excited to learn. That's a great mindset that you should strive to preserve. Don't take it for granted. Train them properly to maintain their enthusiasm, and you'll quickly get them into the Blue. Don't do that, and they're likely to drop into the Yellow.

Characteristics of Someone in the Yellow

Like someone in the Green, an employee in the Yellow has a low skill set. What differentiates them is their mindset, which is also low. They're no longer enthusiastic or confident. They probably were when they first started, but not anymore, which is a huge problem. It's harder to learn when your mindset is low—there's too much self-talk and doubt, too many thoughts bouncing around your head. If you could hear their thoughts, training might sound something like this:

"OK, when a new delivery arrives, click 'Receive Shipment' and then scan the UPC."

Wait, where's "Receive Shipment"? What's a UPC? I'm confused.

"Then pull up the WRO . . ."

WRO?

" . . . click 'Confirm Inventory,' and compare the order to the SKUs on the boxes."

Huh? Where's the SKU? Is that on the purchase order or the boxes? What's the difference between the SKU and the UPC? This is so much harder than I thought.

"Once you've confirmed accuracy, count the boxes and check for damage. Don't let them tell you just to count the pallets. They make mistakes all the time. Any questions so far?"

I don't understand any of this. I'm totally lost. "No, I got it."

"Great. Once the order is confirmed, we need to move the shipment off the dock into the warehouse. So here's what you do . . ."

I really don't know if this is for me.

As the supervisor focuses on skill set, the new employee experiences a drop in mindset. Each additional instruction contributes to their feeling of being overwhelmed. Once they're in this state, training isn't enough. Their trainer must now also rescue their mindset. Their confidence and enthusiasm will eventually increase once they've mastered the skill, but it'll take longer—in many cases, too long.

An employee in the Yellow is likely to hide their feelings because they're still trying to please you. They may not ask questions for fear of looking incompetent, and they may not share their self-doubt or frustration. That's why you really need to watch closely during training. Pay attention to their body language, and ask them how they're feeling. Make it OK for them to have feelings. Then offer encouragement. You don't need to completely reinstate their confidence or enthusiasm. You just need to boost them a little, enough to get them through training. They'll feel better once they've learned the task.

Many retention problems are a result of employees spending too much time in the Yellow. It feels horrible to be undertrained and inadequately supported. No one enjoys being bad at their job, so if that's how they feel, they won't stick around long.

Few things are more important than properly training employees. Busyness is an unacceptable excuse. Properly trained employees will save you time.

TOP-PERFORMANCE SPOTLIGHT

CATANIA OILS
Ayer, Massachusetts

Catania Oils is as committed to building and maintaining their team as they are to manufacturing premium oils. The company is family-run, operated by the great-grandchildren of their original founder. But it's their 200 employees who keep the oil flowing. Annemarie Abdo, Catania's vice president of human resources, shared with me everything they do to operationalize their core value "We are family" and continue the family legacy.

Recruitment in manufacturing can be difficult, so Catania Oils plays the long game. They're active in the community. They make presentations at high schools and offer tours of their facility. They

TOP-PERFORMANCE SPOTLIGHT, continued

know some students aren't college bound, so they help young people see the long-term opportunities manufacturing work can provide. They market job opportunities by posting fun videos on social media highlighting their positive work environment.

The company takes advantage of available government programs to enhance the work experience. They've received grants from the state to fund employee training. Where available, they've also arranged state-funded transportation for workers without cars.

But it's the company's internal programs that really make the difference. One initiative, called "Walk in My Shoes," allows employees to spend a day in another department, getting to see what others do and share a meal with them. Another program, "Supermarket Safari," takes employees on a field trip to local stores that sell their products. Seeing their oils on the shelves gives them a sense of pride and a wider understanding of their work.

The company does a lot to show appreciation to their team. During "Employee Appreciation Month," team members are treated to meals, snacks, and company-branded swag. They also have extended meals to socialize and connect. Year-round team members who are spotted making a difference to the company, co-workers, or customers are honored with the "Impact Award."

To ensure these initiatives are working, Catania measures employee engagement. Three times a year they conduct surveys and solicit feedback. Among organizations using the same engagement survey platform, Catania Oils ranks in the 75th percentile, "which is still lower than we want," Annemarie told me. They aim to be in the top 20 percent of all workplaces and use the data they collect to continuously improve. Employees can anonymously provide feedback, ask questions, or express concerns in the survey, and managers are required to write a response.

TOP-PERFORMANCE SPOTLIGHT, continued

The company starts employees at 120 percent of local minimum wage for entry-level positions and conducts compensation studies twice a year to ensure they remain competitive. Employees receive 401(k) matching after 30 days on the job and profit sharing after one year. Their average tenure with the company is 6.5 years, though their goal is 10 years (compared to a manufacturing industry average of 5.2 years). Annual retention is an impressive 89 percent (and that's after COVID), compared to the manufacturing industry average of 60 percent.

Founder Giuseppe Basile came to the U.S. from Sicily in 1900 in search of opportunity. Three generations later, his descendants are providing opportunities for hundreds of workers who are part of the extended family.

Top-Performance Takeaways:

> Build community relationships to create awareness for potential future employees.
> Look for government grants to supplement training costs, transportation, or other employee services.
> Allow employees to learn about other roles in the company.
> Formally express appreciation to employees and recognize those making an impact.
> Give employees a higher sense of purpose (visionary leadership) by allowing them to see your products and services from the customer's perspective.
> Track employee engagement and solicit feedback for improvement.
> Conduct compensation studies to ensure your wages are competitive.

Training in the Green and Yellow

Training is as much a reflection of the manager's competence as it is the employee's. If the employee doesn't acquire the necessary job skills, it's usually because they were trained improperly. It's possible they're not suited for the position, but it's more likely they weren't prepared well. Training itself is a skill set. If the manager hasn't been trained on how to train others, they may be doing it poorly. That leads to common problems, such as:

> ≫ Training too quickly
> ≫ Making assumptions about what the employee knows
> ≫ Focusing on one learning style
> ≫ Overloading with information
> ≫ Not checking for mastery
> ≫ Not explaining the "why"
> ≫ Focusing more on the task than the person

Training communicates your level of care for employees. Rushed, incomplete training says you're too busy to look after their soft needs. This time isn't just about passing on a skill set. It's also an expression of your culture. The impression you make here will set the tone for your working relationship. You want them to know you've got their back, that you care as much about their growth and well-being as you do their work. If they feel cared about, they'll care more about their work. Training is an upfront investment of your time that will save you time on the back end by preventing mistakes. It's the quickest path to top performance.

Making Training Stick

In the late 19th century, German psychologist Hermann Ebbinghaus developed what's known as "the forgetting curve," which describes the rate at which we forget learned information if it's not reviewed and reinforced. The curve shows a rapid decline in memory retention within the first few hours or days, as you can see in Figure 9.1.

Figure 9.1. The Forgetting Curve

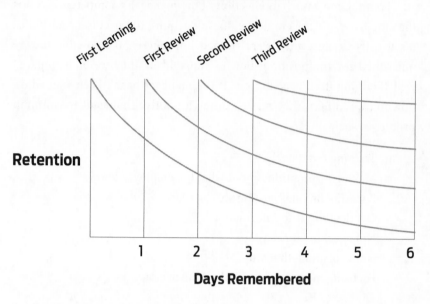

People often learn things temporarily, long enough to pass a test. But they may not remember it long enough to put it to practical use. You must combat this tendency through reinforcement. As the subsequent curves in Figure 9.1 above show, information is retained longer with repeated exposure. According to a 2017 article on educational website Edutopia, "Without any reinforcement or connections to prior knowledge, information is quickly forgotten—roughly 56 percent in one hour, 66 percent after a day, and 75 percent after six days." Employees may be able to demonstrate mastery of a task during training, but what good is that if they've forgotten how to do it a week later?

The implications of memory loss after training are most significant for hourly workers, who are less likely to have "prior knowledge." Their initial training won't be a reinforcement or enhancement of what they already know. Hourly workers are also more likely to be performing repetitive tasks and be expected to adhere to specific procedures or guidelines—so there's a lot to forget. The rushed training and speed with which they're sent to the floor, combined with shift-based scheduling, makes it harder to retrain them. Much of what they learn, they learn by doing on their own, and too often doing the wrong thing.

That means training must occur over time. Give your workers a good enough skill set to get them started, and then help them maintain and expand it. Fortunately, there are ways to make your initial training stick.

Training Their Brains

When my daughter was 5 years old, she asked me to teach her to ride a bike. I found an amazing technique that had her confidently riding on her own within an hour. Instead of overwhelming her with all the steps, I had her ride in a circle with me helping her stay up for 15 minutes. All she had to do was pedal and get used to the motion in that one direction. Then we switched directions and did the same exercise for another 15 minutes. We repeated both circles again, and then we tried the straightaway. Miraculously, after just a few tries, she was able to stay up without my help. She rode straight, turned, and could go wherever she wanted without falling. I can't explain exactly how she acquired the skill, but something about riding in circles made an impression on her cerebellum, something that stuck.

When you train a person on something they've never done before, you're not just showing them how to do it. You're literally rewiring their brain—and you're stimulating various regions of their brain that work in different ways. For example, their hippocampus consolidates information into long-term memory. Their prefrontal cortex helps them understand and apply new information. Their motor cortex controls physical movements. New connections form between their neurons through synaptic plasticity. When you train an employee, you're facilitating a complex process involving the formation and strengthening of neural connections, the release of neurotransmitters, and the coordination of different brain regions. And you thought you were just teaching them how to work the register!

You don't need to understand all this stuff to do it well. But you do need to appreciate the complexity of passing on skills. It's easy when you're busy to see struggling employees as incompetent, but people are more complicated than that. Much of it has to do with brain development. We discussed this in Chapter 1 when we talked about teenagers.

Teaching is not the same thing as facilitating learning. It's not enough to provide information. You must ensure your workers acquire it, remember it, and apply it.

Let's look at a four-step process to do this more thoughtfully.

Tell, Show, Watch, Review

Busy managers just show people how to do things, which is fine for simple tasks, like how to turn on the lights in the walk-in freezer. But if you need to show them how to deice the walk-in freezer's drain line, a more formal training procedure is needed.

The problem is that when we've been doing something for a while, we forget how hard it once was, and we project our competence onto the person we're training. We quickly explain the steps and assume they're absorbing them as fast as we're explaining them. As we confidently discuss the task and tell them how easy it is, we make it harder for them to admit they're confused. They may be too embarrassed to say they don't understand. It doesn't feel good to struggle with something others say is easy. Alternatively, reassuring them how easy the task is might make them too confident before they've had to try it unsupervised.

It's important to have a training process that overcomes these dynamics. It's not enough to go over something. You must pass on a skill set and confirm the employee has mastered it. You must be accountable for training them on the task before you hold them accountable for performing it.

Figure 9.2. Tell, Show, Watch, Review

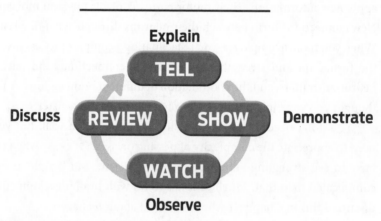

Tell, Show, Watch, Review (see Figure 9.2, above) is a multisensory training method that covers a variety of learning styles. The approach helps the person you're training encode, store, and retrieve information. Here are the four steps:

Tell

This is a verbal description of how to perform a task. This approach is helpful for people who are auditory learners, those who learn best by listening. Methodically explain each step in the process. Remember that part of having a high skill set is being able to state the steps. Explain them in order many times to help the employee learn them, and ask the employee to repeat them back to you. Also use this time to explain the purpose of this task and perhaps the reason for the most important steps. Why do these things matter? How does this task fit into the greater operation? Give your employee some context for their work.

Your verbal instructions are triggering specific regions of the worker's brain that are involved in language processing and comprehension. By repeating verbal instructions, you can strengthen neural connections associated with language acquisition and understanding, enhancing their ability to remember and use the information accurately.

Show

After explaining the steps, visually demonstrate them. When your worker sees you perform a task, it activates mirror neurons in their brain and strengthens the neural pathways associated with the activity you demonstrated, allowing them to better understand and imitate you. This is a different process from the one that happens during the Tell stage, so it's another way to help them remember.

Training videos are a common way to demonstrate a task and can be helpful when part of a more extensive training program. Many organizations have their employees log into a learning management system (LMS) to read instructions and watch videos. They must answer questions correctly before moving on to the next module. This is an efficient way to demonstrate tasks and ensure all steps are described thoroughly, although keep in mind that a video can't observe the employee's facial expressions and body language to gauge their reaction. Another concern is that the worker may focus more on passing the assessments than on actually learning the task. The LMS also prevents some of the bonding that takes place between colleagues when one mentors another. If you're going to use one of these systems, be sure to reinforce them with discussion and human interaction (especially if you're training them on culture). Don't assume your employee has mastered a skill set just because they've completed a module.

Watch

This is sometimes called "Do" rather than "Watch," because in this step you have the employee do the task. But the names of the other three steps describe what the *trainer* is doing. Your role here is to *watch* as they perform the task.

Kinesthetic learners benefit from hands-on experience. Unlike passively listening or observing, doing something gives their brain more sensory feedback. You can read about swimming or watch someone else do it, but there's nothing like feeling the water on your skin or noticing the way your body reacts to paddling and kicking. The tactile experience awakens the motor cortex (controlling physical movement), the somatosensory cortex (processing your senses), and the cerebellum (controlling balance and coordination). Doing something is the only way to really know how good you are at it and what you need to adjust to improve.

Many managers prefer employees learn this way. They put them on the floor so they can learn by doing (and get the work done). They will learn quickly this way, but they won't become top performers. Their focus will be on survival, and without the other elements of good training, they'll hit a performance ceiling.

My dad never learned to type, and then the computer age came along. He quickly taught himself two-fingered typing and has gotten good at it. But his speed will never measure up to someone who's learned proper typing. I'm going through the same thing teaching myself to play guitar. I've hit a certain level of competency, but then I get stuck. I can play the main riff of "Enter Sandman." But the solo? Forget about it. Self-teaching has its advantages, but it's a longer, tougher path to mastery.

Give your employee a chance to try out the task, but only after you explain and demonstrate the proper steps. You want them to experience the right way of doing it, and the challenges that go with doing it right.

Review

Reviewing performance is crucial for excellence. Playing a game is educational, but most learning happens afterward in the locker room and looking at the game tape the next day. Performance must be reviewed to be improved.

After you watch the employee complete the task, talk about what happened. Start by asking them questions: "How'd you feel about that?" "How do you think you did?" "What did you do well?" "Where did you struggle?" "What can you do to improve?" You probably already know the answers to these questions, but you're not trying to teach them—you're facilitating learning. They'll benefit more from what they realize than from what you say.

Knowing their mindset is fragile when learning something new, I like to begin the review process by asking them what they did well. It takes their mind off their mistakes and forces them to give themselves some credit. Then I ask prompting questions to guide them toward improving. Don't provide the answers in the form of a question ("Do you think it would have been better if you started with the right side and worked your way to the left?"). Giving them solutions is not as useful as helping them problem solve, which engages their prefrontal cortex. You're trying to make an impression on their brain so they remember what they learn, and encouraging them to find the solutions will help. If they don't get there on their own, then offer your tips. Be careful with how much feedback you give. Too much information will limit their overall recall.

Once you've reviewed their performance with them, start over. Tell them the steps, show them how, watch them do them, then review and repeat. Keep doing this until they can verbally state the steps and consistently demonstrate them. Do not allow them to work on this task unsupervised until their skill set is high. Keep training. As we've discussed, repetition and reinforcement is your best defense against the forgetting curve. It's also the quickest way to get them into the Blue.

I know you're eager to get your employees working, and I appreciate that your time is limited. But there are few things more important than setting up your workers to succeed. If you train them well from the start, they'll save you time and make your operation run much smoother.

Who Should Do the Training?

I prefer to have employees with a high skill set train those who are still learning—that way everyone benefits. The new person gets guidance from someone who has mastered the task. Your experienced employees are likely better at the task than you are, and asking them to train is a flattering nod to their skill mastery.

Co-worker training is also a great way to promote teamwork. Employees should be elevating each other every chance they get. It should be a cultural norm. Make them responsible for each other's growth.

While your top performers help new employees improve their skill set, you should be close by, monitoring the new people's mindset and making sure they're not slipping into the Yellow. Check in with them throughout the process to ensure they're still enthusiastic.

When having experienced workers conduct training, keep in mind that training itself is a skill set. Just because they can perform a task doesn't mean they can teach it well. If they haven't trained someone before, they're in the Green for training. Explain "Tell, Show, Watch, Review" to them. Demonstrate it. Watch them do it. Then review how they did. Get them into the Blue for training before putting them in charge of someone in the Green.

How to Encourage Someone in the Yellow

Employees in the Green and Yellow both need help with their skill set, but employees in the Yellow also need help with their mindset.

In Chapter 1, we talked about teens being driven by emotion. But even mature adults are vulnerable to stress and fear. Events that "trigger" us activate our amygdala, the region of the brain that processes emotion, especially fear and anxiety. This is a safety mechanism that puts us on high alert when we sense danger. It doesn't take much to stimulate the amygdala—even a little stress can activate this part of the brain. This is a problem, because when it's active, it blocks the neural pathways to the prefrontal cortex, the part of the brain we need for logic, reason, and problem solving. According to neurobiologists and psychiatrists from Yale University in a 2012 article in *Scientific American*, "Neural circuits responsible for conscious self-control are highly vulnerable to even mild stress. When they shut down, primal impulses go unchecked and mental paralysis sets in."

That "mental paralysis" describes what it's like for an employee in the Yellow. They're too "triggered" to learn and too distracted by thoughts and feelings to acquire skills. Your job, therefore, is to watch them closely during training and gauge their mental state. When the stress and self-doubt set in, you need to calm them down and encourage them. Help them disengage their amygdala and reengage their prefrontal cortex. If you don't, Tell, Show, Watch, Review won't make much impact.

Encouragement entails adding a bit more of a human touch to your training. As you move through the four steps, you're also working to improve their confidence and enthusiasm. It'll help if you begin training by telling the employee to anticipate feeling frustrated and confused. Reassure them that it's normal and explain that if these feelings come up, it may be your fault for moving too fast or for not explaining things well. Tell them to let you know when they start to struggle so you can adjust on your end.

This conversation will set a positive tone for training. It takes some of the burden off them and makes it safe for them to feel and express their feelings. All this is important to promote confidence. They'll also appreciate feeling seen as a person with emotions and like having you on their side. Remember, you're not just passing on a skill set. You're building a relationship. If they trust you enough to reveal how they're feeling, you'll have a better idea when to stop training and start encouraging.

Still, you shouldn't rely on them to tell you when they're confused or anxious. Check in with them throughout training and ask how they're doing. Don't ask if they're OK—they'll just say yes. Instead, ask open-ended questions that prompt them to talk, such as:

"OK, what are you thinking now?"

"Tell me what you're feeling."

"How are you doing so far, honestly?"

"All right, let's pause for a second. I've given you a lot so far. Tell me where I've confused you."

"I really want you to feel OK with this, so tell me where you're feeling the most nervous."

For easier tasks or more experienced employees training new ones, you won't have to do this as much. Adjust your approach for the person you're training. But do incorporate a discussion of how they're doing into your training to ensure their mindset remains high enough to continue focusing on their skill set.

As needed, break down the task into small, bite-size steps so they won't feel overwhelmed. Set them up for easy wins. As they master each step, praise them, and make sure they see their progress.

When an employee is in the Yellow, there's also an opportunity to boost your culture. Recruit team members to help encourage them. It'll feel incredible to have co-workers help them succeed.

One of the requirements my son was expected to meet before reporting for his first practice of college basketball was a timed run. He was told to arrive on campus ready to run two miles in 13 minutes. When he reported for the first test, however, he couldn't do it. He came in dead last. That meant he missed strength training and had to spend weeks working on endurance to prepare for another test in front of the entire team. After the second test, he called home to tell us what happened.

His pace had started well, but as the minutes ticked by, breathing became harder, and he started to slow. At the 12th minute, he still had a lot of distance to cover, and he felt a sense of dread. But then something happened he hadn't expected. As he approached the final stretch, the entire team came onto the track to support him. They ran with him, screamed for him, and offered enough encouragement to get him across the finish line. The coach's stopwatch read 12 minutes and 59 seconds. The team went nuts. Their support compensated for my son's self-doubt. As he told us the story, we could tell the crossing of the finish line wasn't just about when he met his endurance requirement. It was the moment his teammates became his brothers. We never forget the people who are there for us when we need them. Get your team in the habit of cheering each other on, especially when someone has a dip in their mindset.

An employee in the Green likes encouragement, but an employee in the Yellow *needs* encouragement. Be there for them to meet that soft need. That's how you get them into the Blue, where you'll get *hard* results.

When Training and Encouragement Don't Work

While many hourly jobs don't require a lot of skills, there's still a basic level of competency needed to do the job. Unfortunately, some people just aren't cut out for certain tasks. It's harder for them than others, and their attempts to get it right just cause frustration for them and everyone else.

You must decide how much time you want to invest in boosting struggling employees. The right person assigned to the right task will learn it quickly and enjoy it. The opposite is also true. Perhaps with enough time, training, and encouragement they'll get where they need to be. But how much time do you have to offer, and how is that time best spent? Is it worth the investment to get them into the Blue, or is your time best spent recruiting and training someone else who will get there faster?

Sometimes you'll hire the wrong person, but that doesn't mean you have to fire them. Perhaps there's a better position or a better task for them. I had many employees at Edible Arrangements who had the same job, but we assigned each different tasks based on their strengths. Some were good at cutting fruit, so that's what they did. Others were slow at cutting but could take that cut fruit and quickly assemble the arrangements. Some were so-so at designing baskets but were great at wrapping the baskets and preparing them for delivery. Everyone was cross-trained, but we put them where they thrived.

Training is an investment of time, so you should get a return on that investment. If you don't, you may need to divest. Don't try to force someone into something for which they're not suited. You're doing them a favor by allowing them to move onto something else that's a better fit. But don't make that decision until you've genuinely given them a chance. Give them patient, loving, thorough training. Only then will you know their potential.

These strategies I've given you are proven ways to help those who are new to tasks succeed. Whether your worker is in the Green or the Yellow, it's your job to coach them into the Blue. Your job then is to keep them there.

CHAPTER 10

Coaching in the Blue

"Hey, Scott. Want to know my approach to good management? I hire great people and stay out of their way!"

I can't tell you how many times I've heard versions of this comment: Hire carefully, train them well, and leave them alone. Great people don't want to be micromanaged. They've earned autonomy. Let them know you're there for them and then let 'em be.

I totally understand this perspective. I also disagree with it. I believe your most important management hours are spent actively coaching your skilled team members. That doesn't mean micromanaging them. It means staying engaged with them and keeping the spark alive. They don't need you to light a fire under them, but they do need you to feed the fire within them.

This is especially true in an hourly work environment. Hourly jobs provide less compensation, less job security, and fewer opportunities for growth. The work may be physically hard, more repetitive, and monotonous. Top-performing hourly workers may aspire to something beyond what you're having them do. They outgrow their jobs. Without the same advantages and motivators that come with salaried work, we can't assume their job satisfaction will last. The very drive that makes them great may also be the drive that makes them want more.

I'm grateful for the many top-performing employees I had at Edible Arrangements. But I'm bummed about the ones who left because I neglected them. I could have done more to keep them. One of my original employees, the first to be promoted to assistant manager, left because she felt overworked and underappreciated. Another customer service employee with the most wonderful outgoing personality left to make a little more money at a nearby cupcake shop. We'd done nothing for either of them to make staying worthwhile. I would have found a way to take better care of them had I realized they were unhappy, but I took them for granted. I lost a lot of great people over the years because I "let 'em be."

Coaching employees into the Blue is important, but keeping them there is just as important. So is coaching them *back* into the Blue when they slip. Passive management won't cut it. Skilled employees need your attention.

In the Blue vs. in the Red

Employees in both the Blue and the Red have a high skill set. They can both verbalize all the steps for performing a specific task and demonstrate them well. What they know about the task isn't the issue. Once someone has made it into the Blue, they've mastered the task, and it's unlikely they'll lose their skills.

What differs is their mindset. When it drops, that high performer is then in the Red for that task. Whereas the needs of employees in the Green or Yellow are similar, employees in the Red need very different handling from those in the Blue. They need help rescuing their mindset and reengagement in their work.

What they don't need is more training, especially if they're already meeting your standards. It's fine if they want to improve. But if not, coaching them on a skill they've already mastered risks driving an employee from the Blue into the Red—or deeper into the Red. That's micromanagement, which no one likes.

Addressing their mindset requires a different approach. An employee in the Blue needs their mindset preserved. An employee in the Red needs their mindset recharged. Either way, you must take an active role.

Characteristics of Someone in the Blue

These are your superstars—your reliable employees who exhibit top performance. They show up, keep up, and step up. They excel with a smile.

But don't let them fool you. Just because they're in the Blue for most things doesn't mean they're in the Blue for *all* things. If you diagnose their performance by task, it's likely they're in a variety of states, each one requiring the corresponding coaching approach. And the diagnosis will change over time. Good people have bad days. Things happen at work and at home that impact their mindset. Sometimes those problems cause their performance to drop for one task, while other times it affects their work across the board.

Managers who focus too much on putting out fires tend to neglect employees in the Blue, which results in many unmet needs. They also dump more work on them because they're reliable. It's like punishing them for being good.

Because top performers are professional, they often conceal their dissatisfaction, so they can slip into the Red without you noticing. As you overlook their low mindset, they look for a new job. How they seem externally matters less than what they feel internally. According to Gallup's "State of the Global Workplace" report for 2023, 59 percent of workers globally are "quiet quitting." These employees "put in the minimum effort required, and they are psychologically disconnected from their employer. Although they are minimally productive, they are more likely to be stressed and burnt out than engaged workers because they feel lost and disconnected from their workplace."

That's why you need to watch your employees closely, have casual check-ins and formal sit-downs, and conduct surveys to measure employee satisfaction. Remain engaged with employees in the Blue to ensure their mindset really is as high as it seems, and then to keep it high.

Characteristics of Someone in the Red

These employees are just as skilled as those in the Blue, but there's been a drop in how they feel. Their mindset—once high—has decreased and their enthusiasm is gone. If their low mindset is apparent, it may present itself in their mood or their work, and that can affect your culture. A low mindset is contagious.

Unlike a skill set, which changes depending on the task, a low mindset often impacts multiple tasks. We've dubbed this *red spill*. Being unhappy about one thing can make you unhappy about many. It can make others unhappy, too.

In an hourly environment, most employee problems occur among those in the Red. They can perform the task, but their work is hampered by attitude problems and a lack of motivation. They don't live up to their potential, and they don't seem to care. Good enough is good enough.

Employees who linger in the Red can be very frustrating to manage. It's harder to coach mindset than skill set, especially when you're unsure why it's low.

I had one team member who was more mature and experienced than my other employees. He learned quickly and showed great promise. He worked well in the kitchen, could sell, and was good at chatting up customers. I believed he was on track for management.

But after a while, things took a bad turn. He started complaining about small things and developed interpersonal problems with his co-workers. Even when his job performance was good, he had a sour look on his face that made the work environment unpleasant for others. There was a lot of red spill going on.

Our sit-downs weren't productive. When I asked what was wrong, he got defensive and blamed others for the tension on the team. He displayed that broad, bad attitude that isn't necessarily egregious but doesn't indicate someone is in the Blue.

This went on for months. We didn't want to fire him (yet), but we definitely couldn't promote him. He must have sensed that, so he came to work one day and started his shift out of uniform. When my manager told him he wasn't getting promoted, he handed her a bag containing his folded uniform and walked out.

I was rooting for this employee. We could have used his skill set, but without the mindset, he was a liability. Perhaps if I had known then what I know now, I could have reengaged him more effectively—or I might have let him go even sooner.

Employees in the Red still have value. You've trained them, so they have experience and a high skill set. Often their drop in mindset is temporary. With a little TLC, they can be coached back into the Blue. Everyone needs occasional redirection. We need to remember their humanity and advocate for them lovingly and patiently.

For a while.

Employees in the Red can also take up a lot of your time—time that might be better spent coaching others. You must decide how much you want to invest in them. Can they be helped? Do they *want* to be helped? Will they respond to your coaching and make an effort in return? These are the tough questions you must tackle as a manager.

The way I see it, employees who are mostly in the Blue save you time, strengthen your team, and make your life easier. They contribute to the operation. Employees in the Red *take* from the operation, and that's not acceptable. Work with them for a while, but not forever.

Too many times, I hung on to underperformers for too long. My loyalty to them affected others on the team who deserved better. They're the ones who should have gotten my attention. I'd rather reinforce high mindsets than reengage low ones. As I got better at building our culture, I became less patient with those who threatened it.

But sometimes employees end up in the Red because their manager pushes them into it. I once assigned one of my managers to oversee our second store, and she took real ownership of its performance. It was her baby, and she thrived there, as did its sales. A few months later, I brought her back to the first store without fully appreciating her attachment to what she had built. She didn't want to complain, but her mood and drop in performance spoke volumes. I treated her like a chess piece. That was on me. Instead of giving her an attitude adjustment, I made a scheduling adjustment and returned her to her preferred location where she once again thrived.

I also learned through an employee satisfaction survey that one of my team members was "no longer feeling it." To my surprise, it was one of my best workers. She was grateful to me and loved our culture, but she was getting bored doing the same work. That also was on me. I sat with her and we explored ways to make things more challenging. I was grateful to learn how she was feeling so I could do something about it before it was too late.

It's dangerous for team members to be in the Red. You need to keep a close watch and rescue them as soon as possible. We'll discuss how to do this in Chapter 11. For now, let's talk about why employees in the Blue end up in the Red.

Why Top Performers Slip into the Red

There are countless reasons, but we've identified six main categories of problems:

1. **Boredom.** People want to feel challenged and want to grow. Hourly work can become monotonous, and even top performers can grow restless and eager to try something new.

2. **Feeling Unappreciated.** My surveys of employees' hard and soft needs have revealed a strong desire for acknowledgment. Most people get far less than they want, which makes them bitter.

3. **Poor Management.** Unfair treatment, disloyalty, disrespect—even an unkind tone of voice can quickly kill their buzz.

4. **Conflict with Co-Workers.** No one likes to come to work and have to battle it out with their colleagues—or even be around people in a bad mood. Ideally your culture will promote harmony. But even the best teams struggle with occasional miscommunication, rivalry, and tension.

5. **Conflict with Customers.** Great employees don't always receive great treatment, especially when a customer is angry. Frontline workers are the face of the company, and angry customers don't always distinguish between the person at fault and the person standing in front of them. They'll take out their feelings on anyone wearing the uniform—and they can be outright abusive.

6. **Personal Problems.** Employees bring their emotions to work, and problems at home may impact their mood, energy level, focus, and even physical health.

Coaching in the Red is about intervention: You're working to resolve these problems. Coaching in the Blue is about prevention: You're working to avoid these problems, which is a better use of your time. You do that by locking in everything they're doing right. Let's look at how to do that.

TOP-PERFORMANCE SPOTLIGHT

GELSON'S MARKETS
Southern California

Gelson's has built a loyal following of discerning shoppers who frequent their 27 grocery stores in Southern California. I'm one of them, primarily because of their extraordinary customer service. I was thrilled to get a sneak peek behind the scenes to learn how they inspire their superstar team of 2,700 (mostly) hourly workers to create their customer experience.

Instead of competing on price, Gelson's competes with premium service. Checkout lines are short and fast. Checkers pull items from carts for their shoppers. The kitchen provides scrumptious food and bright smiles. It's truly an unparalleled shopping experience that's enabled the chain to thrive for more than 70 years.

Consumer Reports ranked Gelson's fourth out of 96 grocers in the U.S. As an employer, they're certified by Great Place to Work, with 78 percent of their employees giving them that rating. This has kept their annual turnover at 27 percent, compared to the retail food industry average of 48 percent. Their average employee tenure is an impressive 11 years. New employees start at up to 120 percent of local minimum wage, consistent with or in excess of union requirements.

TOP-PERFORMANCE SPOTLIGHT, continued

I spoke with their senior vice president, operations, Tim Mahoney. He has been with Gelson's for 45 years, starting his career as a teenager bagging groceries. I asked why they're able to outperform other grocery chains.

"It's the people," he told me. "Anyone can sell a can of beans. We sell service and quality. You get the best results when you focus on the people more than anything else."

HeeSook Alden, vice president, team development and public affairs (who also started as a store-level worker), echoed these sentiments, sharing the original four pillars the company was founded on in 1951: quality products and people, cleanliness, convenience, and personalized service. She was quick to point out the difference between "personalized" service and "customer" service: "Every shopper has different needs. Our job is to personalize the experience to ensure those needs are met."

Gelson's has moved away from its old mission statement and replaced it with a shorter purpose statement: "Nourish. Connect. Inspire." Ongoing discussion of this statement has proved useful to convey the company's culture. "It's more important to us that team members embrace our values rather than memorize a long statement," HeeSook told me. "Shifting their focus onto our four pillars and new purpose statement are all we need to keep our culture alive."

Gelson's has a robust leadership and employee development program, offering everything from executive programs at the USC Marshall School of Business for selected high-potential leaders to English-language programs for employees who are non-native speakers. Gelson's tries to promote from within and create growth opportunities for anyone willing to work for them.

The company has a smaller manager-to-employee ratio than other chains. Senior directors of operations oversee fewer stores,

TOP-PERFORMANCE SPOTLIGHT, continued

allowing them more face time (and better relationships) with team members. It's common practice for employees' immediate supervisors to accompany them on service improvement feedback opportunities so they can work together on boosting performance.

Team members from each store nominate one co-worker for the president's award, and these nominees spend a year on the president's advisory board. The winner among all nominees earns their store a BBQ luncheon served by executive leadership. The executive team also appears on site at each store to honor employees' milestone work anniversaries. In addition to a public banner celebrating these team members, the stores have a "wow board," where management posts extraordinary customer feedback and photos of the team members who earned it.

New employees are trained on culture and assigned a "buddy" to look after them on the job. Store directors are instructed to actively engage all team members, personally checking in with them on a regular basis.

The company acknowledges employees' special occasions, and their president personally signs all birthday cards. If an employee loses a loved one, a member of the leadership team steps in to offer support, and the company sends funeral flowers.

Gelson's celebrates an annual employee appreciation day, provides food during the holidays, and sponsors pizza parties and other events for team members. Employees have access to a variety of discounts, prizes, and performance-based awards. The company also unites team members through community events and charity fundraisers.

Employee work-life balance is another important element of the grocer's long-term strategy. They choose not to be open 24 hours and only schedule night crews for a few days during the holidays. The stores

TOP-PERFORMANCE SPOTLIGHT, continued

close on Christmas and are open for limited hours on other holidays so team members can join their families. They also strive to accommodate school schedules and even work schedules for other jobs. They also do their best to work with employees who need leaves of absence.

That strong support of employees leads directly to a superior customer experience. The stores feel clean and efficient. Workers seem dignified and content. You can feel their joy as you walk the aisles. Because it's a great place to work, it's a great place to shop.

I asked Tim why he's stayed with Gelson's for almost half a century. He responded with certainty that there's nowhere else he'd rather have devoted his life to. "We're a family culture," he said. "I love it here, and I've never wondered about doing something different."

Top-Performance Takeaways:

- ▷ Focus less on a mission statement and more on the ideals that matter most.
- ▷ Invest in ongoing professional growth for both management and team members.
- ▷ Promote from within and give employees a path to growth.
- ▷ Give employees as much face time as possible with multiple levels of management.
- ▷ Allow employees to award co-workers and give those people a platform to contribute ideas.
- ▷ Post positive customer reviews and acknowledge the team members responsible for them.
- ▷ Assign new employees a "buddy."
- ▷ Acknowledge team members' professional and personal milestones.
- ▷ Host social events and offer gifts and prizes.
- ▷ Honor employee work-life balance.

Reinforcing Top Performance

The most important work you do as a manager is locking in top performance. That means shining a light on great behavior. When your worst employees do great things, be all over that greatness—if you want to see more of it.

Your best employees, those who are in the Blue for most tasks, also need their top performance reinforced. They need to be encouraged to continue and rewarded when they do. This is important, because when people aren't pushed forward, they slide backward. Like a birthday party bouncy house, they need a constant flow of fresh energy to keep them inflated.

Reinforcement is about reteaching behavior. It reminds employees what they're supposed to do. Positive reinforcement triggers a release of dopamine, which strengthens the neural connections related to the good behavior. That increases the chances your employee will repeat the behavior. In other words, if something makes them happy, their brain will encourage them to keep doing the thing that created that feeling. It may sound like giving them a dog treat during training, but when it comes to the dopamine effect, we're not much different from our pets. We want to feel good, and we'll keep doing things that make us feel that way.

Coaching an employee in the Blue is about triggering a dopamine release while addressing the areas where they are most vulnerable. Some ways to do this:

Praise and Recognition

Not only does this make employees feel good, but it also prevents them from feeling unappreciated. Most people don't feel adequately recognized, especially at work. According to one 2023 study by Blueboard Inc. and Wakefield Research, 67 percent of Americans don't always feel appreciated at work for what they do. Those who do are four times more likely to be fully engaged in their work, and seven times more likely to feel secure in their jobs. In other words, they're more likely to be in the Blue.

Praise your workers. Praise them a lot. Praise them publicly and praise them one-on-one. Recognize them verbally and sometimes in writing. Vary the ways you acknowledge them.

Give them awards. Give them *rewards* (they don't have to be expensive). Often emotional value exceeds monetary value. Also keep the praise proportional to what they've done. Some work is best acknowledged with a pat on the back, but bigger accomplishments deserve bigger gestures.

Remember, don't praise who people are; praise what they *do*. Celebrate the behavior. And phrases like "good job" and "well done" won't cut it. Be specific about what you're acknowledging. Let them know how their behaviors help the organization, the operation, and the team.

If you want to create a more powerful acknowledgment, be present. Stop everything else you're doing and stop their work as well. Make eye contact as you speak, and pause after you're done. Give it a moment to sink in. That's when the dopamine is released. You want them to really feel the praise.

No matter how you praise them, make it genuine. If it's too big, too often, or too hard to believe, it won't work. Also, don't use this chance to assign more work. That'll make the acknowledgment seem like you were just buttering them up when what you really wanted was to delegate a new task.

Keep in mind that public recognition can trigger people who aren't being recognized. The best way to handle that is to catch everyone doing something right at some point. Look for moments of high mindset and skill set. Give everyone a taste of that dopamine release. Play favorites with behavior, not with people. Everyone should know recognition is available to them, when it's earned.

Even better, have your team recognize each other. Create rituals that encourage them to express gratitude. It could be part of your daily huddle or a monthly meeting. The more recognition you have flowing through your organization, the more dopamine you'll have flowing through your team. That will help lock in top performance.

Map Job Growth

One of the biggest soft needs of hourly workers is a feeling that they're progressing. They want to feel that they're developing on the job and in their lives as opposed to just punching in and cashing out. Even small steps forward make a big difference. A number of the top-performing work environments profiled in this book have formal progress paths mapped out for employees, and their team members appreciate the opportunity.

My son felt deep pride every time he reached a new level at In-N-Out Burger as part of their Associate Levels of Development program. He had no aspirations to become a manager, but he still enjoyed feeling like he was progressing somewhere. Each level gave him additional compensation, more tasks to learn, and new goals to achieve.

Consider creating micro-promotions. Just as the military uses ranks and stripes to recognize advancement, so can you. You can create a progression of tiers or jobs. Some companies do it with numeric levels. Others use job titles: leads, swings, trainers, mentors, captains, shift managers, shift supervisors, department managers, assistant managers—all before becoming an actual manager. Each of these comes with more responsibility, compensation, and perks. Give your teams goals and explain what they must do to achieve them. Everyone needs something to chase after.

Promote Continuous Improvement

Workers like to learn. They also like to get better at what they do, especially when they have a say in the matter. Find new things to teach them, and ask them what they'd like to learn about. Offer to cross-train them, start an optional book club, or add a learning element to your regular meetings. You can even ask employees to do the teaching. The subject matter can be directly related to their work, or it can be broader information that will help them in their lives. You're not just trying to promote hard skills—you're meeting a soft need, which is their desire to learn.

For workers in the Blue for a task, recognize their excellent performance and ask if they're interested in upping their game: "You're really great at this, a total 10 out of 10. Think you could get even better?" Make this sound like encouragement, not criticism. They've already mastered the task, so this is about challenging them to set a new standard, to prove to themselves and others what's possible. Keep the discussion positive and motivating. The purpose isn't really to push them beyond 10 out of 10—you're just making sure they don't slide to a five. You're creating an opportunity to boost their aptitude to preserve their attitude.

If they choose to learn something new, they'll be in the Green for that new task, and they'll need training. But the new challenge will keep them in the Blue for tasks they've already mastered by preserving their mindset.

Chapter 10 / Coaching in the Blue

Promote Autonomy

This doesn't mean leaving them to work alone—it means empowering them with some control. If they're already at a 10 and want to get to a 15, ask them how they can accomplish that. If there's a special project they're well-suited to handle, ask them to set goals and create a plan to achieve them. Empowerment leads to engagement. Find ways to put them in charge in areas where they have the skill set to lead.

Solicit Their Input

An experienced employee with a high skill set can provide meaningful contributions to strategy. Ask for their feedback and ideas. Treat them as colleagues and make them feel like the experts they are. They're also great resources when it comes to their co-workers. They may have ideas for elevating their teammates into the Blue—and they may be the best choices to execute those ideas.

Have Them Train Others

This is a great experience for everyone. Those with a low skill set benefit from the other employee's mastery of the task, and those in the Blue feel recognized for their skills. They also get to feel the satisfaction of enabling others to succeed, which promotes better teamwork. It also frees you from having to do the training. But teach them how to train first.

Be Willing to Let Them Go

My heart broke every time one of my top performers gave notice. Some of that was personal: We were a family. A lot of it, however, was about the operation. It was hard to imagine we could continue without them, but we always did. And their departure created opportunities for new people to step up. As long as our culture remained intact, people could come and go with minimal problems.

Consider it an honor to have made good people better. If you've done your job, you've equipped them to succeed beyond your business. Like kids, they're not yours forever. Enjoy them while you can and wish them well when the time comes for them to leave.

Most employers aren't doing enough to reinforce their employees' performance. They just put people to work, say an occasional "Good job," and buy them pizza and a birthday cake once a year. Sometimes they throw cash or gift cards at them. Then they leave them alone and go deal with other problems. That just won't cut it. You must be more deliberate about meeting their soft needs to preserve their soft skills. Mindset must be managed.

Having said that, your top employees are still human. Your best coaching won't stop their mindset from occasionally slipping out of the Blue. That's why you need to be prepared to coach them out of the Red.

Coaching in the Red

E ven if you do everything I recommended in Chapter 10 to preserve an employee's high mindset, some things remain out of your control. Conflicts with co-workers and customers can't be completely avoided. Neither can personal problems. Employees don't stop being human just because they're on the clock.

But they should be professional. You should hold them accountable for performing well and strengthening your culture. Your goal is to help facilitate that process. No matter how great their skills are or how long their tenure, underperformance and bad attitudes aren't OK. It's their job to be in the Blue, and when they slide, it's *your* job to bring them back. You can coach them back to the Blue, or at some point they'll have to leave. When it comes to being in the Red, however, I have a no loitering policy. They can go into the Red for a bit, but they can't stay there. That must change immediately, or else the employee needs to go.

If you're short-staffed, you'll probably have to be more patient. But it also means you'll need to work even harder to salvage those people who've slipped into the Red. Good coaching on your part should help—and it'll buy you time if you need to start looking for possible replacements. Hopefully that won't be necessary.

Reengaging employees can be tricky when you don't know why their mindset dropped. That's one of the reasons it's important to forge a good relationship with them. You can remain professional and set boundaries while still building trust. Drops in mindset are symptoms of other issues, and you need to know what those issues are so you can intervene accordingly.

If you focus only on their behavior and not on *them*, you're likely to push them deeper into the Red. Your intervention won't help. Their mindset won't improve. They may pretend to be OK to stay out of trouble, but festering internal issues are bound to worsen and create more problems.

Your own mindset is crucial when it comes to improving theirs. In Chapter 2 we discussed the importance of self-reflection. Keep your thoughts and feelings in check, and remind yourself that your people are human. What seems like an attitude problem might really be some major issues in their personal lives.

We grew frustrated with one of our team members, who seemed to stop caring about her work. She always reported for her shifts, but her performance was subpar. Then we learned she was overwhelmed as a single mom who had also had to take on the burden of caring for her aging parents. A friend of mine who manages a Starbucks shared with me her frustration when an underperforming barista developed a sour attitude. She learned from other employees he was struggling to cope with his mom's alcoholism. Personal problems don't excuse low performance, of course, but knowing the full story might inform your coaching. You don't need all the details, and you certainly don't want to pry. But if you approach struggling employees with compassion and understanding, your interventions will be more constructive.

I like to begin conversations with employees in the Red by acknowledging their skill set, which lowers the likelihood of making them defensive. Then I express concern rather than anger. I want them to feel that I'm advocating for them, not disciplining them. I find that leads to better discussions. The conversation might start with something like:

"Michael, you're one of our top salespeople, but your numbers have slipped. I just wanted to make sure you're OK. Tell me what's happening."

Or "Tina, it seems like you're not your usual energetic self today. What's going on?"

Again, you're addressing their mindset, so choose your words carefully. You want them to feel cared about and believe that you're on their side. You are—or you should be.

This isn't about coddling them, it's about influencing them. You're trying to make them feel it's OK to open up about what's really going on.

If they don't offer additional insights during this conversation, you need to make some decisions. If their performance is fine but they just seem a little down, hopefully checking in with them will help. Give them some time and check in again later. There's no exact timing or methodology here. Go with your instincts and just be there for them. Often they'll climb out of their rut on their own. But they'll appreciate that you expressed concern.

If their performance isn't up to standards, or if their mood is affecting others, you need to stand up for your operation and defend your culture.

In the Red vs. in the Yellow

Before you coach team members in the Red, make sure they're not in the Yellow. Managers often confuse these two states. Misdiagnosis leads to mismanagement, so it's important to understand the difference.

Employees in the Red and Yellow both have a low mindset. If that's all you notice, you can't properly diagnose them. What differs is their skill set. Employees in the Red can state the steps to complete a task and demonstrate them. Those in the Yellow can't.

I once laid into my son for not working hard enough in his math class: "Your grades have dropped because you spend all your time playing Madden and not studying!"

"I have been studying!" he protested.

"Oh yeah, what have you done?" I asked.

"I read the chapter three times," he said.

He thought studying meant reading through the chapter repeatedly. He didn't know about engaging with the material, doing practice problems, or asking for help if he was struggling. I thought my son was being lazy, that he had an attitude problem. But in fact he just didn't know how to study. I thought he had a high skill set, but I was wrong. I misdiagnosed him. I didn't help his skill set, and I worsened his mindset. I drove him deep into the Yellow.

Unless you're certain you've seen an underperforming worker do a task correctly multiple times, don't assume they can. Give them a quick test: Ask them to tell you the steps and then perform them. If they get it right, be sure to praise them. "Thanks, I knew you could do it. I might need you to train some others." Now you know: That employee is in the Red. Your compliment may help their mindset and hopefully compensate for what they may feel was doubt about their abilities.

If they can't do the task, that lack of knowledge combined with the low mindset means they're in the Yellow. They need both training and encouragement.

Reprimanding Employees

If it's the first time you're addressing an issue, and the employee isn't revealing any additional information to explain the slide, address their underperformance directly. Remind them of your expectations, and let them know how their performance is affecting the operation and the team. Restate your need for them to be their best selves, and give them some time to return to the Blue. Hopefully your redirection will be enough to get them back on track.

If problems continue, your conversations need to escalate and your love will have to get tougher. It's time to warn them of possible repercussions.

Always have these conversations in private, never in front of co-workers. If you humiliate them, their anger at you will supersede anything you say to them.

Reprimanding employees quickly triggers a number of mechanisms in their brain—in addition to negative emotions such as fear, anger, and embarrassment, there's a release of stress hormones. Before your worker can process what you say, they *feel* it. Those feelings are important—they're part of the encoding process in the brain. Just as you should pause to let them feel your praise, you should also give them a moment to take in this conversation.

But the goal isn't to make them feel bad. It may make you feel good to tell them off, but that will only drive them deeper into the Red, and they'll focus more on your behavior than on their own. To help them back into the Blue, follow your reprimand with a discussion about new behaviors. Express your gratitude for them and your belief in their ability to get back on track. Ask what they need from you to make that happen. Let them know you're on their side.

TOP-PERFORMANCE SPOTLIGHT

ANDROSCOGGIN BANK
Maine

Neil Kiely was working in wind and solar energy development and serving on the board of the 150-year-old Androscoggin Bank when the CEO at the time asked him to step into management and ultimately run the bank. Neil agreed, on the condition that his work could begin with redefining the cultural ecosystem of the organization. He saw the massive sea change happening in the banking industry (which he specified as "new technologies, new competitors and increasing regulatory complexity") and felt internal culture was key to staying relevant. "I wanted to create an environment that attracted and inspired talent and promoted their autonomy," he told me. "We needed to become a bank that clients could connect with, and that meant building a happy, engaged team with a growth mindset."

The process began with a deep dive into understanding what aspects of the culture resonated most with employees. They sat with team members and conducted surveys, identifying the elements of the company that mattered most and others to which they could aspire. That inspired a new mission, vision, and value system that today drives every aspect of the organization, including employee evaluations.

TOP-PERFORMANCE SPOTLIGHT, continued

They worked to become one of only a handful of banks with "B Corp certification," a designation given to organizations that meet high standards for social and environmental impact. Since they achieved B Corp status, most of their new hires have cited that designation as a primary reason for joining the company.

That makes them sound like a nonprofit, but they're anything but. Their 11 branches and three offices are thriving. Neil attributed this to the grass-roots collaboration that defines their operation. He shared one story in which the bank saw an opportunity to increase its mortgage business, which at the time was around $29 million annually. They convened a team of salaried and hourly employees, who spent six months strategizing how to double that number. Although a consultant insisted it couldn't be done, within a year their mortgage business had hit the $97 million mark.

The bank employs around 200 team members, a little more than half of whom are hourly employees working as tellers and back-office support staff. New employees start at approximately 135 percent of local minimum wage. (Those who come with more experience start a bit higher.) All employees, including hourly employees, are eligible for and are typically awarded a bonus. In addition to matching 401(k) contributions, the bank adds another 3 percent of their earnings into their retirement account on every payroll, whether or not they are contributing to that account themselves.

The company enjoys high employee retention, and 80 percent of new hires are recruited by current employees—an important metric, as there will always be a need to replace great talent. "If we're doing our job, many of our people will outgrow theirs," Neil pointed out. "Our culture ensures we can replace them with more good people."

The bank actively monitors employee engagement via third-party surveys. The average employee participation rate for most

TOP-PERFORMANCE SPOTLIGHT, continued

organizations is around 60 to 65 percent. At Androscoggin Bank, 91 percent of employees participate, which in itself is an indicator of engagement. As that engagement has increased, so has the bank's Employee Net Promoter Score (see Chapter 13). This was Neil's plan from the beginning.

One of the ways the bank engages team members is by offering a volunteer individualized development plan. Employees are invited to meet with human resources and their managers to discuss their professional goals. HR then provides training and job shadowing opportunities that align with those goals. Half of their workforce has a personalized training program. The company also provides professional growth and certification through "AB University," where team members can learn about business writing, PowerPoint, public speaking, personal brand development, and other professional skills.

The bank sponsors two "weeks of giving." During these weeks, employees from different departments volunteer during business hours for animal shelters, soup kitchens, and other local charities. Employees are also paid for up to 20 hours of volunteer work on their own time.

"Getting our employees to collaborate for these causes has made a huge impact on their own internal bonds," said Neil. "It's a great way to promote teamwork."

Another way the bank promotes camaraderie is through its "Values & Action" program, which allows team members to formally recognize co-workers. The feedback is sent to the co-worker as well as to managers and is used to nominate employees for awards. Employees can add this peer-to-peer recognition to their file to be used in their annual self-evaluation.

Neil told me that empowerment and autonomy are a vital part of their cultural ecosystem. Employees earn raises and promotions as

TOP-PERFORMANCE SPOTLIGHT, continued

they hit predefined professional benchmarks within the company. "If they want to move up, they know exactly what to do to get there."

On the surface, a banking operation has little to do with other organizations, especially small businesses. I asked Neil what advice he'd give to a niece managing an ice cream store.

"Pay more attention to the intangible drivers of your employees," he told me. "Be thoughtful about your culture. A good culture won't just happen. Ask your employees to help you define that culture. Pretty soon it'll be the culture that maintains performance, so you don't have to."

Top-Performance Takeaways:

> Seek and encourage a growth mindset with your team.
> Assess what matters most to your employees and use that to inspire your workplace ecosystem.
> Work toward high standards defined and recognized by an outside organization.
> Solicit the involvement of employees at all levels to set and achieve goals.
> Measure employee engagement.
> Provide customized training for your employees to help them achieve their own goals.
> Use volunteering to connect with the public and strengthen your team.
> Empower team members with a clear path for promotion.

Addressing the Main Mindset Pitfalls

Ideally, your employee *will* open up to you and explain the reason behind their decline. With a little back-and-forth, hopefully you can find out which of the six reasons discussed in Chapter 10 applies (boredom, feeling unappreciated, poor management, conflict with co-workers, conflict with customers, or personal problems). It's always better when you can address the specific circumstances. Here are a few thoughts on each:

Boredom

Bored employees disengage and start taking their work for granted, and that's when their performance dips. It's also when they start thinking about transitioning to a more interesting work environment. Offering hard incentives like more money might get them to endure the boredom a little longer, but it won't buy you much time. Money meets a hard need, not a soft one.

A bored employee needs fresh challenges. Consider giving them new goals to work toward, ones they can measure. Perhaps it's increasing their speed, productivity, sales, or customer service reviews. Even better, ask *them* what would make their job more interesting. Find out what they'd like to do or learn. You can also offer to cross-train them, give them a new project to lead, or have them train others.

Feeling Unappreciated

If you haven't praised them when they've legitimately earned recognition, apologize. Assure them they deserve acknowledgment without having to ask for it. Explain why you failed to do this earlier, but don't make excuses. And don't try to justify withholding recognition for one task because they're struggling with another. Just give them the recognition they deserve by letting them know they are seen and valued. Use the praise tips discussed earlier in Chapter 10, and make sure you continue to praise them as they earn it.

Poor Management (Yours)

This is another case where you need to humble yourself. If you did something wrong, such as speaking rudely or blaming them for something they didn't do, apologize. You won't seem weak—you'll seem decent, and they'll respect you more for it. No one likes a boss who never admits when they're wrong. If you take responsibility for your shortcomings, they'll follow your lead. Thank them for bringing the issue to your attention, own up to whatever you did wrong, and commit to doing better. Don't find a way to criticize them in return. If you do, it'll weaken your apology. Address any problems on their end at another time. This moment is about reengaging them for whatever you did that drove them into the Red.

Conflict with Co-Workers

Chronic infighting among your team is symptomatic of an unhealthy culture. Fixing things at the macro level is the best way to maintain harmony. Most employee conflicts at Edible Arrangements occurred during the early years. As we got better at hiring, training, and maintaining our culture, this problem mostly took care of itself. We had a better match of personalities, and our team members knew what was expected of them. We were a family, and everyone felt inclined to get along.

Still, they were only human, so I occasionally had to mediate conflicts. Sometimes one employee felt like another wasn't doing their part, or they misinterpreted a joke. One team member complained about another who wouldn't stop talking about her personal problems. Things came up, as they do with any group of people, and they would sometimes pull an otherwise skilled employee deep into the Red.

Employee conflicts were always very triggering for me. With everything else on my plate, the last thing I needed was a member of my team coming to me with interpersonal conflicts. I already had to referee my two children's disputes. Why can't they just do their work?

The answer is that there's more going on than work. Employees also want respect, fairness, social acceptance, and other soft needs. They're spending many hours at their jobs and living their lives among their co-workers—who are defining their experience of work. These relationships matter.

It's reasonable to expect your team members to be professional. They should honor the culture and work things out among themselves. But many hourly workers may not have the communication and social skills to do this. Many come from toxic home lives where conflict is the prevailing dynamic, and empathy and contrition are unfamiliar concepts. They probably haven't heard of "When you . . . I feel" statements.

As a manager, it is your responsibility to help resolve conflict. As a coach, you have an opportunity to teach conflict resolution and use these moments to promote personal growth. That might sound like a bit much when you're just trying to get them to stock shelves, but reframing the situation might make you less resentful. Again, top performance starts with you.

Begin by listening without judgment to all parties involved (and keep it between them). Gather as much information as you can while staying impartial. You can validate their feelings and make sure everyone feels heard without taking sides. Focus on behaviors, not personalities.

If the conflict is a result of miscommunication, a misunderstanding, or different perspectives, try to help them see each other's point of view and seek mutual understanding rather than victory. Too often we fight to win rather than try to understand. Debating the facts rarely helps, since what actually happened matters less than people's perceptions. That's what informs their feelings. Try to steer the conversation away from the facts and manage those perceptions.

What people need most in conflict isn't to have the other person change their mind or agree—it's to feel heard. In a good culture, you don't win arguments: You win friends. Try to guide their conversation to shed light on all points of view, have them articulate each other's perception to ensure they understand it, and discuss appropriate next steps. Always refer back to your culture and hold them accountable to it.

Some employees are incompatible, of course. They just can't get along. This is hard to manage. I once thought I was being clever by assigning two feuding co-workers to do some charity work together on the clock, thinking the shared experience and focus on a higher purpose might help them rise above their petty squabbles. Both said it went well, but I think they were just telling me what I wanted to hear. They just endured the experience, and they certainly didn't grow any closer.

If two employees have a lot to offer your organization but can't coexist, the best thing to do is separate them. Put them in different positions and/ or schedule them at different times. This may not always be practical, but do the best you can. Even then, you may end up having to let one or both go. In the end, you need to decide if their contributions to your culture outweigh the problems they cause.

Sometimes one person is clearly in the wrong—in that case, you need to help them see that. Allow them to share their perspective. They may have something else going on in their lives that caused them to start this conflict. Provide appropriate support, but make sure they understand that there's no excuse for putting your culture in jeopardy.

Other cases are more cut-and-dried. I had one assistant manager who repeatedly came to work hungover and would call in another employee to help open up while she slept in the office. That other employee eventually said something to my general manager. This wasn't a question of mediating conflict between co-workers. I had to let the assistant manager go.

Protect employees who want to do the right thing and get rid of those who don't. Behaviors that impact others negatively shouldn't be tolerated. Abuse (physical or emotional), bullying, sexual harassment, stealing— these are a one-way ticket out the door. So is total disregard for basic professionalism. You shouldn't waste time coaching people who threaten your culture or operation.

I won't pretend that resolving employee conflict is easy. Every situation is different, and as an employer, you must be very careful not to violate any labor laws or cross lines into appropriate behavior. If your organization has an HR department, adhere to their standards and turn to them for advice when necessary. If that's not available to you, consider seeking outside professional advice when needed.

Most of my attempts to mediate among clashing employees rarely made a difference. You can try the above tactics to help your team members be their best selves and promote the best in others. But avoid doing too much refereeing. Document everything, and don't be afraid to make tough decisions that protect your culture.

Conflict with Customers

Every case of employee conflict with customers is different. Sometimes employees blow it. They make mistakes, or they're rude to customers. If they do something egregious, act accordingly. If they use poor judgment but can learn from it, use it as a teaching moment. (And obviously make it right with the customer.)

Often the customers create the conflict. Employees should be trained on how to deal with angry guests: remain professional, do what they must to make the customer happy, and make decisions that align with your values. They definitely shouldn't take things personally.

But they do. Sometimes it's hard not to. One angry customer called one of my top employees a "fat b**ch." She wasn't even responsible for the problem, but he still lashed out at her. She maintained her composure, got through the transaction, and burst into tears once he left. I wasn't in the store at the time. Had I been, I don't think I would've been as professional as she was.

Be there for your team when they're mistreated. They come first, not the customer, and they need you to have their back. That doesn't mean you should argue with customers. They may have their own (inexcusable) reasons for their behavior. But you need to appreciate the impact on your employees' mindset and offer your support.

Most angry customers aren't abusive—they're just rude and unpleasant to your workers. Train your team to listen to them without arguing. Talk about what happened and what could have been done differently. Validate your employee's feelings but avoid criticizing the customer. You always want to encourage feeling love and empathy for your customers, so help your employee find some grace. The customer may not deserve it, but seeing them with empathy might reduce your employee's hurt feelings. At the same time, assure the employee you're on their side. Thank them for their professionalism. Again, what people need most when they're upset is to feel seen and heard, so acknowledge what they went through and express your appreciation for them. Ultimately, how *you* treat them is more important than how the customer does.

Personal Problems

Over the 10 years I owned my stores, we had employees who struggled with health issues, addiction, domestic abuse, immigration issues, child care, legal problems, financial crises, breakups, and other problems. Many of these employees had a high skill set and loved their jobs. But sometimes their personal issues came to work with them.

Hourly workers cope with increased income volatility and have fewer resources with which to manage problems. Even with the best intentions, they may not be able to prevent these matters from impacting their job performance. In other cases, they may not have the maturity or emotional skills to balance their personal problems with their professional responsibilities. Sometimes they need a hand.

You may not be interested in charity work or being anyone's therapist, but you do want to increase productivity and reduce absenteeism. Both require supporting people through challenges.

Many organizations have employee assistance programs (EAPs), which provide free or low-cost resources to help team members manage child-care or elder-care issues, substance abuse, financial or legal problems, and other challenges. At McDonald's, for example, employees can call their "McResource Line" for advice on the above issues. Walmart, in addition to its own extensive EAP, has set up the "Associates in Critical Need Trust" to provide financial assistance to employees facing an unexpected financial crisis. Check to see what programs your organization has available or consider creating one. Many EAPs are set up by third-party providers; consider contracting with one that can create an appropriate plan for your organization.

However, even if you do go with an outside contractor (and it may not be practical for you), you're still your team's supervisor, and you need to be there for them. They'll remember how you reacted in their time of need. This is an opportunity to do the right thing and win their loyalty.

Just as employees have hard and soft needs for their job, they also have hard and soft needs for their personal problems. It's important to understand the difference so you can offer effective and appropriate help. Most hard needs associated with problems are related to money and time. They might need an advance on their paycheck, more flexibility in their schedule, or time off. They might need to occasionally step off the floor to call a doctor or their child's school. In a salaried work environment, this wouldn't be an issue, but when there's a time clock involved, attending to personal matters is often frowned upon.

It's a judgment call to determine how flexible to be and how much to get involved. It's not always easy to balance benevolence and smart HR policy. Some of the employers I interviewed for this book have been shockingly generous with employees and have gotten heavily involved in their lives. I definitely did a few favors for certain team members and tried to be flexible where I could, but I always maintained firm boundaries.

Where we can all be more helpful—perhaps *most* helpful—is in meeting their *soft* needs. That means providing emotional support when your employees are feeling down. Problems are always accompanied by emotions. Before people can solve their problems, they need to get their emotions in check and clear their heads.

Coping is the part they usually need help with, not solving the problem. They just want someone to listen and help them process their feelings. Think about it: When was the last time anyone has taken your advice? When my wife is upset about something, she rarely wants me to tell her what to do. She just wants me to listen. I'm a "doer," so that's tough for me, but that's what helps her. When someone you care about falls into a pit, your instinct might be to reach down and pull them out. But what they really need is for you to stay with them while they find their own way out. Empathy is really just being there and creating a safe space for others to deal with their emotions. If you'd like to treat yourself to a good laugh about this concept, go on YouTube and watch "It's Not About the Nail."

"Just being there" seems passive, but it directly helps their brain. As they get their emotions out, they calm their amygdala and reengage the problem-solving region, the prefrontal cortex. That'll help them find their own solutions. By helping them cope, you're empowering them to problem solve. You may not actually know how to solve their problems, but you can be an empathetic listener. Most of the time, that's all you need to be.

As with any employee in the Red, start your conversation with a positive comment about their skill set and express concern about what's going on. When they reveal the personal issue, practice active listening. Thank them for sharing and let them know you care and will be there if they need anything, including time to deal with whatever is going on. Also remind them that you still need their very best while they're at work. If they can't provide it right now, offer to give them some time off to take care of things.

Chapter 11 / Coaching in the Red

While my intention here is to share ways to help employees who may be struggling personally, I'm not encouraging you to get overinvolved. Be sure to maintain professional boundaries and operate within the guidelines of your HR department, if you have one. Don't get in over your head, and don't make promises you can't keep. Don't ignore serious signs of distress—and don't try to be a therapist. Escalate the matter to HR or connect them with someone qualified to help them. And definitely keep things confidential.

You're managing a professional environment. Every person on the floor should be able to meet company standards, lift up their teammates, and provide exceptional service to customers. If they can't, they shouldn't be at work. You have a whole team to manage. Their personal problems can take up a lot of time and space, and you don't have much of either. Be supportive, but never lower your expectations or standards.

We can't resolve every reason why top performers slide into the Red, but we can usually do more. Each of the above issues is very different and needs to be addressed accordingly. If all you do for employees in the Red is tell them to step up, you won't be dealing with the real problem.

30-Second Leadership isn't a solution for all employee problems. It's a tool. Used properly, it can help you focus on where the employee needs help. We've already discussed the process for diagnosing and the corresponding coaching methods for each of the four performance states. Now let's spend some time practicing so you can see it in action.

CHAPTER 12

Putting 30-Second Leadership to Work

"Scott, I've got a question. I've got one employee who always . . ." Invariably someone in my workshops asks how to deal with a particular person in their organization who's not performing well. They almost never ask how to keep a great person great. I believe preserving your best talent is as important as managing low performers. But I'm happy to hear about their situation and discuss how 30-Second Leadership might help. The process is always the same:

1. Check yourself to ensure you're in the best state to coach.
2. Clarify what task you're going to diagnose and address.
3. Determine if the issue is what the employee knows, what they feel, or both.
4. Address their skill set and/or mindset accordingly and separately.

Practice Coaching

Let's try that now with the situations you responded to in the Coaching Quiz in Chapter 8. Not much information is being given in each scenario, but hopefully applying the tool to these fictional employees will help you apply it to yours. Refer to the 30-Second Leadership model in Chapter 8 (Figure 8.2) for guidance if needed. We'll start with Scenario 1, shown in Figure 12.1 below.

Figure 12.1. Scenario 1

Situation	Your Response
A new automotive service tech is struggling to understand the shop's safety protocols. He's eager to learn and motivated to improve.	a. Provide positive reinforcement for his enthusiasm and suggest he continue learning the protocols as time allows. b. Schedule a one-on-one training session with a more experienced tech to teach him the system. c. Explain the importance of paying more attention during training and ask him to learn it as he goes. d. Empower him with some time and space to learn the protocols as he works.

First, let's diagnose the service tech. He's new and struggling with a task. His skill set is low, but he's eager and motivated, so his mindset is high. Low skill set and high mindset tell us he's in the Green. He needs training. Option A focuses more on how he feels and then leaves him alone to work. That would be OK if he were in the Blue, but it won't help now. Option B matches him with someone else who knows the safety protocols and can give him the information he needs. This is probably the best approach. But let's look at the remaining choices. Option C sounds like a reprimand. It doesn't teach him any skills—it just chastises him. Telling him to "pay attention" will ruin his good attitude and send him into the Yellow. Option D is just bad management. Expecting him to learn safety standards as he goes isn't empowerment—you're just turning him loose without critical information. That's irresponsible. The service tech is in the Green and needs training, so Option B is the way to go.

Now let's take a look at Scenario 2, shown in Figure 12.2 below.

Figure 12.2. Scenario 2

Situation	Your Response
An employee came to work today with a rumpled uniform and bloodshot eyes. His customer service is worse than usual and not up to standard.	a. Write him up and send him home with a warning. b. Keep an eye on him and give him some time to work it out. c. Acknowledge his customer service skills and express concern for his appearance and his drop in performance. d. Keep the conversation focused on work and offer additional training on customer service.

This is the kind of situation that might anger you, so notice your emotional response and make sure your mindset is OK before addressing him. He's demonstrated good customer service in the past, so we know he has the skills. The issue isn't what he knows—it's how he feels. Something is causing him to look below par and provide poor service. With a high skill set and low mindset, he's in the Red. He needs reengagement. But before you try coaching him, assess his physical state to determine if any conversation will be constructive. If not, he's probably not up for working, either. Send him home to get some sleep.

If he can sustain a conversation, you need to find out what's going on. Option A is pure discipline, not conversation. It deals with the symptom, but it doesn't address the problem. It's unlikely to boost his mindset. Option B is more passive. If this employee is typically in the Blue and doesn't usually come to work like this, he's having a bad day, and a quick check-in might be all that's needed. But his customer service is subpar, and that's never OK. He's representing your company and your customers will remember and talk about how he treats them, so you need to coach him more actively. Option C is the classic combination: acknowledge his skill set and express your concern. It's a great way to begin talking to someone who's in the Red. Option D doesn't address the real issue. He knows how to serve customers, so more knowledge won't solve the problem—you need to deal with his mindset. Go with option C and find out why he looks the way he does. He could be partying too much, struggling with a noisy roommate, or having personal problems that are taking a toll on his physical health. If you can determine what's going on, offer appropriate support. If not, express your concern and remind him of your expectations. He can't come to work like this.

Now let's take a look at the situation in Figure 12.3 below:

Figure 12.3. Scenario 3

Situation	Your Response
You just promoted one of your custodial staff to night manager. She's thrilled for the new position.	a. Congratulate her and tell her to come to you with any questions. b. Encourage her to spend some time learning about management. c. Buy her some books on leadership. d. Assign her some shifts shadowing a night manager at another facility.

If you've promoted her, she's probably in the Blue—for custodial work. But now she's a manager, which is entirely different. Even though she has a high mindset for the new position, you still need to develop what's probably a low skill set. For management, she's in the Green and needs training. Option A doesn't give her any. Options B and C are telling her to learn more, but that's too passive. It's not enough for her to learn on her own. Someone needs to actively supervise and train her. Option D is the best choice.

Let's look at Figure 12.4 next:

Figure 12.4. Scenario 4

Situation	Your Response
A new line cook isn't keeping up with the speed and complexity of the kitchen during peak hours. He's feeling overwhelmed and discouraged.	a. Assign him another role in the restaurant. b. Offer encouragement and remind him of his potential. c. Spend a few shifts retraining him and offer encouragement. d. Restate your expectations and give him a set period of time to get up to speed.

Is the problem what he knows (skill set) or how he feels (mindset)? It appears both are low, which means he's in the Yellow. We're looking for an option that provides training and encouragement. Option A removes him from the task altogether. If you invest a lot of time in working with his skill set and mindset and he continues to struggle, assigning him a new role may be something to consider. Sometimes people just aren't a good match for a position, even if they're a good fit for your culture. But it's too early to decide that at this point—give him a chance to master his current position before moving him. Option B addresses his mindset without helping his skill set, but that won't help someone in the Yellow. Option C addresses both what he knows and how he feels, which is probably the best way to go. Option D may be a bit harsh for someone new. He doesn't need threats—he needs coaching.

Now let's try Scenario 5, shown in Figure 12.5:

Figure 12.5. Scenario 5

Situation	Your Response
You just received another complaint about one of your experienced bank tellers from a co-worker you trust, who's accused her of gossiping about a new employee.	a. Stay out of it and let the team work it out among themselves. b. Solicit feedback from the experienced employee about the new one to see if there's any truth to the gossip you may need to respond to. c. Ask the co-worker who complained to speak directly with the experienced teller about her concerns. d. Confront the experienced teller to remind her of your culture and issue her a warning.

Gossip is bad for a work environment and a serious threat to your culture. It needs to be named as an unacceptable behavior. In this case, the source is a bank teller who's done it in the past, and there've been complaints. If you've addressed this issue with her before, she knows better. Honestly, in this case, I'm not inclined to use 30-Second Leadership. I'm just calling her out. Option A doesn't do this. If the team could work this out on their own, they wouldn't be complaining to management. Option B makes the situation about the new employee, the subject of the gossip. It's possible there's something going on there that needs to be addressed, but gossiping about it more isn't helpful. Right now, the issue is the gossip itself. Option C is not unreasonable, especially if hearing feedback from a co-worker about the issue might make an impression. But again, the trusted employee came to you, so they probably want your involvement. I like Option D. It's direct and appropriate.

However, as damaging as gossip is, it's very common. People like to talk about people. They may not realize they're doing it, or how destructive it can be. This is especially true if it's someone younger or less mature. If you sense that's the case, your reprimand may need to include an informative discussion about what gossip is and why it's not welcome in your workplace. Really help them understand how it impacts the whole team.

But something good is also happening here: Employees are expressing their displeasure with gossip. They recognize it's not good for the team, and they want to protect their culture. Be sure to reinforce their willingness to say something to you about it. You want to celebrate that choice.

Let's look at Figure 12.6 below:

Figure 12.6. Scenario 6

Situation	Your Response
Your caregiver with the most tenure continues to enjoy her job and just got another stellar review from a client.	a. Buy her a gift card. b. Acknowledge her and ask in what ways she'd like to grow and get even better. c. Keep her humbled and empowered by keeping some distance. d. Share the review with your other caregivers and explain this is what you expect from all of them.

This is an experienced team member with a high skill set and a high mindset. That puts her into the Blue. There are a few good options here. Based on what you know about her, and on how you've already reinforced her performance, you must decide what's best at this moment. Option A is a decent reward that will make her feel appreciated. Option B is a way to challenge her, which would be good if you sense she'd like to get even better at her job (and might be at risk of growing bored). Option C is a poor choice. It's better to over-acknowledge than leave someone feeling unappreciated.

Option D risks making your other employees feel bad. Public recognition can be used to teach and inspire, but the comparison could push others into the Red if it sounds like they're being criticized. Be aware of how your choices could impact your team members' mindset.

TOP-PERFORMANCE SPOTLIGHT

SUPERCUTS
Pennsylvania, New Jersey, Delaware

While most hourly work environments employ lower-skilled workers, that's not the case in the hair salon industry. Stylists must complete cosmetology school and accumulate a thousand hours or more of training to get a state license. That limits the pool of available workers in a competitive industry that is in dire need of more staff. In spite of the great lengths stylists go through to enter the profession, salons struggle with high turnover. Many leave salon jobs to go out on their own, and others leave the business altogether. The industry is constantly working to refine best practices for recruitment and retention.

Gary Robins has cracked the code. The owner of 66 Supercuts salons in the northeastern U.S., Gary retains more than 70 percent of his stylists annually, well above the industry average of 50 to 60 percent. Many come directly from cosmetology school, starting at 125 to 200 percent of local minimum wage (supplemented by tips and bonuses). With the help of more than 400 employees, Gary has been awarded "Franchisee of the Year" by the International Franchise Association, as well as multiple wins of "Franchisee of the Year" within the Supercuts system. He's also served as president of the Supercuts Franchisee Association.

Gary sees himself as being in the people business more than the haircut business. His job is to boost self-esteem, and great haircuts boost customers' confidence. Gary trains his managers to elevate the

TOP-PERFORMANCE SPOTLIGHT, continued

self-esteem of their stylists as well. "Many of these people don't get a lot of emotional support," he said. "That's our unique opportunity—to let our people know they're appreciated and valued." He personally handwrites cards every month for employees celebrating birthdays and posts their special occasions and work anniversaries on the company Facebook page.

Another way the company makes stylists feel appreciated is by hanging a banner at each of their stations. Managers reward stylists with acknowledgment pins to attach to their banners, similar to the helmet stickers given to football players to recognize performance. The visible record also makes it easier for Gary to see who's doing well when he visits salons.

During these visits, he avoids discussing anything operational with stylists, leaving that to managers. But there is one area where he will intervene directly: "If I see someone committing a cultural violation, I say something immediately. They're going to hear from me if they're not living up to our mission and way of doing things." Gary personally meets with every new employee upon hiring to discuss their culture, so it's no surprise he would want to hold them accountable.

Whereas other organizations focus on culture as a way to promote teamwork, Gary sees it as a condition for individual excellence. "It's important for employees to believe what you believe," he said. "They need a culture that activates five key characteristics." The five characteristics he sees as essential in his organization are:

1. Honesty ethic
2. Work ethic
3. Demonstration of commitment (rather than showing interest)
4. Putting others first
5. Taking responsibility (rather than just doing a job)

TOP-PERFORMANCE SPOTLIGHT, continued

He's not looking for perfection among his team. "Mistakes are OK," he said. "Not knowing is OK. Not caring is not OK." For those who don't care, he prescribes what he calls "CDE," which stands for "career development elsewhere." For those who do, he puts them on a path for growth within his organization. It's his primary reason for continued expansion. "I don't need any more salons," he told me. "But I do need to create opportunities for those who've earned them."

The company relies heavily on providing these opportunities and promoting employee growth. "We're good at cuts and coloring, but we have some strong competition out there for stylists," he admitted. "How can we beat them? We're a beacon where stylists can grow personally and professionally. We want to be the best at that. We're a development company—that's where we shine."

Top-Performance Takeaways:

> ▷ Work to boost the confidence of employees.
> ▷ Create visual forms of acknowledgment.
> ▷ Build a culture around the characteristics you want in team members.
> ▷ Embrace employees who care and let go of those who don't.
> ▷ Create opportunities for employees' professional and personal growth.

Figure 12.7. Scenario 7

Situation	Your Response
A seasoned factory worker is asked to learn a new machine. He's not excited about it and feels uneasy about the change.	a. Praise his previous success and remind him that this is an opportunity to learn a new skill. b. Respect his feelings and allow him to return to his previous role, where he feels more comfortable. c. Explain your need for him to switch machines with a better attitude. d. Acknowledge his concerns and ask a supervisor to work with him until he's comfortable.

This worker is experienced in the factory (see Figure 12.7), but his skill set for the new machine is low. He also lacks enthusiasm and confidence to learn it, so his mindset is also low. He's in the Yellow. He needs more than a push—he needs someone to train him and offer encouragement. It's likely his attitude will improve as he gains aptitude. Option A only addresses attitude. Option B allows him to disengage from learning the new machine altogether. You may have a good reason to respect his wishes on this. But usually when people don't want to do something new, they're just nervous. It's probably worth pushing him a little to see what he can do. Option C, like Option A, just addresses mindset. Option D normalizes his feelings and makes him feel heard, but it also addresses his skill set. This approach is best for someone in the Yellow and will be the quickest way to get him into the Blue.

Now let's take a look at Scenario 8, in Figure 12.8:

Figure 12.8. Scenario 8

Situation	Your Response
Your lead hotel housekeeper has some initial resistance to new procedures for sanitizing rooms. Once she's got them down, she's enthusiastic about contributing to a safer guest experience.	a. She's doing well with the new procedures, so allow her to continue working without interruption. b. Let her know there will always be improvements to the system, and you need her to lean into them without pushback. c. Thank her for her open mind and ask if she has any ideas to refine the procedures. d. Continue training her on the new procedures and offer feedback on other cleaning practices to ensure she continues to improve.

This housekeeper started in the Yellow for the new procedures. She had a low skill set and mindset. Now they're both high, so she's in the Blue. That's often how things go when learning something new. Good coaching hastens the process. Now we need good coaching to keep her in the Blue. Option A is OK for a bit, but at some point, she'll need outside reinforcement to ensure she continues to perform well. Option B is addressing an attitude problem she no longer has. If you want to prepare her for future changes, put more emphasis on what she did right. Thank her for hanging in there to learn the new sanitization procedures, and let her know you'd love to see the same perseverance and willingness to learn moving forward. Option C is a good response for someone in the Blue. Not only does it give her praise, but it also shows respect and empowers her by asking her to contribute ideas. It's certainly better than Option D, which is micromanagement. An employee in the Blue doesn't need help with their skill set, and additional training on something she already knows how to do risks lowering her mindset.

Let's look next at Figure 12.9 below:

Figure 12.9. Scenario 9

Situation	Your Response
You recently lost your temper at one of your bussers who broke a glass. He's experienced and should know better.	a. Ask him why he thinks you lost your temper and what he could have done to prevent that from happening. b. Apologize, but remind him it costs the restaurant money when dishes are broken. c. Compose yourself and continue managing him with a more professional demeanor. d. Apologize for your outburst.

Breaking a glass is bad, but breaking a mindset is worse, and that's what happens when you lose control of yourself. It was an accident. If the busser constantly has accidents, then there's a problem somewhere that you need to figure out and address. He may be doing things wrong, which is a skill set problem. Or maybe there are other issues impacting his mindset, such as personal problems or conflict that might be distracting him. Whatever it is, adjust your coaching accordingly.

Losing your temper is never OK. Always try to manage using your prefrontal cortex (logic and reason), not your amygdala (emotion). Think about how many times you've been in an argument and the conversation diverted from the actual subject to how one person treated the other during the argument: "Don't speak to me like that!" You want to leave your employee thinking about their behavior, not about how you treated them.

If the accident was an isolated incident and the busser is typically in the Blue, it probably doesn't require a reprimand, so make sure they're OK and get the glass cleaned up safely. If it's happened a few times, see if the issue is what the busser knows or how they feel and adjust your coaching style. (Also consider if there's a problem with the procedure itself.)

You need to address yelling at the employee separately. You did something wrong, so you need to own that. Doing so will boost their mindset and repair any damage to your relationship. They'll respect you more for the apology, and it'll make it easier for them to acknowledge their own mistakes.

Option A lacks humility. Even though you're acknowledging your loss of temper, it still puts the blame for it on them. So does Option B, which doesn't sound like a real apology, since it keeps the focus on the cost of the broken glass. Right now, you should be addressing your temper. Option C pretends the incident never happened. You can forget about it, but the employee won't. Option D is the correct response. You need to apologize. If the accident needs to be addressed, do so in a separate conversation.

Now let's try the options in Figure 12.10 below:

Figure 12.10. Scenario 10

Situation	Your Response
A loyal employee informs you that one of the team members who leads the closing shift took home a tub of ice cream without paying for it.	a. Confront the employee who took the ice cream and explain that you're going to take the cost of the ice cream out of their next check. Tell them to pay in advance next time. b. Fire the employee. c. Write up a warning and explain that as a shift lead, you expect more from them. d. Gather your staff for a meeting to discuss the incident and reprimand the employee publicly so everyone can learn from what happened and hold their co-workers accountable.

Confirm if it is true. If so, there's no need to coach the shift lead. Go with Option B: fire them. I'll coach for skill set and mindset, but not for basic morality. Be sure to thank the employee who told you to reinforce their loyalty (and address any guilt they may feel around the other employee losing their job).

Figure 12.11, below, is next:

Figure 12.11. Scenario 11

Situation	Your Response
One of your top delivery drivers seems down lately. His work is getting done, but he's not demonstrating his usual enthusiasm.	a. Check in with him to see if he's OK and ask if there's anything he needs. b. As long as work is being completed to standards, leave him alone. c. Before things worsen, explain that attitude matters and you need him to step up. d. Surprise him with tickets to a sporting event.

With a high skill set and low mindset, he's in the Red, and you need to reengage him. Options B and D don't address the problem. Option C is a bit insensitive. It assumes he has an attitude problem when his mood might stem from something else, like issues in his personal life. You should approach from a place of concern, so Option A is probably the best place to start. If he offers an explanation, give him appropriate support. If he doesn't explain but his work is up to standard and his mindset isn't impacting the team, give him a little time, keep a close eye on him, and check back with him frequently.

The final scenario is below, in Figure 12.12:

Figure 12.12. Scenario 12

Situation	Your Response
A manager who's been working for you for 10 years has been struggling for the past two. She seems to be totally disengaged from her job, and you've spoken with her about it multiple times. She agrees things aren't going as well as they used to, but she can't explain why.	a. Thank her for her service and let her go. b. Write up a warning, restating your expectations. c. Give her more time in hopes she can break out of her funk. d. Promote her to a new role to light a fire under her.

A hotel owner came to me once with this exact situation. I didn't have all the details, so I didn't feel comfortable telling her what to do. But we did look at the situation together through the 30-Second Leadership lens, and we didn't even need 30 seconds to determine this manager is in the Red. She knows what to do, she just no longer feels like doing it and hasn't for two years. I asked the owner if she would hire this manager today with her current mindset. "Absolutely not," she replied. I asked if she'd keep her if she only worked for six months before slipping into this state. "Probably not," she admitted.

I appreciate loyalty, and I understand the comfort of a known quantity like an employee who's been around for 10 years. My concern is that this loyalty is coming at a cost. It may be keeping both parties stuck in a situation that's no longer working. Sometimes things run their course.

It's hard to imagine Option B would awaken any enthusiasm. Option C is basically doing nothing. Option D is inappropriate for someone who's underperforming. Moving her to a different job may help, but a promotion just isn't called for. Depending on the owner's circumstances and willingness to find a new manager, it may be time for Option A.

As this last example demonstrates, not every situation is black and white. Sometimes you need to make tough decisions with the information you have. 30-Second Leadership isn't a complete solution. Nothing is. But hopefully it's a useful tool to get you thinking differently. If you do nothing other than separate skill set and mindset when evaluating employees, you'll already be ahead of most managers.

Coaching Tips

» To get the best results, coach consistently and often.

» Coach all employees on all tasks on a regular basis, based on the state they're in for each task.

» Always diagnose for a specific task, not for an employee's overall performance.

» Use the phrase "In the . . ." when communicating what color they're in for a task as a reminder that it is a temporary state.

» All coaching is important, but your most essential coaching is keeping star employees in the Blue.

» Be careful about misdiagnosing someone as in the Red when they're actually in the Yellow. Always confirm they have the skill set.

» Remember that superstar employees always start off in the Green when they're assigned a new task or promoted to a new role. Don't assume that because they're great at one thing they'll be great at another.

» Keep a record of your diagnoses and coaching, and track employees' performance over time to ensure they're making progress.

» If multiple employees struggle with the same task, consider refining the task.

» Don't allow busyness to prevent you from coaching. Helping employees grow is the most important work a manager can do. Making time for them will boost their performance and independence, resulting in more free time for you.

» While 30-Second Leadership can aid in the evaluation process, its real purpose is to inform how employees are coached in real time. Use it to boost employee performance, not just measure it.

» Share this tool with other managers so you can apply it consistently and use the same terminology to evaluate employees. I wouldn't recommend sharing it with employees, however, as they'll pay too much attention to the labels instead of your actual coaching.

With good coaching, you can boost your team's performance into the Blue and see great things happen. As we move into the final chapters of this book, our objective will be to maintain top performance.

PART 4

MAINTAINING TOP PERFORMANCE

CHAPTER 13

Motivating Your Team

C an you motivate someone?

I've heard many people, including motivational speakers, say that you can't. They claim motivation must come from within. Some distinguish motivation from inspiration, saying it's not enough to make people do things. You must make them want to do them.

I call BS.

To motivate is to give someone a cause or reason to act. It means getting someone to do something. When my business is under pressure, the difference between "motivating" and "inspiring" my team isn't important. I just need them to finish the fruit baskets by 10:00 a.m. I don't need them to be passionate about it—hell, I'm not passionate about it. Stuff just needs to get done, and my job is to get them to do theirs. Is that motivating them or inspiring them? In that moment, it doesn't matter. I'd love for them to love the work, but sometimes, I just need them to *do* the work.

When I was a kid, my family came home one afternoon to find the carcass of a rabbit on the side of our house—presumably the victim of a neighborhood coyote. My mom asked me to clean it up, but I refused. It was disgusting, and this wasn't one of my normal weekly chores. She pleaded, but I held my ground.

"What if I let you pick out two full-size candies at the store later?" she wheedled.

Now she was speaking my language. I grabbed some gloves and a trash bag and disposed of the body.

My mom gave me motivation. She got me to act. She didn't inspire me or make me want to do it. She made me *willing* to do it.

Inspiration is a kind of motivation. It makes us want to do things. But sometimes work must be done whether we want to do it or not. I don't want to scoop my cat's litter box, do my taxes, or floss. I didn't want to do many of the things I've done for my kids, such as changing diapers. I'd rather clean up 10 dead rabbits than help build another shoebox diorama. And do you know how many episodes of *Yo Gabba Gabba!* I've had to sit through? I don't want to do this stuff, but I'm willing to because desire isn't the only thing that drives me. There's also responsibility, love, and honor (as well as a fear of cavities and Child Protective Services).

A lot of hourly work isn't inspiring. It can be hard, dirty, monotonous, and unfulfilling. It's not reasonable to expect your employees to want to do these things. Sometimes the best you can hope for is that they're willing to do them. They may need you to motivate them to act.

But getting them to act isn't enough—you need them to keep doing it. You want sustained motivation. There's no use lighting their fire if they're just going to burn out.

A good work environment can promote both action and desire. You can find the right people, match them with the right tasks, and help them find some joy in their work. And you can lessen the grind and make things a little less painful. Motivation works best when it transcends the push for top performance and promotes top feelings. That means it appeals to one's soft needs. When an employee derives satisfaction from their work, they're more internally driven to do it. If they're satisfied with some of their work, they'll be more committed to all of it.

It'd be great if you could motivate your team by offering them candy, like dangling a carrot in front of a donkey. But candy and carrots only work to a point, just like sticks and other forms of punishment. There's so much more to motivation. Humans are complex, with changing needs and desires. What gets us to act in one moment may not work in the next, and what excites one person may not have meaning for another. You need different types of motivation in your arsenal, and knowing how and when to use these approaches will make you a better manager.

Throughout this book, we've already touched upon many concepts that will help motivate your workers, including getting to know them individually, tapping into their values, and creating a culture they care about. This chapter is about more tangible takeaways, ways to get your team to do the things you need them to do. We're going to look at motivation from several angles, and hopefully you'll acquire a few extra tools for your toolbox.

Intrinsic and Extrinsic Motivation

Employees are driven by two forces, one external and the other internal. Each serves a different purpose. You can focus on either to help stimulate the behaviors you want.

Extrinsic Motivation

My high school physics teacher taught us about Isaac Newton's law of inertia, which says that a body in motion will stay in motion and a body at rest will remain at rest unless acted upon by an external force. That means that if left alone, bodies will remain in their current state, whether that's moving or standing still.

The "external force" is a great way to think about extrinsic motivation. People tend to keep doing what they're doing unless something or someone else gets them to do it differently. All the ways bosses get workers to act are extrinsic motivators: rewards like more money, awards, gifts, and praise, as well as unpleasant things like write-ups and reprimands. In other words, they're all the carrots and sticks. Most managers rely exclusively on these motivators. They pay more, offer stuff, or threaten stuff, and hope that's enough to boost performance.

In some cases, it is. Extrinsic motivation is useful for inspiring short-term bursts of activity. New incentives are exciting. They catch people's attention. The candy my mom offered me wasn't on the table before, which made it compelling. The same goes for signing bonuses or the possibility of promotion.

But after a while, external motivators lose their luster. I once offered bonuses to my employees for increasing their average ticket size over a week. That generated lots of excitement, and they all earned the bonus. When I extended the program for another week, only two earned the bonus. The prize was the same, but it was no longer as compelling. Candy is less tempting after you've already had some. Psychologists call this phenomenon *hedonic adaptation*.

While you should map a clear path for growth within your organization, the external motivators you offer along the way need to be varied and less predictable. That's why you need to mix up how you praise and reinforce employees in the Blue by finding fresh ways to maintain their enthusiasm.

Another concern is that too much external motivation can dampen a worker's mindset around the things you want them to do. Studies have shown that an excess of external stimuli can reduce people's intrinsic motivation by making an otherwise enjoyable activity seem more like work. This is called the *overjustification effect*.

You don't want to encourage a "What's in it for me?" attitude, which makes the work transactional. By definition, of course, all paid work is transactional. But offering additional incentives implies the work is otherwise not worth doing. You're encouraging employees to expect something extra in return, which promotes entitlement and limits autonomy. If an employee relies on your external input to do something, they're less motivated to do it on their own.

Use extrinsic motivation to inspire short-term spikes of action, such as when you're recruiting applicants and getting employees to engage in new tasks, optional work, and special projects. Keep positive reinforcement special by changing when and how you do it.

Intrinsic Motivation

According to a 2022 article from the journal *Psychological Medicine*, "Not all actions are driven by tangible external stimuli or outcomes, known as 'extrinsic' motivation, but are driven by more internal drivers, known as 'intrinsic' motivation, where the activity is perceived as its own outcome." In other words, some things we do just because we want to. The activity itself is the reward, and we don't need outside stimuli to get us to act.

I don't get compensated to play with my dog or need encouragement to volunteer in my community. I'm not contractually obligated to take a later flight after a presentation so I can stay and talk with people—I just really like the interaction. I do these things because I enjoy them. Even when they require effort, they're intrinsically satisfying.

Because intrinsic motivation is self-generated, you can't instill it in someone. But you can create the conditions that cultivate it. That's harder in an hourly work environment, where people are more likely pursuing a paycheck than their interests, so you can't rely on their love of the work. That's why you need to be more deliberate about creating a workplace that inspires your employees. Here are a few ways to do that:

⟩ **Create a positive work environment.** We've discussed this at length. A positive workplace is an inspiring one.

⟩ **Give employees more autonomy.** Let them have a say in their work (when they're in the Blue). The personal investment will deepen their engagement.

⟩ **Help employees track their progress.** People like forward movement. They like to increase their score. Find ways to quantify their work and encourage them to set goals for improvement.

⟩ **Match people with the right work.** My employee Eileen wasn't great at sales or at arranging fruit baskets, but she was a master at wrapping the baskets and preparing them for delivery. She took pride in that and worked harder because of it. It feels good to excel at something, and people excel when they feel good. Assign workers to the tasks for which they're best suited.

⟩ **Connect people's work to their broader goals.** Help them see how the skills they're acquiring will be useful for future endeavors.

I tried to help my team understand that many of the techniques we taught them for selling gift baskets could also be used to sell medical devices, real estate, or corporate accounts. I said similar things about customer service. I tried to link all their work to more important work, and they liked feeling that this job was preparing them for bigger things. Find out during onboarding what their career goals are so you can speak in terms of preparing them for those jobs.

▷ **Connect people's work to a higher purpose.** In Chapter 4, we talked about defining your "why." Having something bigger than oneself to focus on can be inspiring. Philosopher Friedrich Nietzsche put it beautifully when he said, "He who has a why to live for can bear with almost any how." Your employees are more likely to power through tough tasks when they see their purpose. Help them see the why behind what they do.

Stop Demotivating Your Employees

Your employees came to you already motivated. They actively pursued the job, went through the interview, and showed up for work. Those who just want to sit at home on the couch are doing so. While you may want to level up your workers' performance, it's just as important to avoid the common management mistakes that have the opposite effect.

Most demotivation results from neglect. Your busyness may prevent you from giving team members the occasional battery recharge they need. You may fail to:

▷ Give them attention
▷ Train them well
▷ Diagnose them properly
▷ Recognize when they're sliding into the Yellow or Red
▷ Acknowledge them
▷ Build trust and a personal connection
▷ Check in with them
▷ Offer the incentives they want
▷ Provide coaching and feedback

You may also do things that drain their batteries, like:

- ⟩ Rely too heavily on extrinsic motivators
- ⟩ Publicly reprimand them
- ⟩ Speak rudely, talk down to them, or have a tone
- ⟩ Lose your temper
- ⟩ Play favorites
- ⟩ Micromanage
- ⟩ Provide inconsistent hours and scheduling
- ⟩ Act as a poor role model
- ⟩ Behave inappropriately

Your behavior directly impacts theirs. If you want to promote intrinsic motivation, you must be motivational, by being and acting a certain way. You must be at your best to inspire their best.

You'll notice that none of these ideas involve candy, carrots, sticks, or punishment. Those are all extrinsic motivators. Intrinsic motivation is about purposefully creating inspiring conditions that tap into your workers' internal drivers, which is where most employers fall short. That's one more way you can outmanage other companies and become an employer of choice.

Extrinsic motivation has its uses, especially for generating short-term activity. As we discussed, there are times when that's the best way to go. But intrinsic motivation lasts longer. It provides sustained job satisfaction, leading to higher retention rates. People stay when they're fulfilled. Intrinsic motivation also encourages employees to take initiative and solve problems, freeing up your time. It's worth investing some time to promote it.

Tipping and Motivation

Tipping is an extrinsic motivation and reward model that employers have increasingly relied on to compensate hourly service employees while controlling labor costs. Here in the U.S., tipping is a huge part of our culture, and it's evolved. At restaurants, 20 percent is the new 15 percent. And whereas tipping was once meant as a reward for providing outstanding service, now it's expected. You used to feel generous for leaving a 20 percent tip. Now you're a jerk if you don't. I recently had a server hand me the payment device after the meal and say, "The gratuity is already set for 20 percent. You just have to tap OK." He didn't seem motivated by the tip; he seemed entitled to it. There are a lot of social dynamics at play here, and they affect the customer experience. And tipping is cropping up in many more types of businesses. Even small ticket retailers are offering a tip option at the counter now.

No doubt tipping can make harder jobs more desirable, and it theoretically still gives consumers the option to reward someone based on the service they receive. It's a form of immediate feedback, and that has emotional impact. Employees like money, but they also like feeling acknowledged. A good tip does both.

But there's a darker side to tipping. In an hourly worker environment, some workers get tips and others don't. Those who serve food are more likely to receive tips than those who cook it or clean it up. Even when servers tip out additional staff, it can breed bitterness. It can also cause employees to provide better service to "better" customers (i.e., bigger tippers). Earlier I shared I was a hotel bellhop. My coworkers and I paid attention to which cars guests drove. Not only would we work harder for those in nicer vehicles, but we fought amongst ourselves to decide who would carry their luggage.

And because we were chasing tips, we'd create situations to collect more of them, even when it wasn't in the best interests of guests. If someone's dry cleaning was done, rather than having it in their rooms when they returned, we waited until they got back and called to let them know we were bringing their laundry up, giving them time to find a few bucks for our tip. Some of my co-workers would remove TV remotes from rooms so guests would have to call down for a replacement—another opportunity for a tip. We were competing predators, and guests were our prey. And because we interacted with guests directly, they felt more compelled to tip us after each transaction, compared with the housekeeping staff, who undoubtedly worked harder than us while guests were away, and were therefore less likely to receive the same financial rewards.

So the question is, how can you maximize employee compensation and motivation while maintaining a strong, customer-focused culture?

Consider a few different tipping models. What I described above is a traditional individual tipping system, in which customers provide gratuities directly to the employees who serve them. Workers receive immediate payment and feedback.

Some workplaces have found success through pooled tipping, or as they say in the UK, a "tronc" system. In this model, gratuities are collected, combined, and shared based on a predetermined distribution formula. Some just split the money evenly among all employees, while others distribute it based on hours worked. Some have a hierarchical compensation structure that distributes tips as a percentage based on position.

A well-managed tipping pool that's transparent and fair may be great for employee motivation. One 2016 study I came across, called "Impact of Tipping on Workers' Motivation: Comparison between the Hospitality and Gaming Industries in Slovenia," found that "employees in the Slovenian companies with a regulated system of tip distribution tend to be better motivated and treat their guests better than their colleagues in unregulated environments. On the other hand, employees in the hospitality industry are less motivated by tips than their colleagues in the gaming industry, despite receiving individual tips directly." One of the reasons they cite is the psychological impact on those who receive one large share of tips given monthly, compared with those who receive daily tips, "who have no direct insight into the monthly sum total of their tips." In other words, one big monthly amount may be more motivational than daily, incremental tips.

Pooled tipping may also be better for your culture. Theoretically, it encourages more teamwork. It rallies everyone around providing a great experience for customers, which may lead to better tips for everyone. This may also make sense if your business model is moving more toward mobile and delivery and relying less on traditional customer service. It also creates more high-five moments when the money is distributed and workers celebrate what they earned as a cohesive unit. I experienced this once as a bellhop, when three of us worked a night shift during a huge event and agreed to pool our tips. It changed the way we interacted and was a lot more fun.

But pooled tipping also has some disadvantages. It removes the sense of immediate feedback and allows those whose service is subpar to receive as much compensation as the top performers, which can create resentment within the team. One restaurant worker told me that at his workplace, people "bully" others to leave if they're not busy to reduce the number of people splitting the tipping pool. The system requires someone to manage it. There may be some legal and tax implications. I've also heard many stories of managers and business owners who don't distribute the entire pool to workers. In most instances, this is illegal. In all instances, this is not cool.

You must decide what will work best for your team. If gratuities are part of your workplace, consider how your current system may be affecting individual workers, your culture, and your customer experience. Look at others in your industry and see what models are working for them—there may be a way to do it better. But whatever you choose, be sure to comply with all laws and regulations in your area.

TOP-PERFORMANCE SPOTLIGHT

BEAVERTAILS
Niagara Falls, Ontario

BeaverTails is an iconic Canadian pastry shop that's been delighting customers since 1978. One of their most popular locations, owned by Zahir Ismail, operates on the bustling Clifton Hill promenade in Niagara Falls, with a small mobile satellite in Niagara-on-the-Lake. Customers come to indulge their cravings for their famous whole-wheat pastries but are also treated to an equally sweet customer experience facilitated by their 22 team members, most of whom are college students. Online customer ratings are spectacular.

In a sector that's lucky to hang onto employees for just a few months, the average tenure here is two to three years. It's remarkable retention for a seasonal workplace. Over the course of a year, employee workweeks may range from 20 to 40 hours. This works well for college students, who have more availability during the busy summer season and less once school starts. But they also stay because they want to remain part of their BeaverTails family.

TOP-PERFORMANCE SPOTLIGHT, continued

Employees start at just a few cents above minimum wage and split tips. The stores display a QR code on their counters inviting customers to post Google reviews and mention employees by name. Each month the employee with the most positive mentions earns a $75 Amazon gift card.

Zahir Ismail prides himself in the care he shows his team. He knows that as college students, his employees are pursuing other ambitions, so he mentors them as much as possible. He's even had meetings with staff on how to open their own business. "I want to help them with their future goals, so I put aside time for that," he said. Many come to Canada to study from overseas, so he also offers assistance navigating the country's immigration system.

Having heard the complaints of so many other employers, I asked Zahir how he feels about today's young workers. "I've heard the complaints, too, but that hasn't been my experience," he said. "We go out of our way to train them well and treat them well. They do great. They can all be motivated if you just make it a priority."

Zahir's management team consists of one GM to oversee both locations, along with two managers and two supervisors divided between the primary store and the satellite. The group meets weekly to review employee performance and discuss operational objectives. In addition to providing team members with consistent on-site coaching, they also conduct weekly one-on-one check-in phone calls. Managers are instructed to make these calls outside the stores so they can focus exclusively on the employee. During these calls, there's no discussion of work performance; instead, they focus on the worker's well-being and ways to support them. The calls are usually short, but employees appreciate the consistent personal attention. "This is one way we look out for them and make sure they don't leave to go work somewhere else," Zahir told me.

TOP-PERFORMANCE SPOTLIGHT, continued

The company recruits new employees through staffing websites as well as team members' word-of-mouth. Their staffing process has three stages. The first entails remote vetting through application reviews, phone calls, and reference checks. Next is the interview. For those they like, the third stage is a walkthrough of the store. Managers show prospects all aspects of the business to give them an accurate, unpolished idea of what the job will be. It's not enough for management to like the candidates—they want to make sure candidates will like the job.

Once they're hired, managers train employees on work tasks, customer service expectations, and sales targets. They watch the numbers closely, hold employees accountable, and offer incentives to hit sales benchmarks.

New employees quickly realize this is a special workplace. That's by design. Zahir told me, "We want a work environment where employees come for the culture and not just for the money." Two to three times a year, the company plans "employee hangouts," usually some kind of interactive game experience to keep team members engaged with one another. They also hold monthly employee appreciation pizza parties.

Zahir emphasized the importance of management's open-door policy: "Communication is everything. We want employees to know we're here for them as much as we expect them to be here for us."

Top-Performance Takeaways:

- ⟩ Encourage customers to recognize employees with online reviews, and offer bonuses to those with good customer feedback.
- ⟩ Mentor employees around their long-term goals.
- ⟩ Hold employees accountable and offer performance incentives.

Theories of Motivation

Motivation in the workplace has been researched ad nauseam. Since industrialization, people have been studying workers, trying to understand and explain how they behave. There are so many theories and models about it that it's easy to fall down the rabbit hole. But underneath the scholarly discourse are some sensible ideas you can actually use.

Let's review a few of the better-known theories of human motivation and try to extract some practical applications. We're only scratching the surface, but hopefully you'll find an idea or two that will help you.

Maslow's Hierarchy of Needs

In his well-known 1943 paper "A Theory of Human Motivation," psychologist Abraham Maslow described what he called a "hierarchy of needs." He discussed five tiers of motivation, as illustrated in Figure 13.1.

Figure 13.1. Maslow's Hierarchy of Needs

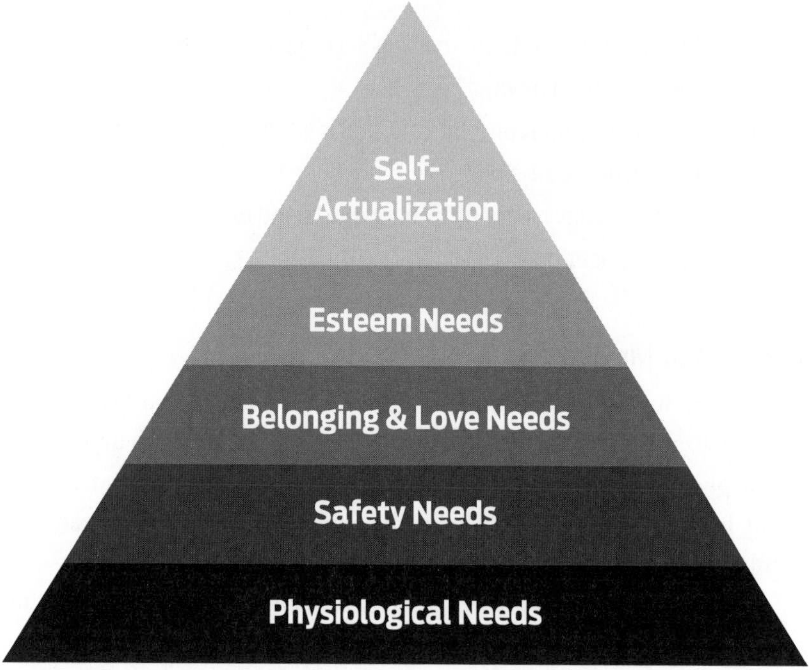

Each level of need is achievable only when the levels below it are satisfied. Once a level is satisfied—in other words, once that need is fulfilled—the person is motivated to fulfill the need on the next level. It makes sense. No one's worried about feeding their soul when they need to feed their stomach. But once their belly is full, they're interested in something more. If you're bothered that some of your strategies for motivating employees aren't working, it might be because you're appealing to them on the wrong level.

The hierarchy starts with the most basic needs of survival and then works its way up to the mental state of self-actualization. The idea of pursuing "self-actualization" while working the counter at a convenience store sounds ridiculous, but when you understand the tiers, you'll see there's something useful here.

Let's look at each one, starting from the bottom of the pyramid.

Physiological Needs

These are all about basic survival, and nothing can else can happen unless these needs are met. They include food, water, air, shelter, and warmth. At work, it means making money, taking breaks, and satisfying their most fundamental personal essentials. If they haven't had a meal in eight hours, praising their performance won't have the effect you're hoping for. Give them a sandwich instead.

Safety Needs

These give people a sense of security and stability. They include a safe living space, income security, access to health care, and protection from threats. At work, they need to be in safe conditions and feel like they can rely on ongoing employment.

Psychological safety is now very much a thing in the workplace, taking precedence over drivers on the higher tiers. If the workplace feels emotionally threatening, employees are less likely to stay.

These first two levels are hard needs: tangible requirements to function in the workplace. As we move up from here, the needs become increasingly soft. They're less tangible, but still deeply meaningful.

Belonging and Love Needs

These are everything social. Family, friends, relationships, romance, community—all the things that make us feel connected to others. These needs are met at work when employees become colleagues and friends, when they feel they're part of a team, and when they feel they have a mentor. If the work environment is toxic, if there's a co-worker they can't stand, or if management mistreats them, a pay raise or a sandwich won't help much. They need a better experience with the people around them. This is where culture becomes really powerful. Lots of people are surviving but live without meaningful human connection. If you can provide it, you'll win more loyalty and higher performance, especially if you can push them to the higher tiers.

Esteem Needs

These are the things that make us feel like we matter: recognition, social status, self-worth, confidence, and a sense of accomplishment. Lower on the pyramid, people are trying to survive. At this level, they're trying to thrive. You can help them do that with recognition, promotion, and asking them to train someone. They feel esteem when customers compliment them or name them in online reviews. The badges, stickers, and symbols we discussed in Chapter 5 also contribute to this feeling.

I lost a number of employees who originally came to our business while they were in survival mode. They just needed a job. Once they were stable, many left for other jobs with a deeper intrinsic payoff. If all your work environment offers is a paycheck, you might lose people when they desire something more.

Money can help provide additional esteem, just as it helps meet physiological and safety needs. This is not just because of its buying power, but also because it shows you recognize the employee's value. At the lower levels, people want to get paid what they need. At the esteem level, they want to get paid what they're worth. But money won't motivate them for long if their social needs aren't met. Again, each level builds on the previous ones.

Self-Actualization

This level is where people reach their full potential and live their values. Life and work are meaningful. They have balance, are fully engaged, and feel profound joy. Workers experience this when they can be creative, work autonomously, or do something they love. They also experience it when they can sink their teeth into a new challenge.

But even if they're lucky enough to achieve self-actualization at work, it's difficult to maintain. They drop lower on the pyramid, either because some of their lower needs are no longer being fulfilled or because they desire more self-actualization than their current job can provide. That's why you need to find ways for them to grow even more—or allow them to move on.

Maslow's hierarchy has been challenged over the years, as is always the case with simple models trying to explain complex things. But I believe there's value in noticing people's priorities. If we can help employees meet their needs and equip them to achieve their wants, maybe we can motivate them to act.

Practical Takeaways:

- Assess your workers' most important needs and start there.
- Push them to the level just above where they currently are.
- Ensure their safety and security and then bring them into your culture.
- Actively make them feel like they matter—that they're not just working, but really excelling.
- Once they've achieved peak performance and joy, find new ways to push them so they can sustain that joy.

Reinforcement Theory of Motivation

Reinforcement theory postulates that behavior is influenced by rewards and punishments. It's all about cause and effect. The theory is most often associated with behavioral psychologist B.F. Skinner. Skinner conducted experiments with animals to see if he could figure out how to influence their behavior. When you picture rats learning to press levers to get a treat, it was B.F. Skinner who taught them.

When applied to human beings, the theory suggests that if we receive a positive outcome or reward after doing something, we're more likely to repeat the action. (That's the dopamine effect we discussed in Chapter 10.) We're less likely to repeat a behavior if we receive a negative outcome. Do your chores, get a cookie. Touch the stove, you get burned.

Reinforcement theory suggests that people have two primary drivers: a desire for pleasure and a resistance to pain. The model in Figure 13.2 shows us four ways to tap into those drivers to motivate employees and shape their behavior. The top two approaches are about encouraging more of the desired behaviors, while the bottom two are about discouraging unwanted behaviors. The approaches on the left side add something to an employee's work experience, and the approaches on the right remove something.

Figure 13.2. Reinforcement Theory

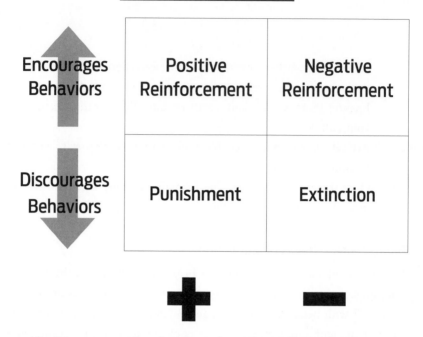

All of these are results of actions taken. The feedback of change to the amount of pleasure or pain is designed to encourage desirable behaviors and discourage unwanted behaviors. Let's look at each one and see how they differ:

> **Positive Reinforcement.** In this approach, you give something or do something for the employee that triggers the dopamine effect. That would include things like rewards, praise, promotion, gifts, and more money. You're actively providing a positive consequence.

> **Negative Reinforcement.** This entails removing something from their work they don't like. Perhaps you reassign them from an unfavorable task to a better one, or reschedule them from a shift they don't like to one they prefer. You're actively removing a source of displeasure.

Both forms of reinforcement are about making the person feel better by either giving or doing something for them that's pleasurable (positive reinforcement) or removing something that feels bad (negative reinforcement).

▷ **Punishment.** This means imposing negative consequences, perhaps the ones you removed through negative reinforcement. You could assign them tasks they don't want or schedule them to come in on their normal day off. You might also suspend them or issue them a warning. You could give them a reprimand. You're actively adding a source of displeasure.

▷ **Extinction.** This means removing a positive consequence. Perhaps you hold back praise, a bonus, or a privilege, or even demote them. You're actively removing a positive part of their work experience.

Punishment and Extinction are about making the person feel worse by either giving or doing something for them that's unpleasant (punishment) or depriving them of something that feels good (extinction).

These four management behaviors rely on extrinsic motivation. They won't promote autonomy, personal satisfaction, or self-motivation. They won't inspire or appeal to your workers' deeper desires. But when you have an occasional need to reinforce someone in the Blue, reengage someone in the Red, quickly encourage a new behavior, or stop one you don't want, one of these approaches may be useful.

Practical Takeaways:

To *encourage* behaviors you want:

▷ Praise your workers when they perform as they should.
▷ Offer rewards, privileges, and other positive consequences that stimulate the dopamine effect.
▷ Remove unpleasant tasks and experiences from the employee's shift to make their workday more pleasant.
▷ Offer flexible scheduling, time off, and breaks to reduce stress.

To *discourage* behaviors you *don't* want:

▷ Withhold praise when your workers don't perform as they should.
▷ Withhold attention.
▷ Reprimand employees who deviate from standards or don't meet expectations.
▷ Assign consequences and issue warnings.
▷ Assign less pleasant tasks and shifts.

McClelland's Theory of Needs

In contrast to reinforcement theory's web of positive and negative motivators, another Harvard psychologist, David McClelland, argued in his 1961 book *The Achieving Society* that people are driven by three intrinsic needs: affiliation, achievement, and power. Each comes with advantages and disadvantages:

- ◈ **Need for affiliation:** Those needing affiliation thrive as part of a unified team. They crave a sense of belonging, do well with collaborative work, and have a lot to offer a positive work culture, as they're very supportive of co-workers. However, they may also resist conflict, which prevents them from asserting themselves. With a need to affiliate comes a need for approval.
- ◈ **Need for achievement:** Employees with this need are often driven to set and seek lofty goals. They work hard and want feedback to help them succeed. They enjoy personal growth and are energized by a sense of accomplishment. But they can also be hard on themselves, and their fear of failure can be extremely stressful. Unlike those needing to affiliate, those needing achievement may step on the toes of anyone in their way.
- ◈ **Need for power:** People with this need like to lead. They want to influence the people and circumstances around them, shape outcomes, help organizations progress, and inspire others to act. But power is easily abused and corrupted, and they may try to fill this need by serving themselves rather than the organization or the culture. The thirst for power can sometimes be the cause of unethical behavior.

Just as you need to adapt your coaching approach based on your diagnosis of an employee's skill set and mindset, if you determine a worker is driven by one of these three needs, you can tap into that to motivate them accordingly.

Practical Takeaways:

For those with a need for **affiliation:**

> ▷ Assign them collaborative, social tasks.
> ▷ Mentor them closely.
> ▷ Encourage them to mentor and train others.
> ▷ Encourage them to express their feelings without fear of judgment.
> ▷ Praise them publicly.
> ▷ Plan team building exercises and social events.

For those with a need for **achievement:**

> ▷ Ask them for their goals and give them the opportunity to seek them.
> ▷ Assign them new tasks and challenges.
> ▷ Provide lots of feedback.
> ▷ Keep an eye on their well-being and help them manage stress.
> ▷ Remind them to look out for co-workers as they pursue their own goals.
> ▷ Encourage them to work toward team success, not just their own.
> ▷ Help restore their mindset if they fail or have a setback.

For those with a need for **power:**

> ▷ Give them autonomy if they're in the Blue for the task.
> ▷ Put them in charge of projects.
> ▷ Ask for their opinions and ideas.
> ▷ Have them mentor and train others.
> ▷ When ready, promote them to leadership roles.
> ▷ Remind them of their responsibility to the culture.
> ▷ Watch their management closely to ensure they're working in the best interests of your organization and those they lead.

McGregor's Theory X and Theory Y

In the 1960s, MIT management theorist Douglas McGregor described two opposing views of employees that require different approaches to management. "Theory X" assumes employees are naturally lazy and dislike work. They require supervision and respond best to external rewards and punishment (aka extrinsic motivation). Because they can't self-manage, management must communicate their expectations and rules and establish lots of structure. Management must also be authoritative, or workers will disengage from their jobs. Theory X workers need to be controlled.

"Theory Y" assumes employees enjoy their work and want to succeed. They're collaborative, self-reliant, and trustworthy. They thrive when they have room to explore and grow. Theory Y workers like to have some control over their jobs. They have intrinsic motivation.

What matters most here is *your* perspective. How do you see your hourly workers, and how does that affect your approach to motivating them? Do you believe in them or disdain them? Do you see them as individuals or have feelings about them as a whole? You probably do have some workers who embody Theory X, but hopefully you also have some who represent Theory Y. Neither theory describes everyone—and that means neither a carrot nor a stick will work across the board.

Fortunately, you don't need to choose just one. A good work environment can accommodate both theories and provide motivation for everyone. Many management scholars have written about the importance of considering the situation and the task when determining how to manage and motivate your employees. They call this *contingency theory*.

But we don't need to delve into the details. Just know that you can provide enough structure and discipline to help those employees who need more supervision, consistent with Theory X, while also creating space for your more self-reliant workers to thrive under your Theory Y guidance.

Practical Takeaways:

For **Theory X** employees:

> ❯ Communicate expectations.
> ❯ Provide structure and guidelines.
> ❯ Enforce policies and procedures.
> ❯ Provide immediate feedback, praise, and discipline.
> ❯ Incentivize them with hard needs such as bonuses and promotions.

For **Theory Y** employees:

> ▷ Promote employee growth and development.
> ▷ Encourage autonomy.
> ▷ Promote a positive work culture.
> ▷ Incentivize them with soft needs such as praise and new challenges.

Motivating the Four Personality Types

In Chapter 7, we talked about Doers, Thinkers, Feelers, and Connectors. Each of these personality types has their own drivers. At this point, you'll probably notice some similarities to McClelland's Theory of Needs. Here, too, you can customize your approach to motivation based on the individual employee.

Practical Takeaways:

For **Doers:**

> ▷ Set clear goals and provide a timeline for completion.
> ▷ Delegate time-sensitive tasks to them.
> ▷ Offer praise and recognition for their hard work and efficiency.
> ▷ Provide lots of tangible feedback.
> ▷ Create opportunities for hands-on, active tasks.

For **Thinkers:**

> ▷ Give them time to analyze and process information.
> ▷ Encourage them to contribute their ideas and insights.
> ▷ Provide a structured and organized work environment.
> ▷ Give them a strong sense of "why" behind the tasks you assign.
> ▷ Explain how their work connects to the larger operation.

For **Feelers:**

> ▷ Show empathy toward their emotions.
> ▷ Express appreciation for their efforts.
> ▷ Offer lots of praise.
> ▷ Choose your words carefully when giving reprimands.
> ▷ Acknowledge the impact of their work on others.

For **Connectors:**

> ▷ Foster a social and inclusive work environment.
> ▷ Recognize and acknowledge their ability to connect with others.
> ▷ Solicit their feedback on culture and team interaction.
> ▷ Assign them to collaborative tasks and allow them to work with customers.
> ▷ Include them in marketing initiatives.

As I said in Chapter 7, these personality types aren't scientific. Your workers may have characteristics of more than one of them, in which case they're likely to respond to more drivers.

This speaks to the larger issue of the theories we've discussed in this chapter. It's tempting to fit human behavior into a clean model. But we're far too complex for any simple descriptions. To me, there's one fundamental takeaway from all these theories that's essential for motivating your employees:

You need to pay attention.

You need to look closely at their individuality. Assess their unique needs and desires, use extrinsic interventions, and awaken their intrinsic motivations.

When to Stop Motivating

Working to boost an employee's mindset can be a real time suck. I'll give them the skill set they need to perform, redirect them a bit when their attitude slides, and help them back into the Blue. But there comes a point of diminishing returns. I'm willing to handle an occasional motivation issue, but I'm not willing to deal with a chronic one. A good employee shouldn't need a constant push. They've been hired to do work, not create it.

If your whole team seems unmotivated, that's a cultural issue—and that's on you. You need to reflect on your management style and remake your work environment. With individuals, something's not right on their end, and hopefully you can identify and rectify it. You may not be able to. They may just be the wrong fit for the organization or the job—or their issues may be beyond your ability to help.

In all my years of managing, I was never able to fix anyone's long-term attitude problem. There were some people I just couldn't motivate, even while I was motivating others just fine. If you've devoted a lot of time and energy to boost an employee's mindset and they're not improving, it may be time to part ways.

Keeping Yourself Motivated

Employees aren't the only ones who burn out. You matter, too. Managing people and an operation can be really taxing, and your mindset might occasionally wane. But who's there to motivate you, praise you, give you feedback, or grab you a sandwich? Who's there to help you achieve top performance and live your best life? There may be no one.

In that case, you have to keep your own batteries charged and set your own goals—not just related to your responsibilities but also your desires. Tap into your intrinsic wants and needs, and look for ways to meet them on the job. Find your own "why." As a manager, you have the opportunity to make a positive impact on others. A higher purpose is built into your job, so be proud of that. When leading people isn't a headache, it's a privilege.

Also eat well, get some sleep, take a break when you can, and get help if you need it. You matter as much as your team, so don't forget to practice a little self-care.

CHAPTER 14

Monitoring and Measuring Performance

When ChatGPT exploded into the public consciousness at the end of 2022, it raised the same question that's come up every time a revolutionary technology has been introduced: Will AI replace humans? I'm not worried—one human job that's not disappearing anytime soon is management. AI can't empathize, read a room, or pick up on subtext and unspoken meaning. It can't pull together a group of strangers and bond them into a united culture. These behaviors are critical for leading people, and while AI can do wondrous things with information, when it comes to facilitating human connection, it's still in the Stone Age.

Emotional intelligence eats artificial intelligence for breakfast. (I asked a chatbot if this was true and it agreed.)

But management isn't just an art—it's also a science. So much of this book has been about feelings, which are real and important in the workplace, but they're messy. Even when we talked about evaluating employees with a hiring matrix in Chapter 7, your scores for each characteristic were subjective. At some point we need real data.

Science relies on observation and measurement, which allows you to determine the impact of new factors. In the workplace, you can't just feel your way forward. Performance must be tracked and quantified—it's the only way to truly know how things are going.

What exactly is "top performance," and how do you know when you've achieved it? *Well, I can just tell. I know when my team feels good and when they don't. We're like a family, so they come to me when there's an issue. As long as work is getting done and I see smiles on their faces, I know we're doing well.* That belief has cost employers a lot of money and a lot of good employees. Feelings matter, but they're nebulous. Sometimes you need hard numbers, which may tell a different and more reliable story.

You can track sales and productivity. You can measure how your workers are doing by choosing key performance indicators (KPIs) like retention, satisfaction, and engagement. You can track employees' confidence in the culture. If you have the courage to ask, you can track their confidence in *you*. Quantifying these things allows you to determine objectively which numbers amount to top performance. Every cheer squad will tell you their team is better. But the only way to know for sure is to look at the scoreboard.

Once you have baseline numbers for these metrics, you determine if things are getting better or worse and act accordingly. You can set goals and work toward higher numbers. You can tie bonuses and rewards to hitting tangible objectives. Tapping into emotions helps boost performance, but tracking numbers helps *measure* performance.

To really stay on top of your team, there are two broad areas you need to monitor: their external performance and their internal experience.

Measuring Employees' External Performance

This is an evaluation of all the tangible and observable parts of an employee's job. During training, they need to understand the criteria for success: what's expected and what will be measured or counted to determine how well they're doing.

Employees appreciate defined goals. They like being able to keep score. There's intrinsic satisfaction in knowing you've met or surpassed a benchmark. Employees want to do well, but you need to clarify for them exactly what success looks like.

I once trained an employee on how to properly cut the peels off sliced cantaloupe wedges (important at Edible Arrangements!). I used the tell, show, watch, review method. Once it seemed like he was in the Blue, I decided to gamify the task by giving him a timed goal. I asked him to peel an entire bucket of wedges in five minutes. If he succeeded, he'd get a candy bar. Go!

Encouraged by his co-workers, he started cutting. He was totally focused, with a little smile on his face, clearly enjoying the challenge. This was monotonous work, but having a goal made it interesting. The tension built as time ticked away. "One minute left!" He was fully engrossed, giving the task everything he had. "Three, two, one, stop!" Five wedges remained unpeeled. "Darn!" he exclaimed, clearly disappointed. That made me happy because it meant he was engaged. Having a measurable goal motivated him. It motivates everyone. I praised him for what he was able to accomplish and gave him the candy bar anyway for his effort. (That probably encouraged a sense of entitlement. My bad.)

Honestly, I don't believe the candy was the prize he wanted. That's an extrinsic incentive. He was chasing an intrinsic payoff, a sense of accomplishment. That's what specific work benchmarks provide for workers. They want to experience their mastery and push to get better. Otherwise they're just passing the time.

Each job has its own unique KPIs. In manufacturing, performance might be measured in products per hour. Call centers measure the average length of calls and the percentage of issues that are resolved in the first call. Retail stores might look at a worker's sales per hour. Quick-service restaurants measure order accuracy, speed, and customer satisfaction.

Other common metrics are safety record, average ticket size, and upselling. Just as you need to operationalize your values by creating specific dos and don'ts, make employee performance more tangible by breaking their job into specific targets they can work toward.

Quality Checks

An important task for any manager is to check their employees' work. Your best people in the Blue for tasks can still get complacent. Step in once in a while to make sure things are up to standard. Give them praise when they are and readjust when they're not. This is important, even for your top employees. The smallest deviation from standards can have big implications.

I spent a day consulting for the owners of an ice cream store. Their P&L showed excessive food costs, so I was searching for the leak. I asked one of their top employees to get me a scoop of ice cream, and then I weighed it. The scoop was two ounces heavier than brand standards. I asked the employee if she knew how much ice cream she was supposed to scoop. She did. The issue wasn't what she knew (skill set). It was what she felt (mindset). She was in the Red for scooping ice cream. She seemed so happy it was easy to misdiagnose her. She didn't have a negative attitude—she'd just gotten a little too comfortable, but that's also a mindset problem. She needed to be re-engaged so she'd pay more attention to her work. All it took was a gentle reminder to watch her scoop size.

But why make a big deal about it? What difference does a little ice cream make? Those two extra ounces, multiplied by the number of scoops they sold per year, amounted to an overage of more than $60,000. To find that, it wasn't enough to eyeball the scoop size. I had to weigh it. I suggested to the owners that they incentivize employees to reduce food costs by offering them a bonus (a tiny fraction of the amount they'd save) tied to this metric.

Employees can also grow complacent when management does. I got too comfortable at my stores when we won that "Best Customer Service" award. Sales were good, the operation felt smooth, morale was high, and things seemed great. But that feeling was the problem. It distracted me from the numbers. My P&L (which I didn't look at often enough) revealed our food waste, and our reports showed a decrease in average ticket size. I let too much time go by before noticing these things.

Don't rely on your feelings alone. Get the data. There's lots of technology to help measure performance, but it's only helpful if you use it and study the numbers. Consistently check your employees' work and monitor their KPIs.

It's also important to verify trust. That may seem counterintuitive: By definition, if you trust someone, you shouldn't need to confirm they're doing the right thing. But trust is often extended a bit generously. Verification keeps you safe and can help deepen trust every time it's confirmed. One of our rituals when we were considering giving an employee a key was what we called the "$20 Test." We'd schedule them to close out the register and slip an extra $20 bill into the till; then we'd wait to see if they reported the discrepancy or keep the $20 and make the numbers add up. We never administered this test to someone who hadn't already earned our trust, and fortunately no one ever failed. It was a great way to confirm they were key-worthy.

Measuring Employees' Internal Experience

We don't just do our work—we feel our work. Most of this book has been about how to boost the way your workers feel because that impacts how they perform. According to Gallup's "State of the Global Workplace: 2022 Report," "Engaged employees are more present and productive; they are more attuned to the needs of customers; and they are more observant of processes, standards, and systems. When taken together, the behaviors of highly engaged business units result in a 23 percent difference in profitability." So we're not just talking about making your workplace pleasant out of kindness. We're talking about running a productive, profitable operation. It's important, therefore, to monitor how your team is doing in their hearts and minds, not just on the floor.

So here, too, you need to collect data, some of it in the form of open-ended feedback. You should ask questions that allow people to express themselves and share ideas. You can gather this information during group meetings, one-on-ones, and surveys.

But it's also important to compile statistics you can quantify and track. Some of the most important internal-experience KPIs to monitor are:

- ▷ **Satisfaction:** How happy are they on the job?
- ▷ **Engagement:** How much do they care about their work?
- ▷ **Retention:** How long do employees stay?
- ▷ **Absenteeism and Calling Out:** How often are they not coming to work (which could be a reflection of low morale or burnout)?
- ▷ **Employee Assistance Program (EAP) Utilization:** How often are employees requesting help for mental health, work-life balance, stress management, and personal well-being?
- ▷ **Connection to Culture:** How connected do they feel to co-workers?
- ▷ **Feelings about Management:** How much do they trust, feel supported, and feel inspired by you?

Your employees' internal experience is a measurement of your external performance. It's your responsibility to train them, engage them, and maintain their satisfaction. It's on you to build a healthy culture, monitor the above KPIs, and work to improve them. You can't determine how well you're managing your team if you don't ask questions and look at the numbers.

I discussed this with a friend of mine, Michelle Rowan, president of data analysis firm Franchise Business Review (FBR). FBR helps franchise brands measure the satisfaction of their independent owners and find opportunities for improvement. They've expanded their services to help them measure employee satisfaction and use that as a primary metric to evaluate managers. Two of FBR's stated values are: "Feedback makes us stronger" and "Build trust through accountability."

"Employees get feedback all the time," Michelle told me. "Managers and business owners, not as much. Without that information, it's harder to improve. Measuring employee satisfaction is the best way to gauge your true impact on them."

In other words, get your team's feedback so you can get better at making them better.

Surveying Your Team

Direct conversations are great, but hourly workers won't always have the courage or communication skills to reveal their feelings. Blind surveys are useful for soliciting their feedback in a safe setting. Surveys also make it easier to measure results by collecting quantifiable data.

There are many third parties and technologies you can use to collect feedback from your team. Several of the top-performing organizations profiled in this book use them to measure employee satisfaction and engagement. If you wish to facilitate these surveys on your own, there are websites and apps that make this easy. Employees can anonymously log into a survey on a company computer or their phone to answer questions, enabling you to get quick, constantly updated data. These platforms also make suggestions for questions and question types to maximize survey completion. Some of them offer randomized prizes to encourage participation—which in itself is worth measuring, as it speaks to employee engagement.

The format of the questions is important when it comes to getting the information you want. Likert scale questions ask about the extent to which someone agrees with a given statement (strongly agree, agree, disagree, and so on). Others ask about feelings on a numeric scale (from 1 to 5, from 1 to 10, etc.). Some are multiple choice. Good survey platforms will suggest formats that encourage response rates and yield the best data.

You should ask questions that test for the specific KPIs you're interested in. Below are a few ideas to get you started.

Engagement Questions:

"I feel motivated to come to work every day. Strongly Agree, Agree, etc.," or "On a scale of 1 to 10, how motivated do you feel coming to work every day?"

"On a scale of 1 to 5, how much do you care about your day-to-day duties?"

"Are you proud to be a part of this organization? (Yes/No)"

Satisfaction Questions:

"Are you happy with the company's commitment to employee well-being and employee support programs? (Yes/No)"

"On a scale of 1 to 5, how satisfied are you with your overall job?"

"I'm happy with how the company treats me. Strongly Agree, Agree, etc."

Team/Culture Questions:

"On a scale of 1 to 5, how connected do you feel to your co-workers?"

"Do you feel that your team has a strong sense of shared goals and a common purpose? (Yes/No)"

"My co-workers and I collaborate well and support each other. Strongly Agree, Agree, etc."

Management Questions:

"On a scale of 1 to 5, how satisfied are you with your relationship with your immediate supervisor/manager?"

"My manager fosters a positive and inclusive work environment for our team. Strongly Agree, Agree, etc."

"Are you satisfied with the overall leadership style and effectiveness of your manager? (Yes/No)"

For each of these, you can add a "comments" section and invite employees to explain their answers. The numbers give you an overall impression of how employees feel, and the comments give you the reasons behind the numbers. Use the numbers to set new goals and the comments to develop new strategies to achieve them.

Employee Net Promoter Score (eNPS)

If you've bought anything in the past 25 years, you've likely been asked some version of the Likert scale question, "On a scale of 0 to 10, how likely are you to recommend our company/product/service to a friend or colleague?" The result is used to calculate your "Net Promoter Score" (NPS). Developed in 2003 by Fred Reichheld at Bain & Company, today the NPS is widely used as a tool to measure loyalty and customer satisfaction.

Depending on how customers answer the question, they're divided into three groups. Those choosing 9-10 are "promoters," the ones who are willing to recommend you. Those choosing 7-8 are "passives," less likely to promote you but also less likely to speak ill of you. Detractors choose 0-6—they may scare people away. Your score is calculated by subtracting the percentage of detractors from the percentage of promoters. The formula is:

NPS = % Promoters - % Detractors

So out of 100 responding customers, if 70 are promoters and 15 are detractors, your NPS is 55. You can use your NPS to see how customer satisfaction compares to other time periods or to others in your industry. Because the NPS is based on only one question, it's one piece of data that should be considered among other forms of feedback.

The NPS has been adapted into an Employee Net Promoter Score (eNPS). It works precisely the same way to gauge employee satisfaction. You simply have to change the question to something like, "On a scale of 0 to 10, how likely are you to recommend our organization as a place to work to a friend or colleague?" If your employees enjoy the job—or if they don't—they're likely to tell others about it. Just like the NPS, this question is one among many you should be asking to get a true picture of how your employees are feeling. It's likely your survey platform already has an eNPS question built in that will calculate the above formula for you.

Measure your eNPS regularly and work to boost your score.

Closing the Feedback Loop

Feedback is part of a healthy communication cycle. Information should flow back to those who provided it so they see it was received and acted upon. You want to empower your employees and show them that their input has the potential to shape their workplace. You don't need to agree with or act on every suggestion. But you do need to let them know their opinions are taken seriously.

Neglecting to respond to feedback sends the opposite message: that they have no voice. That can lower morale and reduce engagement. The lack of response can reduce trust and lower their motivation to provide feedback in the future.

If you conduct a survey, thank your team for responding and assure them you're studying their responses. Be willing to report the results to them. If the data is good, celebrate that with them, but if it's not, own that. Acknowledge their concerns and let them know you're committed to making adjustments. Invite them to brainstorm solutions. The more involved they are in the improvements, the more likely it is they'll embrace them. When you're ready to announce any changes as a result of the survey, show them how their feedback led to this new plan of action. This isn't just about appeasing them—it's about responding to a group that's qualified to point out your blind spots and encouraging them to continue expressing their opinions. Like everything else your employees do, giving you honest feedback is a behavior—and one you want to reinforce.

All the above also applies to any feedback given about you. Thank them for their input, acknowledge your opportunity to improve, and then make the improvements. Model the way feedback should be taken. If they see you're committed to top performance, they'll be more committed, too.

TOP-PERFORMANCE SPOTLIGHT

KIDDIE ACADEMY EDUCATIONAL CHILD CARE
Fort Wayne, Indiana

Early childhood education is a high-stakes endeavor. Not only are you caring for the safety and minds of children but also the hopes, dreams, and fears of their parents. Then there's the other group that needs nurturing: your staff, committed hourly workers entrusted with the sacred act of caring for someone else's child. It's hard, important work. Together, this community is defined by its vulnerability and mutual support. The entire operation must be fueled by a love for loving people.

In Fort Wayne, Indiana, no one loves people more than Kiddie Academy Educational Child Care—and the feeling is mutual. For four years running, they've been selected as the number-one child-care company by the Fort Wayne Newspapers Readers' Choice Awards. The two-academy operation has stellar online reviews and a loyal following of families. Their original academy ranks among the top 5 percent within the entire franchise system, and their new location is already performing in the top 15 percent.

TOP-PERFORMANCE SPOTLIGHT, continued

While Kiddie Academy offers excellent facilities and a research-based educational framework for teachers, what matters most is the experience created *by* the teachers. "We rely on them to provide the best classroom experience possible for the children," said owner Hajira Khan. "To ensure that happens, we need to provide them with the best *work* experience."

Each academy employs 30 people, all but managers being paid on an hourly basis. New assistant teachers start at 179 percent of the Indiana minimum wage. Pay increases after a 90-day probation period. Teachers are supported by assistant teachers, including flex staff who fill in during breaks, absences, and any time teachers need a moment.

Hajira explained that while the teams at both academies are extremely collaborative, their cultures are slightly different, since her new academy has a younger staff that wants more personal time. She's improved retention (which is difficult in early childhood education) by offering them four 10-hour shifts per week, while teachers at her original academy prefer the traditional five-day schedule.

Staffing can be tough in this industry. New applicants must go through background checks and drug screens and meet other stringent requirements. Lead teachers must have certification or a degree in childhood development. All this limits the pool of hourly talent. In Fort Wayne, Kiddie Academy has given itself an edge by creating an attractive workplace. Many of its best applicants have been referred by current teachers.

Hajira has resisted the trend of offering hiring bonuses. "Why should I offer bonuses to people I don't even know rather than to the teachers I already have?" she asked. She's chosen instead to invest those dollars into reinforcing the performance of her current team. "I'd rather offer incentives and rewards to my proven teachers to make them want to stay." She also invests more in onboarding, providing a full two weeks of training with a mentor teacher.

TOP-PERFORMANCE SPOTLIGHT, continued

Once on staff, new teachers join a culture that, by design, feels like family. The entire team meets regularly to acknowledge special occasions, anniversaries, social media shout-outs, and consistent positive visits from state regulators. Managers build personal relationships with teachers and check in often to see what they need.

Teachers are also set up to support each other. The school divides them into pods led by a team mentor who encourages them to share ideas and facilitate fun activities among their classes, such as door decorating contests and charity drives. Within each classroom, teachers are empowered to build their own culture within the Kiddie Academy framework. The teachers appreciate the autonomy.

They also appreciate the opportunity to grow. Hajira reimburses teachers for enrollment in child development certification online and offers a raise upon completion, putting them on the path to become a lead teacher. For those who commit to stay at the academy, the company supplements an Indiana scholarship to pursue associate or bachelor's degrees in early childhood education. All teachers receive ongoing (and paid) training to accumulate state-required education credits.

The company remains active in the community. Though teachers can't leave the academy during the day, their participation in book and food drives and other charitable initiatives allows them to feel connected to a greater purpose beyond their already very meaningful work.

I asked Hajira if there's a connection between caring for children and caring for her team, and she shared a few interesting parallels. The first was mapping out progress. "Kids like a visual timeline so they know how the day will progress," she said. "They like knowing when to expect reading time, snack, nap, and playtime. Our teachers also like an agenda. They appreciate understanding how training will unfold and what the expectations are." She also talked about how kids in

TOP-PERFORMANCE SPOTLIGHT, continued

the classroom like to have jobs and special assignments, such as snack helper and door helper. "Our teachers also like to take on challenges and new tasks. These extra responsibilities keep them engaged."

When asked to describe the culture of her academies, Hajira repeated the word "engaged," which also encompasses her approach to ownership. She plays an active role in both academies, visiting both sites daily to connect with parents, students, and her teams. She works tirelessly to advance her own skills and improve the operation. "I'm not perfect," she said. "I believe we should never stop learning. Be willing to try new ideas."

Her example tells us that a good leader is a continuous learner.

Top-Performance Takeaways:

> Create a best-in-class customer experience by creating a best-in-class employee experience.
> Offer a four-day workweek and hire flex staff who can fill in when needed.
> Consider offering retention bonuses instead of hiring bonuses.
> Hold regular meetings to ritualize acknowledgment and appreciation.
> Give proven team members autonomy within the framework of your company standards.
> Encourage and help sponsor professional growth.
> Find ways to connect your team to the community.
> Communicate clear agendas and objectives for training and meetings.
> Keep employees engaged with new roles and tasks.
> Remain active and visible in your organization.

Tracking 30-Second Leadership Diagnosis

The 30-Second Leadership system is designed to be a coaching tool, not an employee evaluation tool. Your diagnosis is based on what's happening in the moment. But if you keep track of your diagnoses, they will tell useful stories over time. You don't even need the details—just knowing which colors they've been in can be quite insightful.

For instance, take a look at Figure 14.1. The column on the left lists the employees by their position in a restaurant, and the other columns show their current diagnosis for a number of different tasks. From just a glance at the data, we can extract a lot of information.

If I'm the manager, I'd be pleased to see that five of the six employees responsible for greeting guests are in the Blue for that task, but I'll want to check in with Monica to see why she's struggling with that. I'm also glad our hosts are doing so well. Maybe I'll bring them a treat today to say thank you. Tommy is clearly new, so we'll keep training him. Diane and Alex are in the Blue for most tasks, so that's also good news. Max has a lot of Red, so I need to follow up on that right away. But before I do, something about cleaning is jumping out at me. All but one person responsible for it are in the Red or Yellow. They have a low mindset for that task. If it were just one or two people, I'd speak with them and try to reengage them. But when I see this many people struggling with the same thing, it makes me think there may be a problem with the task itself. Maybe we should change our cleaning procedures.

Figure 14.1. Team Performance Grid

	Cleaning	Greeting Guests	Taking Orders	Upselling
SERVERS				
Steve				
Monica				
Maisy				
Aaron				

BUSSERS	Cleaning	Greeting Guests	Taking Orders	Upselling
Andre				
Max				
Sarah				

HOSTS	Reservations	Greeting Guests		
Rebecca				
Angela				

COOKS	Cleaning	Food Prep	Plating Meals	Order Accuracy
Tommy				
Alex				
Diane				

Recording data visually in this way tells me a lot, indicating where specifically I need to coach my team members.

But let's take a deeper look at Max. I've also tracked all his diagnoses since hiring him, as displayed in Figure 14.2.

Figure 14.2. Employee Performance Grid

MAX										
BUSSER										
DATE:	12/13	12/1	11/16	11/3	10/18	10/9	9/21	9/9	9/4	9/2
TASKS:										
Cleaning										HIRED
Setting Tables										HIRED
Washing Dishes										HIRED
Stocking										HIRED

We'd expect to see a lot of Green and Yellow during training, followed by an upward trend into the Blue—and we do. But then we start to see a lot of Red. That's not top performance. He's slipping, and he has been for a while. He needs re-engagement right away.

One more thing stands out: On 10/9 he was diagnosed as in the Yellow for stocking. But a couple of weeks earlier he was in the Blue. How could he have lost his skill set so quickly? One of those diagnoses was wrong. He's in the Blue now for that task, so I won't worry too much. But I might talk to the manager who diagnosed him back then (if it wasn't my mistake) to ensure they're evaluating performance accurately.

More investigation is needed to understand what's happening behind the colors. But the collective data over time can be very useful to get a sense of what's going on.

Measurement is a critical part of management. It goes beyond simply observing or relying on intuition to reveal the truth. Numbers don't tell the whole story, but they tell a lot of it. Keep a close eye on your team and be sure everyone knows precisely what you're looking for. Top performance isn't an abstraction—it's a focal point employees can work toward. Coaching them to achieve clear goals is much more effective than just telling them to do their best.

CHAPTER 15

Final Thoughts

anaging hourly workers isn't easy, and nothing I've shared here is meant to suggest otherwise. You're never going to prevent all issues. I know what it feels like when you think you've tried everything, but I'd like to suggest that maybe you haven't. Perhaps there are a few things you can do differently. You probably started this book hoping to figure out how to get your employees to perform better. I hope you're here at the end thinking about how *you* might perform better. Performance ends with your team, but it starts with you.

When I get into conversations about managing hourly workers, it's hard to avoid talking politics. I dislike dealing with politics in my work. Like any culture, if we share the same beliefs, it connects us. If we don't, it divides us.

There are many political questions when it comes to hourly workers, where they work, and how they should be compensated. Some believe hourly work was never meant to support a family. Others believe every worker should be able to earn a livable wage. Some see hourly work environments

263

as a means to provide health insurance to as many people as possible. Others worry about labor costs and the sustainability of the organization.

I don't want to risk losing any bonds I may have been fortunate enough to create with you. But there are some fundamental principles about managing employees that I do wish to stand up for, and I think you should, too.

- Everyone deserves respect.
- Everyone's time is valuable.
- Everyone should be held accountable.
- Everyone is replaceable.
- Employees are entitled to nothing. Neither are employers.
- Everyone should be judged by *who* they are, not *what* they are.
- Employing different kinds of people will bring in more skills, more perspectives, and more value to your workplace.
- Every interaction should build stronger relationships and bring people closer together.
- People need feedback.
- People need an opportunity to advance.
- Every person should make your culture stronger.
- Life outside of work is important.
- The workplace should be safe in every way.
- Leadership is a privilege.
- There is no greater success than helping someone else succeed.

If you read something you liked in the book, please post it on social media and tag me! You can find me on all the major social media platforms.

I'd also love to be of ongoing help to you. I can give live keynote presentations and workshops to your organization as well as one-on-one coaching. Visit www.ScottGreenberg.com for more information. I also have an online manager training course based on the content of this book, along with videos, exercises, worksheets, and tools, that'll help you build and manage a top-performing team. Information on that can be found at www.StopTheShiftShow.com.

My perspective isn't just that of an employer. I'm also a father. It just so happens that as I write this, tomorrow I'm driving my daughter to

Universal Studios, where she's interviewing for her first job. If she gets it, I'm entrusting their managers with the welfare of my baby girl. I don't want them to see her as a number or a faceless tool for profit. I want them to see *her*. I want them to treat her as a partner whom they can develop for the good of everyone in the Universal Studios family. I want them to honor their stated values of putting "safety first," being "team players," doing "the right thing," being "innovators," working to "drive results," valuing their "community," and having "fun." I want them to create a place where she can thrive by helping them thrive.

They may not hire her, but maybe *you* will. I wrote this book envisioning you as the person who someday will manage either of my kids. You will have more face time with them than I will. You may have more influence than I do. That weighs heavily on me. And even if you don't hire my kids, you've hired someone else's. You're in charge of people's babies and will make a permanent imprint on them, for better or for worse. It is my great hope that you'll achieve top performance by working to improve the world, one hourly son or daughter at a time.

A Final Farewell Story

In a verdant forest, there existed two neighboring villages, each led by an elder. The first elder, Kavi, was known for her profound wisdom and guidance. The second elder, Dagan, was infamous for his insatiable thirst for riches and power. Each accompanied by their eldest child, the two embarked on a quest to reach a fabled tree that bore a precious fruit. This fruit was said to possess extraordinary qualities and grant great wisdom to those who ate from it.

As Kavi approached the towering tree, she observed that the fruit grew from its tallest branches. She reassuringly nodded to her daughter before lifting her upon her own shoulders. The child extended her hand as far as she could, but the fruit remained out of reach. Kavi stood on her toes and carefully lifted her daughter even higher, their bond a testament to their mutual trust.

As Dagan approached the tree, he commanded his son to climb. The boy had a difficult time getting his footing. Multiple times he slipped off the lower branches. With each fall, the boy's frustration grew, but Dagan showed little regard for his son's struggles, driven solely by his desire to obtain the fruit's power. He commanded his son to try harder.

Kavi lifted her daughter as high as she could, helping the child reach the pinnacle of the tree. The child extended her hand, delicately plucked the fruit, and lowered it to her mother, their unity culminating in success. Kavi carefully helped her daughter back down to the forest floor. Together they enjoyed the fruit, embracing the wisdom it held, their bond strengthened by the shared journey.

Dagan's son remained distant from the highest branches, unable to reach the fruit no matter how hard he tried or how loud his father commanded. Eventually they gave up, returning to their village disappointed and empty-handed.

You and your hourly workers can stop the shift show and reach extraordinary heights, but they need to stand on your shoulders. The taller you stand, the farther they can reach. You need to be at your best for them to be at theirs. That entails a little less pushing, and a lot more lifting.

Acknowledgments

This was the last and most stressful part of the book to write, mainly out of fear of leaving someone out, which I'm certain I have. There are so many people who've helped. My editor pushed me to get this done and I wrote this under duress. If I've failed to name you here, please accept my apologies and blame him.

To my agent, Wendy Keller, you believed in me before I wrote one word of any book. You're a professional dream maker and I'm deeply grateful to have you representing me.

To my primary collaborator at Entrepreneur Press, Sean Strain, you've been a consummate professional, a huge advocate for the book, and an absolute pleasure to work with. Thanks for believing in the project and for investing in its success.

To my copy editor, Wyn Hilty, your fine-tooth comb has the finest teeth, which you used to tighten my words and check my facts. If I sound smart, it's because I was smart enough to take your suggestions. To my production project manager, Mackenzie Truman, thanks for getting the book to the finish line. And to Andrew Welyczko, people will judge the book by its cover. I judge you by the cover, and my opinion couldn't be higher.

To the rest of the team at Entrepreneur, including Ryan Shea, Bill Shaw, Charles Muselli, and Jason Feifer, you do great work and it's an honor to have your name on the book's spine.

To my manager, Denise Wehle, if I sometimes complain about how busy and tired I am, it's partially because you're so great at your job. Thanks for keeping me out there. I'm so grateful for our partnership. We've got some exciting times ahead!

To Katrina Mitchell, Aletha McManama, and Jessica Cadriel from the Franchise Speakers Bureau, you've opened too many doors to count. No one does it better, and few are better friends.

To my good friend and 30-Second Leadership co-creator, Mario del Pero, Bro, did you ever believe our model would go this far? OK, I did, too. Here's to keeping each other in the Blue.

To my close friend, Steve Callaghan, we've discussed every detail of adulting, usually while we're on a trail. Thanks for sharing, for listening, and for waiting for me to retie my shoelaces.

To my former business partner and longtime friend, Adam Nathan, thanks for the unwavering support, encouragement, and talks off the ledge. Underneath our brotherly jabs is nothing but love and admiration. No joke.

To my dear friend and former Edible Arrangements manager, Jennifer Satzman, and my former top-performing team members, thanks for being living proof that hourly greatness is possible.

To the many top-performing leaders profiled throughout the book who were kind enough to share their philosophy and tactics, including Amy Hudson, Amrit Dhaliwal, Ed Cote, Justin Stewart, Shawn Basseri, Vanessa Ellis, Ray Howell, Sean Riley, Annemarie Abdo, Tim Mahoney, HeeSook Alden, Zahir Ismail, Jonathan Weathington, Neil Kiely, Gary Robins, Hajira Khan, and Jim Cochonour.

Thanks to so many other friends and colleagues who've supported the project and me in a number of ways that have earned you a place in my heart and in these acknowledgments, including Rodel Delfin, Lee Broekman, Erin Fisher, Liane Caruso, Jennifer Cassetta, Kathleen Gosser, PhD., Pino Di Ioia, Jenn Johnston, Evan Katz, Whitney Knight, Ross Kramer, Emily

Lawrence, Kristin Selmeczy, Angela Coté, Yvonne Manganaro, Michelle Rowan, Trevlor Rappleye, Marietta Snetsinger, Nicole Salla, Amanda Barker, Chris Thomes, Mike Norkin, Renée Boudakian, Julie Turner, Cathy Susie, Caroline Susie, and my peeps from the Franchise Lean In Group: Jack Monson, Alesia Visconti, Brynn Gibbs, Mark Spencer, Michael Minitelli, Fernando Meza, Karen Wenning, Derrick Ableman, Kater Danford, Cassidy Ford, Prit Sen, Ty Brewster, Amanda Dempsey, Hope Alteri, Karen Booze, Abby Schmidt, Ingrid Schneider, Emily George, Kim Lucey, Ali Kraus, Amy Layne, and Patti Rother.

To my brother, Brent, once again, you were the first reader of the first draft, and you still liked the book. Since we were kids, I've wanted to show off in front of my cool older brother. That hasn't changed.

To my sister, Kelli, it's unlikely you'll ever read this book, but just in case you come across a copy at Mom and Dad's and flip to the back to see if I mentioned you, here you go. You'll say you read the book and loved it. I love you, liar.

To my nephew and fellow UCLA Bruin, Cameron, thanks for reading through the book and keeping me out of trouble with Generation Z. I'll do my best to keep you out of trouble with Generation X. You really should listen to our music.

To my in-laws, Ron and Diane Andersen, I'm still trying to be worthy of your daughter. Thanks for your love and support.

To my dad, another early reader, my role model, and my biggest cheerleader. The best part of my Edible Arrangements experience was talking shop with you. I'll always cherish that. I hope I can be half the father to Bailey and Peyton as you've been to me.

To my mom, where do I start? Your unconditional love and support for everything I've ever done has demonstrated what perfect parenting is. I'm so grateful for you. I'm sorry I've now written two books, but Brent and Kelli have written none.

To my kids, Bailey and Peyton. I wrote this book with you two in mind. May you have bosses who lead you like the top performers in this book. Even better, may you become bosses who lead like them. You two inspire everything I do. I hope you both have kids of your own someday so you can understand how much I love you.

And finally, to Rachel, I have more to say about how much I love and appreciate you than I do about managing hourly workers. There's just not enough room here, nor do I think my agent could sell a book about that. You're always here with me, and always there for me. In fact, I'm so caught up as I write this, I'm going to step away from my keyboard to give you a kiss. So hang on a second… OK, that was nice.

Acknowledgments

About the Author

S cott Greenberg is an internationally recognized speaker, author, and consultant who helps leaders and teams improve their performance and grow their organizations. He's given presentations in all 50 states in the U.S. and throughout the world with clients that include McDonald's, Great Clips, Anytime Fitness, Nike, the U.S. Air Force, Allstate, RE/MAX, Young Presidents' Organization, the U.S. Department of the Interior, and countless others. For ten years, Scott was a multi-unit franchisee with Edible Arrangements. In addition to building a top-ranked flagship store in Los Angeles, Scott acquired a second struggling location and made it profitable within a year. His operation won the Edible Arrangements "Best Customer Service" and "Manager of the Year" awards out of more than 1000 locations worldwide. Scott is a contributing writer for Entprepreneur.com and *Nation's Restaurant News*, and is the author of the book *The Wealthy Franchisee: Game-Changing Steps to Becoming a Thriving Franchise Superstar*. He lives in Los Angeles. More information at www.ScottGreenberg.com.

Index